THE NOTE-BOOKS OF SAMUEL BUTLER

By
SAMUEL BUTLER

The Note-Books Of Samuel Butler

by **Samuel Butler**

ISBN: 978-93-57488-77-8

Published by

DOUBLE 9 BOOKS

2/13-B, Ansari Road, Daryaganj
New Delhi – 110002
info@double9books.com
www.double9books.com
Tel. 011-40042856

ABOUT THE AUTHOR

Butler was the grandson of Samuel Butler, the principal of Shrewsbury School and afterwards the bishop of Lichfield. He was the son of the Reverend Thomas Butler. The young Samuel transferred to St. John's College in Cambridge after spending six years at Shrewsbury, where he graduated in 1858. In order to prepare for holy orders, young Butler even went so far as to do a little "slumming" in a London parish because his father wanted him to become a clergyman. He was being pulled away from all his father stood for, including his family, the church, and Christianity itself — or at least what it had seemed to imply at Langar Rectory — by the current of his fierce independence and heresy. After an unpleasant incident with his father, Butler left Cambridge, the church, and his home and emigrated to New Zealand, where (using money provided by his father) he established a sheep run in the Canterbury settlement. Butler then returned to Cambridge and continued his musical studies and drawing. After doubling his money in New Zealand, Butler left for England in 1864 and moved into the Clifford's Inn apartment that would serve as his permanent residence. The Way of All Flesh, which was released in 1903, the year after Butler passed away, is widely regarded as his best work. It undoubtedly encompasses a lot of the essential elements of Butlerism.

CONTENTS

Preface

Early in his life Samuel Butler began to carry a note-book and to write down in it anything he wanted to remember; it might be something he heard some one say, more commonly it was something he said himself. In one of these notes he gives a reason for making them:

"One's thoughts fly so fast that one must shoot them; it is no use trying to put salt on their tails."

So he bagged as many as he could hit and preserved them, re-written on loose sheets of paper which constituted a sort of museum stored with the wise, beautiful, and strange creatures that were continually winging their way across the field of his vision. As he became a more expert marksman his collection increased and his museum grew so crowded that he wanted a catalogue. In 1874 he started an index, and this led to his reconsidering the notes, destroying those that he remembered having used in his published books and re-writing the remainder. The re-writing shortened some but it lengthened others and suggested so many new ones that the index was soon of little use and there seemed to be no finality about it ("Making Notes," post). In 1891 he attached the problem afresh and made it a rule to spend an hour every morning re-editing his notes and keeping his index up to date. At his death, in 1902, he left five bound volumes, with the contents dated and indexed, about 225 pages of closely written sermon paper to each volume, and more than enough unbound and unindexed sheets to made a sixth volume of equal size.

In accordance with his own advice to a young writer (post), he wrote the notes in copying ink and kept a pressed copy with me as a precaution against fire; but during his lifetime, unless he wanted to refer to something while he was in my chambers, I never looked at them. After his death I took them down and went through them. I knew in a general way what I should find, but I was not prepared for such a multitude and variety of thoughts, reflections, conversations, incidents. There are entries about his early life at Langar, Handel, school days at Shrewsbury, Cambridge, Christianity, literature, New Zealand, sheep-farming, philosophy, painting, money, evolution, morality, Italy, speculation, photography, music, natural history, archæology, botany, religion, book-keeping, psychology, metaphysics, the *Iliad*, the *Odyssey*, Sicily, architecture, ethics, the *Sonnets* of Shakespeare. I thought of publishing the books just as they stand, but too many of the entries are of no general interest and too many are of a kind that must wait if they are ever to be published. In addition to these objections the confusion is very great. One would look in the earlier volumes for entries about New Zealand and evolution and in the later ones for entries about the *Odyssey* and the *Sonnets*, but there is no attempt at arrangement and anywhere one may come upon something about Handel, or a philosophical reflection, between a note giving the name of the best hotel in an Italian town and another about Harry Nicholls and Herbert Campbell as the Babes in the Wood in the pantomime at the Grecian Theatre. This confusion has a charm, but it is a charm that would not, I fear, survive in print and, personally, I find that it makes the books distracting for continuous reading. Moreover they were not intended to be published as they stand ("Preface to Vol. II," post), they were intended for his own private use as a quarry from which to take material for his writing, and it is remarkable that in practice he scarcely ever used them in this way ("These Notes," post). When he had written and re-written a note and spoken it and repeated it in conversation, it became so much a part of him that, if he wanted to introduce it in a book, it was less trouble to re-state it again from memory than to search through his "precious indexes" for it and copy it ("Gadshill and Trapani,", "At Piora," post). But he could not have re-stated a note from memory if he had not learnt it by writing it, so that it may be said that he did use the notes for his books, though not precisely in the way he originally intended. And the constant re-writing and re-considering were useful also by forcing him to settle exactly what he thought and to state it as clearly and tersely as possible. In this way the making of the notes must have had an influence on the formation of his style — though here again he had no such idea in his mind when writing them ("Style," post)

In one of the notes he says:

"A man may make, as it were, cash entries of himself in a day-book, but the entries in the ledger and the balancing of the accounts should be done by others."

When I began to write the Memoir of Butler on which I am still engaged, I marked all the more autobiographical notes and had them copied; again I was struck by the interest, the variety, and the confusion of those I left untouched. It seemed to me that any one who undertook to become Butler's accountant and to post his entries upon himself would have to settle first how many and what accounts to open in the ledger, and this could not be done until it had been settled which items were to be selected for posting. It was the difficulty of those who dare not go into the water until after they have learnt to swim. I doubt whether I should ever have made the plunge if it had not been for the interest which Mr. Desmond MacCarthy took in Butler and his writings. He had occasionally browsed on my copy of the books, and when he became editor of a review, the *New Quarterly*, he asked for some of the notes for publication, thus providing a practical and simple way of entering upon the business without any very alarming plunge. I talked his proposal over with Mr. R. A. Streatfeild, Butler's literary executor, and, having obtained his approval, set to work. From November 1907 to May 1910, inclusive, the *New Quarterly* published six groups of notes and the long note on "Genius" (post). The experience gained in selecting, arranging, and editing these items has been of great use to me and I thank the proprietor and editor of the *New Quarterly* for permission to republish such of the notes as appeared in their review.

In preparing this book I began by going through the notes again and marking all that seemed to fall within certain groups roughly indicated by the arrangement in the review. I had these selected items copied, distributed them among those which were already in print, shuffled them and turned them over, meditating on them, familiarising myself with them and tentatively forming new groups. While doing this I was continually gleaning from the books more notes which I had overlooked, and making such verbal alterations as seemed necessary to avoid repetition, to correct obvious errors and to remove causes of reasonable offence. The ease with which two or more notes would condense into one was sometimes surprising, but there were cases in which the language had to be varied and others in which a few words had to be added to bridge over a gap; as a rule, however, the necessary words were lying ready in some other note. I also reconsidered the titles and provided titles for many notes which had none. In making these verbal alterations I bore in mind Butler's own views on the subject which I found in a note about editing letters:

"Granted that an editor, like a translator, should keep as religiously close to the original text as he reasonably can, and, in every alteration, should consider what the writer would have wished and done if he or she could have been consulted, yet, subject to these limitations, he should be free to alter according to his discretion or indiscretion."

My "discretion or indiscretion" was less seriously strained in making textual changes than in determining how many, and what, groups to have and which notes, in what order, to include in each group. Here is a note Butler made about classification:

"Fighting about words is like fighting about accounts, and all classification is like accounts. Sometimes it is easy to see which way the balance of convenience lies, sometimes it is very hard to know whether an item should be carried to one account or to another."

Except in the group headed "Higgledy-Piggledy," I have endeavoured to post each note to a suitable account, but some of Butler's leading ideas, expressed in different forms, will be found posted to more than one account, and this kind of repetition is in accordance with his habit in conversation. It would probably be correct to say that I have heard him speak the substance of every note many times in different contexts. In seeking for the most characteristic context, I have shifted and shifted the notes and considered and re-considered them under different aspects, taking hints from the delicate chameleon changes of significance that came over them as they harmonised or discorded with their new surroundings. Presently I caught myself restoring notes to positions they had previously occupied instead of finding new places for them, and the increasing frequency with which difficulties were solved by these restorations at last forced me to the conclusion, which I accepted only with very great regret, that my labours were at an end.

I do not expect every one to approve of the result. If I had been trying to please every one, I should have made only a very short and unrepresentative selection which Mr. Fifield would have refused to publish. I have tried to make suck a book as I believe would have pleased Butler. That is to say, I have tried to please one who, by reason of his intimate knowledge of the subject and of the difficulties, would have looked with indulgence upon the many mistakes which it is now too late to correct, even if knew how to correct them. Had it been possible for him to see what I have done, he would have detected all my sins, both of omission and of commission, and I like to imagine that he would have used some such consoling words as these: "Well, never mind; one cannot have everything; and, after all, 'Le mieux est l'ennemi du bien.'"

Here will be found much of what he used to say as he talked with one or two intimate friends in his own chambers or in mine at the close of the day, or on a Sunday walk in the country round London, or as we wandered together through Italy and Sicily; and I would it were possible to charge these pages with some echo of his voice and with some reflection of his manner. But, again; one cannot have everything.

> "Men's work we have," quoth one, "but we want them —
> Them palpable to touch and clear to view."
> Is it so nothing, then, to have the gem
> But we must cry to have the setting too?

In the *New Quarterly* each note was headed with a reference to its place in the Note-Books. This has not been done here because, on consideration, it seemed useless, and even irritating, to keep on putting before the reader references which he could not verify. I intend to give to the British Museum a copy of this volume wherein each note will show where the material of which it is composed can be found; thus, if the original Note-Books are also some day given to the Museum, any one sufficiently interested will be able to see exactly what I have done in selecting, omitting, editing, condensing and classifying.

Some items are included that are not actually in the Note-Books; the longest of these are the two New Zealand articles "Darwin among the Machines" and "Lucubratio Ebria" as to which something is said in the Prefatory Note to "The Germs of Erewhon and of *Life and Habit*" (post). In that Prefatory Note a Dialogue on Species by Butler and an autograph letter from Charles Darwin are mentioned. Since the note was in type I have received from New Zealand a copy of the Weekly Press of 19th June, 1912, containing the Dialogue again reprinted and a facsimile reproduction of Darwin's letter. I thank Mr. W. H. Triggs, the present editor of the Press, Christchurch, New Zealand, also Miss Colborne-Veel and the members of the staff for their industry and perseverance in searching for and identifying Butler's early contributions to the newspaper.

The other principal items not actually in the Note-Books, the letter to T. W. G. Butler (post), "A Psalm of Montreal" (post) and "The Righteous Man" (post). I suppose Butler kept all these out of his notes because he considered that they had served their purpose; but they have not hitherto appeared in a form now accessible to the general reader.

All the footnotes are mine and so are all those prefatory notes which are printed in italics and the explanatory remarks in square brackets which occur occasionally in the text. I have also preserved, in square brackets, the date of a note when anything seemed to turn on it. And I have made the index.

The Biographical Statement is founded on a skeleton Diary which is in the Note-Books. It is intended to show, among other things, how intimately the great variety of subjects touched upon in the notes entered into and formed part of Butler's working life. It does not stop at the 18th of June, 1902, because, as he says (post), "Death is not more the end of some than it is the beginning of others"; and, again (post), for those who come to the true birth the life we live beyond the grave is our truest life. The Biographical Statement has accordingly been carried on to the present time so as to include the principal events that have occurred during the opening period of the "good average three-score years and ten of immortality" which he modestly hoped he might inherit in the life of the world to come.

Henry Festing Jones.

Mount Eryx,
Trapani, Sicily,
August, 1912.

I
Lord, What is Man?

Man

i

We are like billiard balls in a game played by unskilful players, continually being nearly sent into a pocket, but hardly ever getting right into one, except by a fluke.

ii

We are like thistle-down blown about by the wind—up and down, here and there—but not one in a thousand ever getting beyond seed-hood.

iii

A man is a passing mood coming and going in the mind of his country; he is the twitching of a nerve, a smile, a frown, a thought of shame or honour, as it may happen.

iv

How loosely our thoughts must hang together when the whiff of a smell, a band playing in the street, a face seen in the fire, or on the gnarled stem of a tree, will lead them into such vagaries at a moment's warning.

v

When I was a boy at school at Shrewsbury, old Mrs. Brown used to keep a tray of spoiled tarts which she sold cheaper. They most of them looked pretty right till you handled them. We are all spoiled tarts.

vi

He is a poor creature who does not believe himself to be better than the whole world else. No matter how ill we may be, or how low we may have fallen, we would not change identity with any other person. Hence our self-conceit sustains and always must sustain us till death takes us and our conceit together so that we need no more sustaining.

Man must always be a consuming fire or be consumed. As for hell, we are in a burning fiery furnace all our lives—for what is life but a process of combustion?

Life

i

We have got into life by stealth and *petitio principii*, by the free use of that contradiction in terms which we declare to be the most outrageous violation of our reason. We have wriggled into it by holding that everything is both one and many, both infinite in time and space and yet finite, both like and unlike to the same thing, both itself and not itself, both free and yet inexorably fettered, both every adjective in the dictionary and at the same time the flat contradiction of every one of them.

ii

The beginning of life is the beginning of an illusion to the effect that there is such a thing as free will and that there is such another thing as necessity— the recognition of the fact that there is an "I can" and an "I cannot," an "I may" and an "I must."

iii

Life is not so much a riddle to be read as a Gordian knot that will get cut sooner or later.

iv

Life is the distribution of an error—or errors.

v

Murray (the publisher) said that my *Life of Dr. Butler* was an omnium gatherum. Yes, but life is an omnium gatherum.

vi

Life is a superstition. But superstitions are not without their value. The snail's shell is a superstition, slugs have no shells and thrive just as well. But a snail without a shell would not be a slug unless it had also the slug's indifference to a shell.

vii

Life is one long process of getting tired.

viii

My days run through me as water through a sieve.

ix

Life is the art of drawing sufficient conclusions from insufficient premises.

x

Life is eight parts cards and two parts play, the unseen world is made manifest to us in the play.

xi

Lizards generally seem to have lost their tails by the time they reach middle life. So have most men.

xii

A sense of humour keen enough to show a man his own absurdities, as well as those of other people, will keep him from the commission of all sins, or nearly all, save those that are worth committing.

xiii

Life is like music, it must be composed by ear, feeling and instinct, not by rule. Nevertheless one had better know the rules, for they sometimes guide in doubtful cases — though not often.

xiv

There are two great rules of life, the one general and the other particular. The first is that every one can, in the end, get what he wants if he only tries. This is the general rule. The particular rule is that every individual is, more or less, an exception to the general rule.

xv

Nature is essentially mean, mediocre. You can have schemes for raising the level of this mean, but not for making every one two inches taller than his neighbour, and this is what people really care about.

xvi

All progress is based upon a universal innate desire on the part of every organism to live beyond its income.

The World

i

The world is a gambling-table so arranged that all who enter the casino must play and all must lose more or less heavily in the long run, though they win occasionally by the way.

ii

We play out our days as we play out cards, taking them as they come, not knowing what they will be, hoping for a lucky card and sometimes getting one, often getting just the wrong one.

iii

The world may not be particularly wise — still, we know of nothing wiser.

iv

The world will always be governed by self-interest. We should not try to stop this, we should try to make the self-interest of cads a little more coincident with that of decent people.

The Individual and the World

There is an eternal antagonism of interest between the individual and the world at large. The individual will not so much care how much he may suffer in this world provided he can live in men's good thoughts long after he has left it. The world at large does not so much care how much suffering the individual may either endure or cause in this life, provided he will take himself clean away out of men's thoughts, whether for good or ill, when he has left it.

My Life

i

I imagine that life can give nothing much better or much worse than what I have myself experienced. I should say I had proved pretty well the extremes of mental pleasure and pain; and so I believe each in his own way does, almost every man.

ii

I have squandered my life as a schoolboy squanders a tip. But then half, or more than half the fun a schoolboy gets out of a tip consists in the mere fact of having something to squander. Squandering is in itself delightful, and so I found it with my life in my younger days. I do not squander it now, but I am not sorry that I have squandered a good deal of it. What a heap of rubbish there would have been if I had not! Had I not better set about squandering what is left of it?

The Life we Live in Others

A man should spend his life or, rather, does spend his life in being born. His life is his birth throes. But most men miscarry and never come to the true birth at all and some live but a very short time in a very little world and none are eternal. Still, the life we live beyond the grave is our truest life, and our happiest, for we pass it in the profoundest sleep as though we were children in our cradles. If we are wronged it hurts us not; if we wrong others, we do not suffer for it; and when we die, as even the Handels and Bellinis and Shakespeares sooner or later do, we die easily, know neither fear nor pain and live anew in the lives of those who have been begotten of our work and who have for the time come up in our room.

An immortal like Shakespeare knows nothing of his own immortality about which we are so keenly conscious. As he knows nothing of it when it is in its highest vitality, centuries, it may be, after his apparent death, so it is best and happiest if during his bodily life he should think little or nothing about it and perhaps hardly suspect that he will live after his death at all.

And yet I do not know—I could not keep myself going at all if I did not believe that I was likely to inherit a good average three-score years and ten of immortality. There are very few workers who are not sustained by this belief, or at least hope, but it may well be doubted whether this is not a sign that they are not going to be immortal—and I am content (or try to be) to fare as my neighbours.

The World Made to Enjoy

When we grumble about the vanity of all human things, inasmuch as even the noblest works are not eternal but must become sooner or later as though they had never been, we should remember that the world, so far as we can see, was made to enjoy rather than to last. Come-and-go pervades everything of which we have knowledge, and though great things go more slowly, they are built up of small ones and must fare as that which makes them.

Are we to have our enjoyment of Handel and Shakespeare weakened because a day will come when there will be no more of either Handel or Shakespeare nor yet of ears to hear them? Is it not enough that they should stir such countless multitudes so profoundly and kindle such intense and affectionate admiration for so many ages as they have done and probably will continue to do? The life of a great thing may be so long as practically to come to immortality even now, but that is not the point. The point is that if anything was aimed at at all when things began to shape or to be shaped, it seems to have been a short life and a merry one, with an extension of time in certain favoured cases, rather than a permanency even of the very best and noblest. And, when one comes to think of it, death and birth are so closely correlated that one could not destroy either without destroying the other at the same time. It is extinction that makes creation possible.

If, however, any work is to have long life it is not enough that it should be good of its kind. Many ephemeral things are perfect in their way. It must be of a durable kind as well.

Living in Others

We had better live in others as much as we can if only because we thus live more in the race, which God really does seem to care about a good deal, and less in the individual, to whom, so far as I can see, he is indifferent. After we are dead it matters not to the life we have led in ourselves what people may say of us, but it matters much to the life we lead in others and this should be our true life.

Karma

When I am inclined to complain about having worked so many years and taken nothing but debt, though I feel the want of money so continually (much more, doubtless, than I ought to feel it), let me remember that I come in free, gratis, to the work of hundreds and thousands of better men than myself who often were much worse paid than I have been. If a man's true self is his karma — the life which his work lives but which he knows very little about and by which he takes nothing — let him remember at least that he can enjoy the karma of others, and this about squares the account — or rather far more than squares it. [1883.]

Birth and Death

i

They are functions one of the other and if you get rid of one you must get rid of the other also. There is birth in death and death in birth. We are always dying and being born again.

ii

Life is the gathering of waves to a head, at death they break into a million fragments each one of which, however, is absorbed at once into the sea of life and helps to form a later generation which comes rolling on till it too breaks.

iii

What happens to you when you die? But what happens to you when you are born? In the one case we are born and in the other we die, but it is not possible to get much further.

iv

We commonly know that we are going to die though we do not know that we are going to be born. But are we sure this is so? We may have had the most gloomy forebodings on this head and forgotten all about them. At any rate we know no more about the very end of our lives than about the very beginning. We come up unconsciously, and go down unconsciously; and we rarely see either birth or death. We see people, as consciousness, between the two extremes.

Reproduction

Its base must be looked for not in the desire of the parents to reproduce but in the discontent of the germs with their surroundings inside those parents, and a desire on their part to have a separate maintenance. [16] [1880.]

Thinking almost Identically

The ova, spermatozoa and embryos not only of all human races but of all things that live, whether animal or vegetable, think little, but that little almost identically on every subject. That "almost" is the little rift within the lute which by and by will give such different character to the music. [1889.]

Is Life Worth Living?

This is a question for an embryo, not for a man. [1883.]

Evacuations

There is a resemblance, greater or less, between the pleasure we derive from all the evacuations. I believe that in all cases the pleasure arises from rest—rest, that is to say, from the considerable, though in most cases unconscious labour of retaining that which it is a relief to us to be rid of.

In ordinary cases the effort whereby we retain those things that we would get rid of is unperceived by the central government, being, I suppose, departmentally made; we—as distinguished from the subordinate personalities of which we are composed—know nothing about it, though the subordinates in question doubtless do. But when the desirability of removing is abnormally great, we know about the effort of retaining perfectly well, and the gradual increase in our perception of the effort suggests strongly that there has been effort all the time, descending to conscious and great through unconscious and normal from unconscious and hardly any at all. The relaxation of this effort is what causes the sense of refreshment that follows all healthy discharges.

All our limbs and sensual organs, in fact our whole body and life, are but an accretion round and a fostering of the spermatozoa. They are the real "He." A man's eyes, ears, tongue, nose, legs and arms are but so many organs and tools that minister to the protection, education, increased intelligence and multiplication of the spermatozoa; so that our whole life is in reality a series of complex efforts in respect of these, conscious or unconscious according to their comparative commonness. They are the central fact in our existence, the point towards which all effort is directed. Relaxation of effort here, therefore, is the most complete and comprehensive of all relaxations and, as such, the supreme gratification—the most complete rest we can have, short of sleep and death.

Man and His Organism

i

Man is but a perambulating tool-box and workshop, or office, fashioned for itself by a piece of very clever slime, as the result of long experience; and truth is but its own most enlarged, general and enduring sense of the coming togetherness or convenience of the various conventional arrangements which, for some reason or other, it has been led to sanction. Hence we speak of man's body as his "trunk."

ii

The body is but a pair of pincers set over a bellows and a stewpan and the whole fixed upon stilts.

iii

A man should see himself as a kind of tool-box; this is simple enough; the difficulty is that it is the tools themselves that make and work the tools. The skill which now guides our organs and us in arts and inventions was at one time exercised upon the invention of these very organs themselves. Tentative bankruptcy acts afford good illustrations of the manner in which organisms have been developed. The ligaments which bind the tendons of our feet or the valves of our blood vessels are the ingenious enterprises of individual cells who saw a want, felt that they could supply it, and have thus won themselves a position among the old aristocracy of the body politic.

The most incorporate tool—as an eye or a tooth or the fist, when a blow is struck with it—has still something of the non-ego about it; and in like manner such a tool as a locomotive engine, apparently entirely separated from the body, must still from time to time, as it were, kiss the soil of the human body and be handled, and thus become incorporate with man, if it is to remain in working order.

Tools

A tool is anything whatsoever which is used by an intelligent being for realising its object. The idea of a desired end is inseparable from a tool. The very essence of a tool is the being an instrument for the achievement of a purpose. We say that a man is the tool of another, meaning that he is being used for the furtherance of that other's ends, and this constitutes him a machine in use. Therefore the word "tool" implies also the existence of a living, intelligent being capable of desiring the end for which the tool is used, for this is involved in the idea of a desired end. And as few tools grow naturally fit for use (for even a stick or a fuller's teasel must be cut from their places and modified to some extent before they can be called tools), the word "tool" implies not only a purpose and a purposer, but a purposer who can see in what manner his purpose can be achieved, and who can contrive (or find ready-made and fetch and employ) the tool which shall achieve it.

Strictly speaking, nothing is a tool unless during actual use. Nevertheless, if a thing has been made for the express purpose of being used as a tool it is commonly called a tool, whether it is in actual use or no. Thus hammers, chisels, etc., are called tools, though lying idle in a tool-box. What is meant is that, though not actually being used as instruments at the present moment, they bear the impress of their object, and are so often in use that we may speak of them as though they always were so. Strictly, a thing is a tool or not a tool just as it may happen to be in use or not. Thus a stone may be picked up and used to hammer a nail with, but the stone is not a tool until picked up with an eye to use; it is a tool as soon as this happens, and, if thrown away immediately the nail has been driven home, the stone is a tool no longer. We see, therefore, matter alternating between a toolish or organic state and an untoolish or inorganic. Where there is intention it is organic, where there is no intention it is inorganic. Perhaps, however, the word "tool" should cover also the remains of a tool so long as there are manifest signs that the object was a tool once.

The simplest tool I can think of is a piece of gravel used for making a road. Nothing is done to it, it owes its being a tool simply to the fact that it subserves a purpose. A broken piece of granite used for macadamising a road is a more complex instrument, about the toolishness of which no doubt can be entertained. It will, however, I think, be held that even a piece of gravel found in situ and left there untouched, provided it is so left because it was deemed suitable for a road which was designed to pass over the spot, would become a tool in virtue of the recognition of its utility, while a similar piece of gravel a yard off on either side the proposed road would not be a tool.

The essence of a tool, therefore, lies in something outside the tool itself. It is not in the head of the hammer, nor in the handle, nor in the combination of the two that the essence of mechanical characteristics exists, but in the recognition of its utility and in the forces directed through it in virtue of this recognition. This appears more plainly when we reflect that a very complex machine, if intended for use by children whose aim is not serious, ceases to rank in our minds as a tool, and becomes a toy. It is seriousness of aim and recognition of suitability for the achievement of that aim, and not anything in the tool itself, that makes the tool.

The goodness or badness, again, of a tool depends not upon anything within the tool as regarded without relation to the user, but upon the ease or difficulty experienced by the person using it in comparison with what he or others of average capacity would experience if they had used a tool of a different kind. Thus the same tool may be good for one man and bad for another.

It seems to me that all tools resolve themselves into the hammer and the lever, and that the lever is only an inverted hammer, or the hammer only an inverted lever, whichever one wills; so that all the problems of mechanics are present to us in the simple stone which may be used as a hammer, or in the stick that may be used as a lever, as much as in the most complicated machine. These are the primordial cells of mechanics. And an organ is only another name for a tool.

Organs and Makeshifts

I have gone out sketching and forgotten my water-dipper; among my traps I always find something that will do, for example, the top of my tin case (for holding pencils). This is how organs come to change their uses and hence their forms, or at any rate partly how.

Joining and DisjoiningThese are the essence of change.

One of the earliest notes I made, when I began to make notes at all, I found not long ago in an old book, since destroyed, which I had in New Zealand. It was to the effect that all things are either of the nature of a piece of string or a knife. That is, they are either for bringing and keeping things together, or for sending and keeping them apart. Nevertheless each kind contains a little of its opposite and some, as the railway train and the hedge, combine many examples of both. Thus the train, on the whole, is used for bringing things together, but it is also used for sending them apart, and its divisions into classes are alike for separating and keeping together. The hedge is also both for joining things (as a flock of sheep) and for disjoining (as for keeping the sheep from getting into corn). These are the more immediate ends. The ulterior ends, both of train and hedge, so far as we are concerned, and so far as anything can have an end, are the bringing or helping to bring meat or dairy produce into contact with man's inside, or wool on to his back, or that he may go in comfort somewhere to converse with people and join his soul on to theirs, or please himself by getting something to come within the range of his senses or imagination.

A piece of string is a thing that, in the main, makes for togetheriness; whereas a knife is, in the main, a thing that makes for splitty-uppiness; still, there is an odour of togetheriness hanging about a knife also, for it tends to bring potatoes into a man's stomach.

In high philosophy one should never look at a knife without considering it also as a piece of string, nor at a piece of string without considering it also as a knife.

Cotton Factories

Surely the work done by the body is, in one way, more its true life than its limbs and organisation are. Which is the more true life of a great cotton factory—the bales of goods which it turns out for the world's wearing or the machinery whereby its ends are achieved? The manufacture is only possible by reason of the machinery; it is produced by this. The machinery only exists in virtue of its being capable of producing the manufacture; it is produced for this. The machinery represents the work done by the factory that turned it out.

Somehow or other when we think of a factory we think rather of the fabric and mechanism than of the work, and so we think of a man's life and living body as constituting himself rather than of the work that the life and living body turn out. The instinct being as strong as it is, I suppose it sound, but it seems as though the life should be held to be quite as much in the work itself as in the tools that produce it—and perhaps more.

Our Trivial Bodies

i

Though we think so much of our body, it is in reality a small part of us. Before birth we get together our tools, in life we use them, and thus fashion our true life which consists not in our tools and tool-box but in the work we have done with our tools. It is Handel's work, not the body with which he did the work, that pulls us half over London. There is not an action of a muscle in a horse's leg upon a winter's night as it drags a carriage to the Albert Hall but is in connection with, and part outcome of, the force generated when Handel sat in his room at Gopsall and wrote the *Messiah*. Think of all the forces which that force has controlled, and think, also, how small was the amount of molecular disturbance from which it proceeded. It is as though we saw a conflagration which a spark had kindled. This is the true Handel, who is a more living power among us one hundred and twenty-two years after his death than during the time he was amongst us in the body.

ii

The whole life of some people is a kind of partial death—a long, lingering death-bed, so to speak, of stagnation and nonentity on which death is but the seal, or solemn signing, as the abnegation of all further act and deed on the part of the signer. Death robs these people of even that little strength which they appeared to have and gives them nothing but repose.

On others, again, death confers a more living kind of life than they can ever possibly have enjoyed while to those about them they seemed to be alive. Look at Shakespeare; can he be properly said to have lived in anything like his real life till a hundred years or so after his death? His physical life was but as a dawn preceding the sunrise of that life of the world to come which he was to enjoy hereafter. True, there was a little stir—a little abiding of shepherds in the fields, keeping watch over their flocks by night—a little buzzing in knots of men waiting to be hired before the daybreak—a little stealthy movement as of a burglar or two here and there—an inchoation of life. But the true life of the man was after death and not before it.

Death is not more the end of some than it is the beginning of others. So he that loses his soul may find it, and he that finds may lose it.

II
Elementary Morality

The Foundations of Morality

i

These are like all other foundations; if you dig too much about them the superstructure will come tumbling down.

ii

The foundations which we would dig about and find are within us, like the Kingdom of Heaven, rather than without.

iii

To attempt to get at the foundations is to try to recover consciousness about things that have passed into the unconscious stage; it is pretty sure to disturb and derange those who try it on too much.

Counsels of Imperfection

It is all very well for mischievous writers to maintain that we cannot serve God and Mammon. Granted that it is not easy, but nothing that is worth doing ever is easy. Easy or difficult, possible or impossible, not only has the thing got to be done, but it is exactly in doing it that the whole duty of man consists. And when the righteous man turneth away from his righteousness that he hath committed and doeth that which is neither quite lawful nor quite right, he will generally be found to have gained in amiability what he has lost in holiness.

If there are two worlds at all (and that there are I have no doubt) it stands to reason that we ought to make the best of both of them, and more particularly of the one with which we are most immediately concerned. It is as immoral to be too good as to be too anything else. The Christian morality is just as immoral as any other. It is at once very moral and very immoral. How often do we not see children ruined through the virtues, real or supposed, of their parents? Truly he visiteth the virtues of the fathers upon the children unto the third and fourth generation. The most that can be said for virtue is that there is a considerable balance in its favour, and that it is a good deal better to be for it than against it; but it lets people in very badly sometimes.

If you wish to understand virtue you must be sub-vicious; for the really virtuous man, who is fully under grace, will be virtuous unconsciously and will know nothing about it. Unless a man is out-and-out virtuous he is sub-vicious.

Virtue is, as it were, the repose of sleep or death. Vice is the awakening to the knowledge of good and evil—without which there is no life worthy of the name. Sleep is, in a way, a happier, more peaceful state than waking and, in a way, death may be said to be better than life, but it is in a very small way. We feel such talk to be blasphemy against good life and, whatever we may say in death's favour, so long as we do not blow our brains out we show that we do not mean to be taken seriously. To know good, other than as a heavy sleeper, we must know vice also. There cannot, as Bacon said, be a "Hold fast that which is good" without a "Prove all things" going before it. There is no knowledge of good without a knowledge of evil also, and this is why all nations have devils as well as gods, and regard them with sneaking kindness. God without the devil is dead, being alone.

Lucifer

We call him at once the Angel of Light and the Angel of Darkness: is this because we instinctively feel that no one can know much till he has sinned much—or because we feel that extremes meet, or how?

The Oracle in *Erewhon*

The answer given by the oracle was originally written concerning any vice—say drunkenness, but it applies to many another—and I wrote not "sins" but "knows": [26]

> He who knows aught
> Knows more than he ought;
> But he who knows nought
> Has much to be taught.

God's Laws

The true laws of God are the laws of our own well-being.

Physical Excellence

The question whether such and such a course of conduct does or does not do physical harm is the safest test by which to try the question whether it is moral or no. If it does no harm to the body we ought to be very chary of calling it immoral, while if it tends towards physical excellence there should be no hesitation in calling it moral. In the case of those who are not forced to over-work themselves — and there are many who work themselves to death from mere inability to restrain the passion for work, which masters them as the craving for drink masters a drunkard — over-work in these cases is as immoral as over-eating or drinking. This, so far as the individual is concerned. With regard to the body politic as a whole, it is, no doubt, well that there should be some men and women so built that they cannot be stopped from working themselves to death, just as it is unquestionably well that there should be some who cannot be stopped from drinking themselves to death, if only that they may keep the horror of the habit well in evidence.

Intellectual Self-Indulgence

Intellectual over-indulgence is the most gratuitous and disgraceful form which excess can take, nor is there any the consequences of which are more disastrous.

Dodging Fatigue

When fatigued, I find it rests me to write very slowly with attention to the formation of each letter. I am often thus able to go on when I could not otherwise do so.

Vice and Virtue

i

Virtue is something which it would be impossible to over-rate if it had not been over-rated. The world can ill spare any vice which has obtained long and largely among civilised people. Such a vice must have some good along with its deformities. The question "How, if every one were to do so and so?" may be met with another "How, if no one were to do it?" We are a body corporate as well as a collection of individuals.

As a matter of private policy I doubt whether the moderately vicious are more unhappy than the moderately virtuous; "Very vicious" is certainly less happy than "Tolerably virtuous," but this is about all. What pass muster as the extremes of virtue probably make people quite as unhappy as extremes of vice do.

The truest virtue has ever inclined toward excess rather than asceticism; that she should do this is reasonable as well as observable, for virtue should be as nice a calculator of chances as other people and will make due allowance for the chance of not being found out. Virtue knows that it is impossible to get on without compromise, and tunes herself, as it were, a trifle sharp to allow for an inevitable fall in playing. So the Psalmist says, "If thou, Lord, wilt be extreme to mark what is done amiss: O Lord who may abide it?" and by this he admits that the highest conceivable form of virtue still leaves room for some compromise with vice. So again Shakespeare writes, "They say, best men are moulded out of faults; And, for the most, become much more the better For being a little bad."

ii

The extremes of vice and virtue are alike detestable; absolute virtue is as sure to kill a man as absolute vice is, let alone the dullnesses of it and the pomposities of it.

iii

God does not intend people, and does not like people, to be too good. He likes them neither too good nor too bad, but a little too bad is more venial with him than a little too good.

iv

As there is less difference than we generally think between the happiness of men who seem to differ widely in fortune, so is there also less between their moral natures; the best are not so much better than the worst, nor the worst so much below the best as we suppose; and the bad are just as important an element in the general progress as the good, or perhaps more so. It is in strife that life lies, and were there no opposing forces there would be neither moral nor immoral, neither victory nor defeat.

v

If virtue had everything her own way she would be as insufferable as dominant factions generally are. It is the function of vice to keep virtue within reasonable bounds.

vi

Virtue has never yet been adequately represented by any who have had any claim to be considered virtuous. It is the sub-vicious who best understand virtue. Let the virtuous people stick to describing vice—which they can do well enough.

My Virtuous Life

I have led a more virtuous life than I intended, or thought I was leading. When I was young I thought I was vicious: now I know that I was not and that my unconscious knowledge was sounder than my conscious. I regret some things that I have done, but not many. I regret that so many should think I did much which I never did, and should know of what I did in so garbled and distorted a fashion as to have done me much mischief. But if things were known as they actually happened, I believe I should have less to be ashamed of than a good many of my neighbours—and less also to be proud of.

Sin

Sin is like a mountain with two aspects according to whether it is viewed before or after it has been reached: yet both aspects are real.

Morality

turns on whether the pleasure precedes or follows the pain. Thus, it is immoral to get drunk because the headache comes after the drinking, but if the headache came first, and the drunkenness afterwards, it would be moral to get drunk.

Change and Immorality

Every discovery and, indeed, every change of any sort is immoral, as tending to unsettle men's minds, and hence their custom and hence their morals, which are the net residuum of their "mores" or customs. Wherefrom it should follow that there is nothing so absolutely moral as stagnation, except for this that, if perfect, it would destroy all mores whatever. So there must always be an immorality in morality and, in like manner, a morality in immorality. For there will be an element of habitual and legitimate custom even in the most unhabitual and detestable things that can be done at all.

Cannibalism

Morality is the custom of one's country and the current feeling of one's peers. Cannibalism is moral in a cannibal country.

Abnormal Developments

If a man can get no other food it is more natural for him to kill another man and eat him than to starve. Our horror is rather at the circumstances that make it natural for the man to do this than at the man himself. So with other things the desire for which is inherited through countless ancestors, it is more natural for men to obtain the nearest thing they can to these, even by the most abnormal means if the ordinary channels are closed, than to forego them altogether. The abnormal growth should be regarded as disease but, nevertheless, as showing more health and vigour than no growth at all would do. I said this in *Life and Habit* (ch. iii.) when I wrote "it is more righteous in a man that he should eat strange food and that his cheek so much as lank not, than that he should starve if the strange food be at his command." [30]

Young People

With regard to sexual matters, the best opinion of our best medical men, the practice of those nations which have proved most vigorous and comely, the evils that have followed this or that, the good that has attended upon the other should be ascertained by men who, being neither moral nor immoral and not caring two straws what the conclusion arrived at might be, should desire only to get hold of the best available information. The result should be written down with some fulness and put before the young of both sexes as soon as they are old enough to understand such matters at all. There should be no mystery or reserve. None but the corrupt will wish to corrupt facts; honest people will accept them eagerly, whatever they may prove to be, and will convey them to others as accurately as they can. On what pretext therefore can it be well that knowledge should be withheld from the universal gaze upon a matter of such universal interest? It cannot be pretended that there is nothing to be known on these matters beyond what unaided boys and girls can be left without risk to find out for themselves. Not one in a hundred who remembers his own boyhood will say this. How, then, are they excusable who have the care of young people and yet leave a matter of such vital importance so almost absolutely to take care of itself, although they well know how common error is, how easy to fall into and how disastrous in its effects both upon the individual and the race?

Next to sexual matters there are none upon which there is such complete reserve between parents and children as on those connected with money. The father keeps his affairs as closely as he can to himself and is most jealous of letting his children into a knowledge of how he manages his money. His children are like monks in a monastery as regards money and he calls this training them up with the strictest regard to principle. Nevertheless he thinks himself ill-used if his son, on entering life, falls a victim to designing persons whose knowledge of how money is made and lost is greater than his own.

The Family

i

I believe that more unhappiness comes from this source than from any other—I mean from the attempt to prolong family connection unduly and to make people hang together artificially who would never naturally do so. The mischief among the lower classes is not so great, but among the middle and upper classes it is killing a large number daily. And the old people do not really like it much better than the young.

ii

On my way down to Shrewsbury some time since I read the Bishop of Carlisle's *Walks in the Regions of Science and Faith,* [31] then just published, and found the following on in the essay which is entitled "Man's Place in Nature." After saying that young sparrows or robins soon lose sight of their fellow-nestlings and leave off caring for them, the bishop continues: —

"Whereas 'children of one family' are constantly found joined together by a love which only grows with years, and they part for their posts of duty in the world with the hope of having joyful meetings from time to time, and of meeting in a higher world when their life on earth is finished."

I am sure my great-grandfather did not look forward to meeting his father in heaven—his father had cut him out of his will; nor can I credit my grandfather with any great longing to rejoin my great-grandfather—a worthy man enough, but one with whom nothing ever prospered. I am certain my father, after he was 40, did not wish to see my grandfather any more—indeed, long before reaching that age he had decided that Dr. Butler's life should not be written, though R. W. Evans would have been only too glad to write it. Speaking for myself, I have no wish to see my father again, and I think it likely that the Bishop of Carlisle would not be more eager to see his than I mine.

Unconscious Humour

"Writing to the Hon. Mrs. Watson in 1856, Charles Dickens says: 'I have always observed within my experience that *the men who have left home very young* have, *many long years afterwards*, had the tenderest regard for it. That's a pleasant thing to think of as one of the wise adjustments of this life of ours.'" [32a]

Homer's *Odyssey*

From the description of the meeting between Ulysses and Telemachus it is plain that Homer considered it quite as dreadful for relations who had long been separated to come together again as for them to separate in the first instance. And this is about true. [32b]

Melchisedec

He was a really happy man. He was without father, without mother and without descent. He was an incarnate bachelor. He was a born orphan.

Bacon for Breakfast

Now [1893] when I am abroad, being older and taking less exercise, I do not want any breakfast beyond coffee and bread and butter, but when this note was written [1880] I liked a modest rasher of bacon in addition, and used to notice the jealous indignation with which heads of families who enjoyed the privilege of Cephas and the brethren of our Lord regarded it. There were they with three or four elderly unmarried daughters as well as old mamma — how could they afford bacon? And there was I, a selfish bachelor —. The appetising, savoury smell of my rasher seemed to drive them mad. I used to feel very uncomfortable, very small and quite aware how low it was of me to have bacon for breakfast and no daughters instead of daughters and no bacon. But when I consulted the oracles of heaven about it, I was always told to stick to my bacon and not to make a fool of myself. I despised myself but have not withered under my own contempt so completely as I ought to have done.

God and Man

To love God is to have good health, good looks, good sense, experience, a kindly nature and a fair balance of cash in hand. "We know that all things work together for good to them that love God." To be loved by God is the same as to love Him. We love Him because He first loved us.

The Homeric Deity and the *Pall Mall Gazette*

A writer in the *Pall Mall Gazette* (I think in 1874 or 1875, and in the autumn months, but I cannot now remember) summed up Homer's conception of a god as that of a "superlatively strong, amorous, beautiful, brave and cunning man." This is pretty much what a good working god ought to be, but he should also be kind and have a strong sense of humour, together with a contempt for the vices of meanness and for the meannesses of virtue. After saying what I have quoted above the writer in the *Pall Mall Gazette* goes on, "An impartial critic can judge for himself how far, if at all, this is elevated above the level of mere fetish worship." Perhaps it is that I am not an impartial critic, but, if I am allowed to be so, I should say that the elevation above mere fetish worship was very considerable.

Good Breeding the Summum Bonum

When people ask what faith we would substitute for that which we would destroy, we answer that we destroy no faith and need substitute none. We hold the glory of God to be the summum bonum, and so do Christians generally. It is on the question of what is the glory of God that we join issue. We say it varies with the varying phases of God as made manifest in his works, but that, so far as we are ourselves concerned, the glory of God is best advanced by advancing that of man. If asked what is the glory of man we answer "Good breeding" — using the words in their double sense and meaning both the continuance of the race and that grace of manner which the words are more commonly taken to signify. The double sense of the words is all the more significant for the unconsciousness with which it is passed over.

Advice to the Young

You will sometimes find your elders laying their heads together and saying what a bad thing it is for young men to come into a little money — that those always do best who have no expectancy, and the like. They will then quote some drivel from one of the Kingsleys about the deadening effect an income of £300 a year will have upon a man. Avoid any one whom you may hear talk in this way. The fault lies not with the legacy (which would certainly be better if there were more of it) but with those who have so mismanaged our education that we go in even greater danger of losing the money than other people are.

Religion

Is there any religion whose followers can be pointed to as distinctly more amiable and trustworthy than those of any other? If so, this should be enough. I find the nicest and best people generally profess no religion at all, but are ready to like the best men of all religions.

Heaven and Hell

Heaven is the work of the best and kindest men and women. Hell is the work of prigs, pedants and professional truth-tellers. The world is an attempt to make the best of both.

Priggishness

The essence of priggishness is setting up to be better than one's neighbour. Better may mean more virtuous, more clever, more agreeable or what not. The worst of it is that one cannot do anything outside eating one's dinner or taking a walk without setting up to know more than one's neighbours. It was this that made me say in *Life and Habit* [close of ch. ii.] that I was among the damned in that I wrote at all. So I am; and I am often very sorry that I was never able to reach those more saintly classes who do not set up as instructors of other people. But one must take one's lot.

Lohengrin

He was a prig. In the bedroom scene with Elsa he should have said that her question put him rather up a tree but that, as she wanted to know who he was, he would tell her and would let the Holy Grail slide.

Swells

People ask complainingly what swells have done, or do, for society that they should be able to live without working. The good swell is the creature towards which all nature has been groaning and travailing together until now. He is an ideal. He shows what may be done in the way of good breeding, health, looks, temper and fortune. He realises men's dreams of themselves, at any rate vicariously. He preaches the gospel of grace. The world is like a spoilt child, it has this good thing given it at great expense and then says it is useless!

Science and Religion

These are reconciled in amiable and sensible people but nowhere else.

Gentleman

If we are asked what is the most essential characteristic that underlies this word, the word itself will guide us to gentleness, to absence of such things as brow-beating, overbearing manners and fuss, and generally to consideration for other people.

The Finest Men

I suppose an Italian peasant or a Breton, Norman or English fisherman, is about the best thing nature does in the way of men—the richer and the poorer being alike mistakes.

On being a Swell all Round

I have never in my life succeeded in being this. Sometimes I get a new suit and am tidy for a while in part, meanwhile the hat, tie, boots, gloves and underclothing all clamour for attention and, before I have got them well in hand, the new suit has lost its freshness. Still, if ever I do get any money, I will try and make myself really spruce all round till I find out, as I probably shall in about a week, that if I give my clothes an inch they will take an ell. [1880.]

Money

is the last enemy that shall never be subdued. While there is flesh there is money—or the want of money; but money is always on the brain so long as there is a brain in reasonable order.

A Luxurious Death

Death in anything like luxury is one of the most expensive things a man can indulge himself in. It costs a lot of money to die comfortably, unless one goes off pretty quickly.

Money, Health and Reputation

Money, if it live at all, that is to say if it be reproductive and put out at any interest, however low, is mortal and doomed to be lost one day, though it may go on living through many generations of one single family if it be taken care of. No man is absolutely safe. It may be said to any man, "Thou fool, this night thy money shall be required of thee." And reputation is like money: it may be required of us without warning. The little unsuspected evil on which we trip may swell up in a moment and prove to be the huge, Janus-like mountain of unpardonable sin. And his health may be required of any fool, any night or any day.

A man will feel loss of money more keenly than loss of bodily health, so long as he can keep his money. Take his money away and deprive him of the means of earning any more, and his health will soon break up; but leave him his money and, even though his health breaks up and he dies, he does not mind it so much as we think. Money losses are the worst, loss of health is next worst and loss of reputation comes in a bad third. All other things are amusements provided money, health and good name are untouched.

Solicitors

A man must not think he can save himself the trouble of being a sensible man and a gentleman by going to his solicitor, any more than he can get himself a sound constitution by going to his doctor; but a solicitor can do more to keep a tolerably well-meaning fool straight than a doctor can do for an invalid. Money is to the solicitor what souls are to the parson or life to the physician. He is our money-doctor.

Doctors

Going to your doctor is having such a row with your cells that you refer them to your solicitor. Sometimes you, as it were, strike against them and stop their food, when they go on strike against yourself. Sometimes you file a bill in Chancery against them and go to bed.

Priests

We may find an argument in favour of priests if we consider whether man is capable of doing for himself in respect of his moral and spiritual welfare (than which nothing can be more difficult and intricate) what it is so clearly better for him to leave to professional advisers in the case of his money and his body which are comparatively simple and unimportant.

III
The Germs of Erewhon and of Life and Habit

Prefatory Note

The Origin of Species was published in the autumn of 1859, and Butler arrived in New Zealand about the same time and read the book soon afterwards. In 1880 he wrote in *Unconscious Memory* (close of Chapter 1): "As a member of the general public, at that time residing eighteen miles from the nearest human habitation, and three days' journey on horseback from a bookseller's shop, I became one of Mr. Darwin's many enthusiastic admirers, and wrote a philosophic dialogue (the most offensive form, except poetry and books of travel into supposed unknown countries, that even literature can assume) upon the *Origin of Species*. This production appeared in the *Press*, Canterbury, New Zealand, in 1861 or 1862, but I have long lost the only copy I had."

The Press was founded by James Edward FitzGerald, the first Superintendent of the Province of Canterbury. Butler was an intimate friend of FitzGerald, was closely associated with the newspaper and frequently wrote for it. The first number appeared 25th May, 1861, and on 25th May, 1911, the Press celebrated its jubilee with a number which contained particulars of its early life, of its editors, and of Butler; it also contained reprints of two of Butler's contributions, viz. *Darwin among the Machines*, which originally appeared in its columns 13 June, 1863; and *Lucubratio Ebria*, which originally appeared 29 July, 1865. The Dialogue was not reprinted because, although the editor knew of its existence and searched for it, he could not find it. At my request, after the appearance of the jubilee number, a further search was made, but the Dialogue was not found and I gave it up for lost.

In March, 1912, Mr. R. A. Streatfeild pointed out to me that Mr. Tregaskis, in Holborn, was advertising for sale an autograph letter by Charles Darwin sending to an unknown editor a Dialogue on Species from a New Zealand newspaper, described in the letter as being "remarkable from its spirit and from giving so clear and accurate a view of Mr. D.'s theory." Having no doubt that this referred to Butler's lost contribution to the *Press*, I bought the autograph letter and sent it to New Zealand, where it now is in the Canterbury Museum, Christchurch. With it I sent a letter to the editor of the *Press*, giving all further information in my possession about the Dialogue. This letter, which appeared 1 June, 1912, together with the presentation of Darwin's autograph, stimulated further search, and in the issue for 20th December, 1862, the Dialogue was found by Miss Colborne-Veel, whose father was editor of the paper at the time Butler was writing for it. The *Press* reprinted the Dialogue 8th June, 1912.

When the Dialogue first appeared it excited a great deal of discussion in the colony and, to quote Butler's words in a letter to Darwin (1865), "called forth a contemptuous rejoinder from (I believe) the Bishop of Wellington." This rejoinder was an article headed "Barrel-Organs," the idea being that there was nothing new in Darwin's book, it was only a grinding out of old tunes with which we were all familiar. Butler alludes to this controversy in a note made on a letter from Darwin which he gave to the British Museum. "I remember answering an attack (in the *Press*, New Zealand) on me by Bishop Abraham, of Wellington, as though I were someone else, and, to keep up the deception, attacking myself also. But it was all very young and silly." The bishop's article and Butler's reply, which was a letter signed A. M. and some of the resulting correspondence were reprinted in the *Press*, 15th June, 1912.

At first I thought of including here the Dialogue, and perhaps the letter signed A. M. They are interesting as showing that Butler was among the earliest to study closely the *Origin of Species*, and also as showing the state of his mind before he began to think for himself, before he wrote *Darwin among the Machines* from which so much followed; but they can hardly be properly considered as germs of *Erewhon* and *Life and Habit*. They rather show the preparation of the soil in which those germs sprouted and grew; and, remembering his last remark on the subject that "it was all very young and silly," I decided to omit them. The Dialogue is no longer lost, and the numbers of the *Press* containing it and the correspondence that ensued can be seen in the British Museum.

Butler's other two contributions to the *Press* mentioned above do contain the germs of the machine chapters in *Erewhon*, and led him to the theory put forward in *Life and Habit*. In 1901 he wrote in the preface to the new and revised edition of *Erewhon*: "The first part of *Erewhon* written was an article headed *Darwin among the Machines* and signed 'Cellarius.' It was written in the Upper Rangitata district of Canterbury Province (as it then was) of New Zealand, and appeared at Christchurch in the *Press* newspaper, June 13, 1863. A copy of this article is indexed under my books in the British Museum catalogue."

The article is in the form of a letter, and the copy spoken of by Butler, as indexed under his name in the British Museum, being defective, the reprint which appeared in the jubilee number of the *Press* has been used in completing the version which follows.

Further on in the preface to the 1901 edition of *Erewhon* he writes: "A second article on the same subject as the one just referred to appeared in the *Press* shortly after the first, but I have no copy. It treated machines from a different point of view and was the basis of -274 of the present edition of *Erewhon*. This view ultimately led me to the theory I put forward in *Life and Habit*, published in November, 1877. [41] I have put a bare outline of this theory (which I believe to be quite sound) into the mouth of an Erewhonian professor in Chapter XXVII of this book."

This second article was *Lucubratio Ebria*, and was sent by Butler from England to the editor of the *Press* in 1865, with a letter from which this is an extract:

> "I send you an article which you can give to FitzGerald or not, just as you think it most expedient—for him. Is not the subject worked out, and are not the Canterbury people tired of Darwinism? For me—is it an article to my credit? I do not send it to FitzGerald because I am sure he would put it into the paper.... I know the undue lenience which he lends to my performances, and believe you to be the sterner critic of the two. That there are some good things in it you will, I think, feel; but I am almost sure that considering *usque ad nauseam* etc., you will think it had better not appear.... I think you and he will like that sentence: 'There was a moral government of the world before man came into it.' There is hardly a sentence in it written without deliberation; but I need hardly say that it was done upon tea, not upon whiskey ...
>
> "P.S. If you are in any doubt about the expediency of the article take it to M.
>
> "P.P.S. Perhaps better take it to him anyhow."

The preface to the 1901 edition of Erewhon contains some further particulars of the genesis of that work, and there are still further particulars in *Unconscious Memory*, Chapter II, "How I wrote *Life and Habit*."

The first tentative sketch of the *Life and Habit* theory occurs in the letter to Thomas William Gale Butler which is given post. This T. W. G. Butler was not related to Butler, they met first as art-students at Heatherley's, and Butler used to speak of him as the most brilliant man he had ever known. He died many years ago. He was the writer of the "letter from a friend now in New Zealand," from which a quotation is given in *Life and Habit*, Chapter V (, 84). Butler kept a copy of his letter to T. W. G. Butler, but it was imperfectly pressed; he afterwards supplied some of the missing words from memory, and gave it to the British Museum.

Darwin among the Machines

[To the Editor of the *Press*, Christchurch, New Zealand — 13 June, 1863.]

Sir — There are few things of which the present generation is more justly proud than of the wonderful improvements which are daily taking place in all sorts of mechanical appliances. And indeed it is matter for great congratulation on many grounds. It is unnecessary to mention these here, for they are sufficiently obvious; our present business lies with considerations which may somewhat tend to humble our pride and to make us think seriously of the future prospects of the human race. If we revert to the earliest primordial types of mechanical life, to the lever, the wedge, the inclined plane, the screw and the pulley, or (for analogy would lead us one step further) to that one primordial type from which all the mechanical kingdom has been developed, we mean to the lever itself, and if we then examine the machinery of the *Great Eastern*, we find ourselves almost awestruck at the vast development of the mechanical world, at the gigantic strides with which it has advanced in comparison with the slow progress of the animal and vegetable kingdom. We shall find it impossible to refrain from asking ourselves what the end of this mighty movement is to be. In what direction is it tending? What will be its upshot? To give a few imperfect hints towards a solution of these questions is the object of the present letter.

We have used the words "mechanical life," "the mechanical kingdom," "the mechanical world" and so forth, and we have done so advisedly, for as the vegetable kingdom was slowly developed from the mineral, and as, in like manner, the animal supervened upon the vegetable, so now, in these last few ages, an entirely new kingdom has sprung up of which we as yet have only seen what will one day be considered the antediluvian prototypes of the race.

We regret deeply that our knowledge both of natural history and of machinery is too small to enable us to undertake the gigantic task of classifying machines into the genera and sub-genera, species, varieties and sub-varieties, and so forth, of tracing the connecting links between machines of widely different characters, of pointing out how subservience to the use of man has played that part among machines which natural selection has performed in the animal and vegetable kingdom, of pointing out rudimentary organs [*see note*] which exist in some few machines, feebly developed and perfectly useless, yet serving to mark descent from some ancestral type which has either perished or been modified into some new phase of mechanical existence. We can only point out this field for investigation; it must be followed by others whose education and talents have been of a much higher order than any which we can lay claim to.

Some few hints we have determined to venture upon, though we do so with the profoundest diffidence. Firstly we would remark that as some of the lowest of the vertebrata attained a far greater size than has descended to their more highly organised living representatives, so a diminution in the size of machines has often attended their development and progress. Take the watch for instance. Examine the beautiful structure of the little animal, watch the intelligent play of the minute members which compose it; yet this little creature is but a development of the cumbrous clocks of the thirteenth century — it is no deterioration from them. The day may come when clocks, which certainly at the present day are not diminishing in bulk, may be entirely superseded by the universal use of watches, in which case clocks will become extinct like the earlier saurians, while the watch (whose tendency has for some years been rather to decrease in size than the contrary) will remain the only existing type of an extinct race.

The views of machinery which we are thus feebly indicating will suggest the solution of one of the greatest and most mysterious questions of the day. We refer to the question: What sort of creature man's next successor in the supremacy of the earth is likely to be. We have often heard this debated; but it appears to us that we are ourselves creating our own successors; we are daily adding to the beauty and delicacy of their physical organisation; we are daily giving them greater power and supplying, by all sorts of ingenious contrivances, that self-regulating, self-acting power which will be to them what intellect has been to the human race. In the course of ages we shall find ourselves the inferior race. Inferior in power, inferior in that moral quality of self-control, we shall look up to them as the acme of all that the best and wisest man can ever dare to aim at. No evil passions, no jealousy, no avarice, no impure desires will disturb the serene might of those glorious creatures. Sin, shame and sorrow will have no place among them. Their minds will be in a state of perpetual calm, the contentment of a spirit that knows no wants, is disturbed by no regrets. Ambition will never torture them. Ingratitude will never cause them the uneasiness of a moment. The guilty conscience, the hope deferred, the pains of exile, the insolence of office and the spurns that patient merit of the unworthy takes — these will be entirely unknown to them. If they want "feeding" (by the use of which very word we betray our recognition of them as living organism) they will be attended by patient slaves whose business and interest it will be to see that they shall want for nothing. If they are out of order they will be promptly attended to by physicians who are thoroughly acquainted with their constitutions; if they die, for even these glorious animals will not be exempt from that necessary and universal consummation, they will immediately enter into a new phase of existence, for what machine dies entirely in every part at one and the same instant?

We take it that when the state of things shall have arrived which we have been above attempting to describe, man will have become to the machine what the horse and the dog are to man. He will continue to exist, nay even to improve, and will be probably better off in his state of domestication under the beneficent rule of the machines than he is in his present wild state. We treat our horses, dogs, cattle and sheep, on the whole, with great kindness, we give them whatever experience teaches us to be best for them, and there can be no doubt that our use of meat has added to the happiness of the lower animals far more than it has detracted from it; in like manner it is reasonable to suppose that the machines will treat us kindly, for their existence is as dependent upon ours as ours is upon the lower animals. They cannot kill us and eat us as we do sheep, they will not only require our services in the parturition of their young (which branch of their economy will remain always in our hands) but also in feeding them, in setting them right if they are sick, and burying their dead or working up their corpses into new machines. It is obvious that if all the animals in Great Britain save man alone were to die, and if at the same time all intercourse with foreign countries were by some sudden catastrophe to be rendered perfectly impossible, it is obvious that under such circumstances the loss of human life would be something fearful to contemplate — in like manner, were mankind to cease, the machines would be as badly off or even worse. The fact is that our interests are inseparable from theirs, and theirs from ours. Each race is dependent upon the other for innumerable benefits, and, until the reproductive organs of the machines have been developed in a manner which we are hardly yet able to conceive, they are entirely dependent upon man for even the continuance of their species. It is true that these organs may be ultimately developed, inasmuch as man's interest lies in that direction; there is nothing which our infatuated race would desire more than to see a fertile union between two steam engines; it is true that machinery is even at this present time employed in begetting machinery, in becoming the parent of machines often after its own kind, but the days of flirtation, courtship and matrimony appear to be very remote and indeed can hardly be realised by our feeble and imperfect imagination.

Day by day, however, the machines are gaining ground upon us; day by day we are becoming more subservient to them; more men are daily bound down as slaves to tend them, more men are daily devoting the energies of their whole lives to the development of mechanical life. The upshot is simply a question of time, but that the time will come when the machines will hold the real supremacy over the world and its inhabitants is what no person of a truly philosophic mind can for a moment question.

Our opinion is that war to the death should be instantly proclaimed against them. Every machine of every sort should be destroyed by the well-wisher of his species. Let there be no exceptions made, no quarter shown; let us at once go back to the primeval condition of the race. If it be urged that this is impossible under the present condition of human affairs, this at once proves that the mischief is already done, that our servitude has commenced in good earnest, that we have raised a race of beings whom it is beyond our power to destroy and that we are not only enslaved but are absolutely acquiescent in our bondage.

For the present we shall leave this subject which we present gratis to the members of the Philosophical Society. Should they consent to avail themselves of the vast field which we have pointed out, we shall endeavour to labour in it ourselves at some future and indefinite period.

I am, Sir, &c.,
Cellarius.

Note.—We were asked by a learned brother philosopher who saw this article in MS. what we meant by alluding to rudimentary organs in machines. Could we, he asked, give any example of such organs? We pointed to the little protuberance at the bottom of the bowl of our tobacco pipe. This organ was originally designed for the same purpose as the rim at the bottom of a tea-cup, which is but another form of the same function. Its purpose was to keep the heat of the pipe from marking the table on which it rested. Originally, as we have seen in very early tobacco pipes, this protuberance was of a very different shape to what it is now. It was broad at the bottom and flat, so that while the pipe was being smoked, the bowl might rest upon the table. Use and disuse have here come into play and served to reduce the function to its present rudimentary condition. That these rudimentary organs are rarer in machinery than in animal life is owing to the more prompt action of the human selection as compared with the slower but even surer operation of natural selection. Man may make mistakes; in the long run nature never does so. We have only given an imperfect example, but the intelligent reader will supply himself with illustrations.

Lucubratio Ebria

[From the *Press*, 29 July, 1865]

There is a period in the evening, or more generally towards the still small hours of the morning, in which we so far unbend as to take a single glass of hot whisky and water. We will neither defend the practice nor excuse it. We state it as a fact which must be borne in mind by the readers of this article; for we know not how, whether it be the inspiration of the drink, or the relief from the harassing work with which the day has been occupied, or from whatever other cause, yet we are certainly liable about this time to such a prophetic influence as we seldom else experience. We are rapt in a dream such as we ourselves know to be a dream, and which, like other dreams, we can hardly embody in a distinct utterance. We know that what we see is but a sort of intellectual Siamese twins, of which one is substance and the other shadow, but we cannot set either free without killing both. We are unable to rudely tear away the veil of phantasy in which the truth is shrouded, so we present the reader with a draped figure, and his own judgment must discriminate between the clothes and the body. A truth's prosperity is like a jest's, it lies in the ear of him that hears it. Some may see our lucubration as we saw it; and others may see nothing but a drunken dream, or the nightmare of a distempered imagination. To ourselves it as the speaking with unknown tongues to the early Corinthians; we cannot fully understand our own speech, and we fear lest there be not a sufficient number of interpreters present to make our utterance edify. But there! (Go on straight to the body of the article.)

The limbs of the lower animals have never been modified by any act of deliberation and forethought on their own part. Recent researches have thrown absolutely no light upon the origin of life—upon the initial force which introduced a sense of identity, and a deliberate faculty into the world; but they do certainly appear to show very clearly that each species of the animal and vegetable kingdom has been moulded into its present shape by chances and changes of many millions of years, by chances and changes over which the creature modified had no control whatever, and concerning whose aim it was alike unconscious and indifferent, by forces which seem insensate to the pain which they inflict, but by whose inexorably beneficent cruelty the brave and strong keep coming to the fore, while the weak and bad drop behind and perish. There was a moral government of this world before man came near it—a moral government suited to the capacities of the governed, and which, unperceived by them, has laid fast the foundations of courage, endurance and cunning. It laid them so fast that they became more and more hereditary. Horace says well, *fortes creantur fortibus et bonis* good men beget good children; the rule held even in the geological period; good ichthyosauri begat good ichthyosauri, and would to our discomfort have gone on doing so to the present time, had not better creatures been begetting better things than ichthyosauri, or famine, or fire, or convulsion put an end to them. Good apes begat good apes, and at last when human intelligence stole like a late spring upon the mimicry of our semi-simious ancestry, the creature learnt how he could, of his own forethought, add extra-corporaneous limbs to the members of his body and become not only a vertebrate mammal, but a vertebrate machinate mammal into the bargain.

It was a wise monkey that first learned to carry a stick and a useful monkey that mimicked him. For the race of man has learned to walk uprightly much as a child learns the same thing. At first he crawls on all fours, then he clambers, laying hold of whatever he can; and lastly he stands upright alone and walks, but for a long time with an unsteady step. So when the human race was in its gorilla-hood it generally carried a stick; from carrying a stick for many million years it became accustomed and modified to an upright position. The stick wherewith it had learned to walk would now serve it to beat its younger brothers and then it found out its service as a lever. Man would thus learn that the limbs of his body were not the only limbs that he could command. His body was already the most versatile in existence, but he could render it more versatile still. With the improvement in his body his mind improved also. He learnt to perceive the moral government under which he held the feudal tenure of his life—perceiving it he symbolised it, and to this day our poets and prophets still strive to symbolise it more and more completely.

The mind grew because the body grew—more things were perceived—more things were handled, and being handled became familiar. But this came about chiefly because there was a hand to handle with; without the hand there would be no handling; and no method of holding and examining is comparable to the human hand. The tail of an opossum is a prehensile thing, but it is too far from his eyes—the elephant's trunk is better, and it is probably to their trunks that the elephants owe their sagacity. It is here that the bee in spite of her wings has failed. She has a high civilisation but it is one whose equilibrium appears to have been already attained; the appearance is a false one, for the bee changes, though more slowly than man can watch her; but the reason of the very gradual nature of the change is chiefly because the physical organisation of the insect changes, but slowly also. She is poorly off for hands, and has never fairly grasped the notion of tacking on other limbs to the limbs of her own body and so, being short-lived to boot, she remains from century to century to human eyes in *statu quo*. Her body never becomes machinate, whereas this new phase of organism, which has been introduced with man into the mundane economy, has made him a very quicksand for the foundation of an unchanging civilisation; certain fundamental principles will always remain, but every century the change in man's physical status, as compared with the elements around him, is greater and greater; he is a shifting basis on which no equilibrium of habit and civilisation can be established; were it not for this constant change in our physical powers, which our mechanical limbs have brought about, man would have long since apparently attained his limit of possibility; he would be a creature of as much fixity as the ants and bees—he would still have advanced but no faster than other animals advance. If there were a race of men without any mechanical appliances we should see this clearly. There are none, nor have there been, so far as we can tell, for millions and millions of years. The lowest Australian savage carries weapons for the fight or the chase, and has his cooking and drinking utensils at home; a race without these things would be completely *ferae naturae* and not men at all. We are unable to point to any example of a race absolutely devoid of extra-corporaneous limbs, but we can see among the Chinese that with the failure to invent new limbs, a civilisation becomes as much fixed as that of the ants; and among savage tribes we observe that few implements involve a state of things scarcely human at all. Such tribes only advance *pari passu* with the creatures upon which they feed.

It is a mistake, then, to take the view adopted by a previous correspondent of this paper; to consider the machines as identities, to animalise them, and to anticipate their final triumph over mankind. They are to be regarded as the mode of development by which human organism is most especially advancing, and every fresh invention is to be considered as an additional member of the resources of the human body. Herein lies the fundamental difference between man and his inferiors. As regards his flesh and blood, his senses, appetites, and affections, the difference is one of degree rather than of kind, but in the deliberate invention of such unity of limbs as is exemplified by the railway train—that seven-leagued foot which five hundred may own at once—he stands quite alone.

In confirmation of the views concerning mechanism which we have been advocating above, it must be remembered that men are not merely the children of their parents, but they are begotten of the institutions of the state of the mechanical sciences under which they are born and bred. These things have made us what we are. We are children of the plough, the spade, and the ship; we are children of the extended liberty and knowledge which the printing press has diffused. Our ancestors added these things to their previously existing members; the new limbs were preserved by natural selection, and incorporated into human society; they descended with modifications, and hence proceeds the difference between our ancestors and ourselves. By the institutions and state of science under which a man is born it is determined whether he shall have the limbs of an Australian savage or those of a nineteenth century Englishman. The former is supplemented with little save a rug and a javelin; the latter varies his physique with the changes of the season, with age, and with advancing or decreasing wealth. If it is wet he is furnished with an organ which is called an umbrella and which seems designed for the purpose of protecting either his clothes or his lungs from the injurious effects of rain. His watch is of more importance to him than a good deal of his hair, at any rate than of his whiskers; besides this he carries a knife, and generally a pencil case. His memory goes in a pocket book. He grows more complex as he becomes older and he will then be seen with a pair of spectacles, perhaps also with false teeth and a wig; but, if he be a really well-developed specimen of the race, he will be furnished with a large box upon wheels, two horses, and a coachman.

Let the reader ponder over these last remarks, and he will see that the principal varieties and sub-varieties of the human race are not now to be looked for among the negroes, the Circassians, the Malays, or the American aborigines, but among the rich and the poor. The difference in physical organisation between these two species of man is far greater than that between the so-called types of humanity. The rich man can go from here to England whenever he feels so inclined. The legs of the other are by an invisible fatality prevented from carrying him beyond certain narrow limits. Neither rich nor poor as yet see the philosophy of the thing, or admit that he who can tack a portion of one of the P. & O. boats on to his identity is a much more highly organised being than one who cannot. Yet the fact is patent enough, if we once think it over, from the mere consideration of the respect with which we so often treat those who are richer than ourselves. We observe men for the most part (admitting however some few abnormal exceptions) to be deeply impressed by the superior organisation of those who have money. It is wrong to attribute this respect to any unworthy motive, for the feeling is strictly legitimate and springs from some of the very highest impulses of our nature. It is the same sort of affectionate reverence which a dog feels for man, and is not infrequently manifested in a similar manner.

We admit that these last sentences are open to question, and we should hardly like to commit ourselves irrecoverably to the sentiments they express; but we will say this much for certain, namely, that the rich man is the true hundred-handed Gyges of the poets. He alone possesses the full complement of limbs who stands at the summit of opulence, and we may assert with strictly scientific accuracy that the Rothschilds are the most astonishing organisms that the world has ever yet seen. For to the nerves or tissues, or whatever it be that answers to the helm of a rich man's desires, there is a whole army of limbs seen and unseen attachable: he may be reckoned by his horse-power — by the number of foot-pounds which he has money enough to set in motion. Who, then, will deny that a man whose will represents the motive power of a thousand horses is a being very different from the one who is equivalent but to the power of a single one?

Henceforward, then, instead of saying that a man is hard up, let us say that his organisation is at a low ebb, or, if we wish him well, let us hope that he will grow plenty of limbs. It must be remembered that we are dealing with physical organisations only. We do not say that the thousand-horse man is better than a one-horse man, we only say that he is more highly organised, and should be recognised as being so by the scientific leaders of the period. A man's will, truth, endurance are part of him also, and may, as in the case of the late Mr. Cobden, have in themselves a power equivalent to all the horse-power which they can influence; but were we to go into this part of the question we should never have done, and we are compelled reluctantly to leave our dream in its present fragmentary condition.

Letter to Thomas William Gale Butler

February 18th, 1876.

My dear Namesake . . .

My present literary business is a little essay some 25 or 30 pp. long, which is still all in the rough and I don't know how it will shape, but the gist of it is somewhat as follows: —

1. Actions which we have acquired with difficulty and now perform almost unconsciously — as in playing a difficult piece of music, reading, talking, walking and the multitude of actions which escape our notice inside other actions, etc. — all this worked out with some detail, say, four or five pages.

General deduction that we never do anything in this unconscious or semi-conscious manner unless we know how to do it exceedingly well and have had long practice.

Also that consciousness is a vanishing quantity and that as soon as we know a thing really well we become unconscious in respect of it — consciousness being of attention and attention of uncertainty — and hence the paradox comes clear, that as long as we know that we know a thing (or do an action knowingly) we do not know it (or do the action with thorough knowledge of our business) and that we only know it when we do not know of our knowledge.

2. Whatever we do in this way is all one and the same in kind — the difference being only in degree. Playing [almost?] unconsciously — writing, more unconsciously (as to each letter) — reading, very unconsciously — talking, still more unconsciously (it is almost impossible for us to notice the action of our tongue in every letter) — walking, much the same — breathing, still to a certain extent within our own control — heart's beating, perceivable but beyond our control — digestion, unperceivable and beyond our control, digestion being the oldest of the . . . habits.

3. A baby, therefore, has known how to grow itself in the womb and has only done it because it wanted to, on a balance of considerations, in the same way as a man who goes into the City to buy Great Northern A Shares . . . It

is only unconscious of these operations because it has done them a very large number of times already. A man may do a thing by a fluke once, but to say that a foetus can perform so difficult an operation as the growth of a pair of eyes out of pure protoplasm without knowing how to do it, and without ever having done it before, is to contradict all human experience. Ipso facto that it does it, it knows how to do it, and ipso facto that it knows how to do it, it has done it before. Its unconsciousness (or speedy loss of memory) is simply the result of over-knowledge, not of under-knowledge. It knows so well and has done it so often that its power of self-analysis is gone. If it knew what it was doing, or was conscious of its own act in oxidising its blood after birth, I should suspect that it had not done it so often before; as it is I am confident that it must have done it more often—much more often—than any act which we perform consciously during our whole lives.

4. When, then, did it do it? Clearly when last it was an impregnate ovum or some still lower form of life which resulted in that impregnate ovum.

5. How is it, then, that it has not gained perceptible experience? Simply because a single repetition makes little or no difference; but go back 20,000 repetitions and you will find that it has gained in experience and modified its performance very materially.

6. But how about the identity? What is identity? Identity of matter? Surely no. There is no identity of matter between me as I now am, and me as an impregnate ovum. Continuity of existence? Then there is identity between me as an impregnate ovum and my father and mother as impregnate ova. Drop out my father's and mother's lives between the dates of their being impregnate ova and the moment when I became an impregnate ovum. See the ova only and consider the second ovum as the first two ova's means not of reproducing themselves but of continuing themselves—repeating themselves—the intermediate lives being nothing but, as it were, a long potato shoot from one eye to the place where it will grow its next tuber.

7. Given a single creature capable of reproducing itself and it must go on reproducing itself for ever, for it would not reproduce itself, unless it reproduced a creature that was going to reproduce itself, and so on ad infinitum.

Then comes Descent with Modification. Similarity tempered with dissimilarity, and dissimilarity tempered with similarity—a contradiction in terms, like almost everything else that is true or useful or indeed intelligible at all. In each case of what we call descent, it is still the first reproducing creature identically the same—doing what it has done before—only with such modifications as the struggle for existence and natural selection have induced. No matter how highly it has been developed, it can never be other than the primordial cell and must always begin as the primordial cell and repeat its last performance most nearly, but also, more or less, all its previous performances.

A begets A' which is A with the additional experience of a dash. A' begets A" which is A with the additional experiences of A' and A"; and so on to An but you can never eliminate the A.

8. Let An stand for a man. He begins as the primordial cell—being verily nothing but the primordial cell which goes on splitting itself up for ever, but gaining continually in experience. Put him in the same position as he was in before and he will do as he did before. First he will do his tadpoles by rote, so to speak, on his head, from long practice; then he does his fish trick; then he grows arms and legs, all unconsciously from the inveteracy of the habit, till he comes to doing his man, and this lesson he has not yet learnt so thoroughly. Some part of it, as the breathing and oxidisation business, he is well up to, inasmuch as they form part of previous roles, but the teeth and hair, the upright position, the power of speech, though all tolerably familiar, give him more trouble—for he is very stupid—a regular dunce in fact. Then comes his newer and more complex environment, and this puzzles him—arrests his attention—whereon consciousness springs into existence, as a spark from a horse's hoof.

To be continued—I see it will have to be more than 30 pp. It is still foggy in parts, but I must clear it a little. It will go on to show that we are all one animal and that death (which was at first voluntary, and has only come to be disliked because those who did not dislike it committed suicide too easily) and reproduction are only phases of the ordinary waste and repair which goes on in our bodies daily.

Always very truly yours,

S. Butler.

IV
Memory and Design

Clergymen and Chickens

[*Extract from a lecture* On Memory as a Key to the Phenomena of Heredity *delivered by Butler at the Working Men's College, Great Ormond Street, on Saturday, 2nd December, 1882.*]

Why, let me ask, should a hen lay an egg which egg can become a chicken in about three weeks and a full-grown hen in less than a twelvemonth, while a clergyman and his wife lay no eggs but give birth to a baby which will take three-and-twenty years before it can become another clergyman? Why should not chickens be born and clergymen be laid and hatched? Or why, at any rate, should not the clergyman be born full grown and in Holy Orders, not to say already beneficed? The present arrangement is not convenient, it is not cheap, it is not free from danger, it is not only not perfect but is so much the reverse that we could hardly find words to express our sense of its awkwardness if we could look upon it with new eyes, or as the cuckoo perhaps observes it.

The explanation usually given is that it is a law of nature that children should be born as they are, but this is like the parched pea which St. Anthony set before the devil when he came to supper with him and of which the devil said that it was good as far as it went. We want more; we want to know with what familiar set of facts we are to connect the one in question which, though in our midst, at present dwells apart as a mysterious stranger of whose belongings, reason for coming amongst us, antecedents, and so forth, we believe ourselves to be ignorant, though we know him by sight and name and have a fair idea what sort of man he is to deal with.

We say it is a phenomenon of heredity that chickens should be laid as eggs in the first instance and clergymen born as babies, but, beyond the fact that we know heredity extremely well to look at and to do business with, we say that we know nothing about it. I have for some years maintained this to be a mistake and have urged, in company with Professor Hering, of Prague, and others, that the connection between memory and heredity is so close that there is no reason for regarding the two as generically different, though for convenience sake it may be well to specify them by different names. If I can persuade you that this is so, I believe I shall be able to make you understand why it is that chickens are hatched as eggs and clergymen born as babies.

When I say I can make you understand why this is so, I only mean that I can answer the first "why" that any one is likely to ask about it, and perhaps a "why" or two behind this. Then I must stop. This is all that is ever meant by those who say they can tell us why a thing is so and so. No one professes to be able to reach back to the last "why" that any one can ask, and to answer it. Fortunately for philosophers, people generally become fatigued after they have heard the answer to two or three "whys" and are glad enough to let the matter drop. If, however, any one will insist on pushing question behind question long enough, he will compel us to admit that we come to the end of our knowledge which is based ultimately upon ignorance. To get knowledge out of ignorance seems almost as hopeless a task as to get something out of any number of nothings, but this in practice is what we have to do and the less fuss we make over it the better.

When, therefore, we say that we know "why" a thing is so and so, we mean that we know its immediate antecedents and connections, and find them familiar to us. I say that the immediate antecedent of, and the phenomenon most closely connected with, heredity is memory. I do not profess to show why anything can remember at all, I only maintain that whereas, to borrow an illustration from mathematics, life was formerly an equation of, say, 100 unknown quantities, it is now one of only, inasmuch as memory and heredity have been shown to be one and the same thing.

Memory

i

Memory is a kind of way (or weight—whichever it should be) that the mind has got upon it, in virtue of which the sensation excited endures a little longer than the cause which excited it. There is thus induced a state of things in which mental images, and even physical sensations (if there can be such a thing as a physical sensation) exist by virtue of association, though the conditions which originally called them into existence no longer continue.

This is as the echo continuing to reverberate after the sound has ceased.

ii

To be is to think and to be thinkable. To live is to continue thinking and to remember having done so. Memory is to mind as viscosity is to protoplasm, it gives a tenacity to thought—a kind of *pied à terre* from which it can, and without which it could not, advance.

Thought, in fact, and memory seem inseparable; no thought, no memory; and no memory, no thought. And, as conscious thought and conscious memory are functions one of another, so also are unconscious thought and unconscious memory. Memory is, as it were, the body of thought, and it is through memory that body and mind are linked together in rhythm or vibration; for body is such as it is by reason of the characteristics of the vibrations that are going on in it, and memory is only due to the fact that the vibrations are of such characteristics as to catch on to and be caught on to by other vibrations that flow into them from without—no catch, no memory.

Antitheses

Memory and forgetfulness are as life and death to one another. To live is to remember and to remember is to live. To die is to forget and to forget is to die. Everything is so much involved in and is so much a process of its opposite that, as it is almost fair to call death a process of life and life a process of death, so it is to call memory a process of forgetting and forgetting a process of remembering. There is never either absolute memory or absolute forgetfulness, absolute life or absolute death. So with light and darkness, heat and cold, you never can get either all the light, or all the heat, out of anything. So with God and the devil; so with everything. Everything is like a door swinging backwards and forwards. Everything has a little of that from which it is most remote and to which it is most opposed and these antitheses serve to explain one another.

Unconscious Memory

A man at the Century Club was falling foul of me the other night for my use of the word "memory." There was no such thing, he said, as "unconscious memory"—memory was always conscious, and so forth. My business is—and I think it can be easily done—to show that they cannot beat me off my unconscious memory without my being able to beat them off their conscious memory; that they cannot deny the legitimacy of my maintaining the phenomena of heredity to be phenomena of memory without my being able to deny the legitimacy of their maintaining the recollection of what they had for dinner yesterday to be a phenomenon of memory. My theory of the unconscious does not lead to universal unconsciousness, but only to pigeon-holing and putting by. We shall always get new things to worry about. If I thought that by learning more and more I should ever arrive at the knowledge of absolute truth, I would leave off studying. But I believe I am pretty safe.

Reproduction and Memory

There is the reproduction of an idea which has been produced once already, and there is the reproduction of a living form which has been produced once already. The first reproduction is certainly an effort of memory. It should not therefore surprise us if the second reproduction should turn out to be an effort of memory also. Indeed all forms of reproduction that we can follow are based directly or indirectly upon memory. It is only the one great act of reproduction that we cannot follow which we disconnect from memory.

Personal Identity

We are so far identical with our ancestors and our contemporaries that it is very rarely we can see anything that they do not see. It is not unjust that the sins of the fathers should be visited upon the children, for the children committed the sins when in the persons of their fathers; they ate the sour grapes before they were born: true, they have forgotten the pleasure now, but so has a man with a sick headache forgotten the pleasure of getting drunk the night before.

Sensations

Our sensations are only distinguishable because we feel them in different places and at different times. If we feel them at very nearly the same time and place we cannot distinguish them.

Cobwebs in the Dark

If you walk at night and your face comes up against a spider's web woven across the road, what a shock that thin line gives you! You fristle through every nerve of your body.

Shocks and Memory

Memory is our sense that we are being shocked now as we were shocked then.

Shocks

Given matter conscious in one part of itself of a shock in another part (i.e. knowing in what part of itself it is shocked) retaining a memory of each shock for a little while afterwards, able to feel whether two shocks are simultaneous or in succession, and able to know whether it has been shocked much or little — given also that association does not stick to the letter of its bond — and the rest will follow.

Design

i

There is often connection but no design, as when I stamp my foot with design and shake something down without design, or as when a man runs up against another in the street and knocks him down without intending it. This is undesign within design.

Fancied insults are felt by people who see design in a connection where they should see little connection, and no design.

Connection with design is sometimes hard to distinguish from connection without design; as when a man treads on another's corns, it is not always easy to say whether he has done so accidentally or on purpose.

Men have been fond in all ages of ascribing connection where there is none. Thus astrology has been believed in. Before last Christmas I said I had neglected the feasts of the Church too much, and that I should probably be more prosperous if I paid more attention to them: so I hung up three pieces of ivy in my rooms on Xmas Eve. A few months afterwards I got the entail cut off my reversion, but I should hardly think there was much connection between the two things. Nevertheless I shall hang some holly up this year.

ii

It seems also designed, ab extra (though who can say whether this is so?), that no one should know anything whatever about the ultimate, or even deeper springs of growth and action. If not designed the result is arrived at as effectually as though it were so.

Accident, Design and Memory

It is right to say either that heredity and memory are one and the same thing, or that heredity is a mode of memory, or that heredity is due to memory, if it is thereby intended that animals can only grow in virtue of being able to recollect. Memory and heredity are the means of preserving experiences, of building them together, of uniting a mass of often confused detail into homogeneous and consistent mind and matter, but they do not originate. The increment in each generation, at the moment of its being an increment, has nothing to do with memory or heredity, it is due to the chances and changes of this mortal state. Design comes in at the moment that a living being either feels a want and forecasts for its gratification, or utilises some waif or stray of accident on the principle, which underlies all development, that enough is a little more than what one has. It is the business of memory and heredity to conserve and to transmit from one generation to another that which has been furnished by design, or by accident designedly turned to account.

It is therefore not right to say, as some have supposed me to mean, that we can do nothing which we do not remember to have done before. We can do nothing very difficult or complicated which we have not done before, unless as by a tour de force, once in a way, under exceptionally favourable circumstances, but our whole conscious life is the performance of acts either imperfectly remembered or not remembered at all. There are rain-drops of new experiences in every life which are not within the hold of our memory or past experience, and, as each one of these rain-drops came originally from something outside, the whole river of our life has in its inception nothing to do with memory, though it is only through memory that the rain-drops of new experience can ever unite to form a full flowing river of variously organised life and intelligence.

Memory and Mistakes

Memory vanishes with extremes of resemblance or difference. Things which put us in mind of others must be neither too like nor too unlike them. It is our sense that a position is not quite the same which makes us find it so nearly the same. We remember by the aid of differences as much as by that of samenesses. If there could be no difference there would be no memory, for the two positions would become absolutely one and the same, and the universe would repeat itself for ever and ever as between these two points.

When ninety-nine hundredths of one set of phenomena are presented while the hundredth is withdrawn without apparent cause, so that we can no longer do something which according to our past experience we ought to find no difficulty in doing, then we may guess what a bee must feel as it goes flying up and down a window-pane. Then we have doubts thrown upon the fundamental axiom of life, i.e. that like antecedents will be followed by like consequents. On this we go mad and die in a short time.

Mistaken memory may be as potent as genuine recollection, so far as its effects go, unless it happens to come more into collision with other and not mistaken memories than it is able to contend against.

Mistakes or delusions occur mainly in two ways.

First, when the circumstances have changed a little but not enough to make us recognise the fact: this may happen either because of want of attention on our part or because of the hidden nature of the alteration, or because of its slightness in itself, the importance depending upon its relations to something else which make a very small change have an importance it would not otherwise have: in these cases the memory reverts to the old circumstances unmodified, a sufficient number of the associated ideas having been reproduced to make us assume the remainder without further inspection, and hence follows a want of harmony between action and circumstances which results in trouble somewhere.

Secondly, through the memory not reverting in full perfection, though the circumstances are reproduced fully and accurately.

Remembering

When asked to remember "something" indefinitely you cannot: you look round at once for something to suggest what you shall try and remember. For thought must be always about some "thing" which thing must either be a thing by courtesy, as an air of Handel's, or else a solid, tangible object, as a piano or an organ, but always the thing must be linked on to matter by a longer or shorter chain as the case may be. I was thinking of this once while walking by the side of the Serpentine and, looking round, saw some ducks alighting on the water; their feet reminded me of the way the sea-birds used to alight when I was going to New Zealand and I set to work recalling attendant facts. Without help from outside I should have remembered nothing.

A Torn Finger-Nail

Henry Hoare [a college friend], when a young man of about five-and-twenty, one day tore the quick of his fingernail—I mean he separated the fleshy part of the finger from the nail—and this reminded him that many years previously, while quite a child, he had done the same thing. Thereon he fell to thinking of that time which was impressed upon his memory partly because there was a great disturbance in the house about a missing five-pound note and partly because it was while he had the scarlet fever.

Following the train of thought aroused by his torn finger, he asked himself how he had torn it, and after a while it came back to him that he had been lying ill in bed as a child of seven at the house of an aunt who lived in Hertfordshire. His arms often hung out of the bed and, as his hands wandered over the wooden frame, he felt that there was a place where nut had come out so that he could put his fingers in. One day, in trying to stuff a piece of paper into this hole, he stuffed it in so far and so tightly that he tore the quick of nail. The whole thing came back vividly and, though he had not thought of it for nearly twenty years, he could see the room in his aunt's house and remembered how his aunt use to sit by his bedside writing at a little table from which he had got the piece of paper which he had stuffed into the hole.

So far so good. But then there flashed upon him an idea that was not so pleasant. I mean it came upon him with irresistible force that the piece of paper, he had stuffed into the hole in the bedstead was the missing five-pound note about which there had been so much disturbance. At that time he was so young that a five-pound note was to him only a piece of paper; when he heard that the money was missing, he had thought it was five sovereigns; or perhaps he was too ill to think anything, or to be questioned; I forget what I was told about this—at any rate he had no idea of the value of the piece of paper he was stuffing into the hole. But now the matter had recurred to him at all he felt so sure that it was the note that he immediately went down to Hertfordshire, where his aunt was still living, and asked, to the surprise of every one, to be allowed to wash his hands in the room he had occupied as a child. He was told that there were friends staying in the house who had the room at present, but, on his saying he had a reason and particularly begging to be allowed to remain alone a little while in this room, he was taken upstairs and left there.

He went to the bed, lifted up the chintz which then covered the frame, and found his old friend the hole. A nut had been supplied and he could no longer get his finger into it. He rang the bell and when the servant came asked for a bed-key. All this time he was rapidly acquiring the reputation of being a lunatic throughout the whole house, but the key was brought, and by the help of it he got the nut off. When he had done so, there, sure enough, by dint of picking with his pocket-knife, he found the missing five-pound note.

See how the return of a given present brings back the presents that have been associated with it.

Unconscious Association

One morning I was whistling to myself the air "In Sweetest Harmony" from *Saul*. Jones heard me and said:

"Do you know why you are whistling that?"

I said I did not.

Then he said: "Did you not hear me, two minutes ago, whistling 'Eagles were not so Swift'?"

I had not noticed his doing so, and it was so long since I had played that chorus myself that I doubt whether I should have consciously recognised it. That I did recognise it unconsciously is tolerably clear from my having gone on with "In Sweetest Harmony," which is the air that follows it.

Association

If you say "Hallelujah" to a cat, it will excite no fixed set of fibres in connection with any other set and the cat will exhibit none of the phenomena of consciousness. But if you say "Me-e-at," the cat will be there in a moment, for the due connection between the sets of fibres has been established.

Language

The reason why words recall ideas is that the word has been artificially introduced among the associated ideas, and the presence of one idea recalls the others.

V
Vibrations

Contributions to Evolution

To me it seems that my contributions to the theory of evolution have been mainly these:

1. The identification of heredity and memory and the corollaries relating to sports, the reversion to remote ancestors, the phenomena of old age, the causes of the sterility of hybrids and the principles underlying longevity — all of which follow as a matter of course. This was *Life and Habit*. [1877.]

2. The re-introduction of teleology into organic life which, to me, seems hardly (if at all) less important than the *Life and Habit* theory. This was *Evolution Old and New*. [1879.]

3. An attempt to suggest an explanation of the physics of memory. I was alarmed by the suggestion and fathered it upon Professor Hering who never, that I can see, meant to say anything of the kind, but I forced my view on him, as it were, by taking hold of a sentence or two in his lecture, on *Memory as a Universal Function of Organised Matter* and thus connected memory with vibrations. This was *Unconscious Memory*. [1880.]

What I want to do now [1885] is to connect vibrations not only with memory but with the physical constitution of that body in which the memory resides, thus adopting Newland's law (sometimes called Mendelejeff's law) that there is only one substance, and that the characteristics of the vibrations going on within it at any given time will determine whether it will appear to us as (say) hydrogen, or sodium, or chicken doing this, or chicken doing the other. [This touched upon in the concluding chapter of *Luck or Cunning?* 1887.]

I would make not only the mind, but the body of the organism to depend on the characteristics of the vibrations going on within it. The same vibrations which remind the chicken that it wants iron for its blood actually turn the pre-existing matter in the egg into the required material. According to this view the form and characteristics of the elements are as much the living expositions of certain vibrations — are as much our manner of perceiving that the vibrations going on in that part of the one universal substance are such and such—as the colour yellow is our perception that a substance is being struck by vibrations of light, so many to the second, or as the action of a man walking about is our mode of perceiving that such and such another combination of vibrations is, for the present, going on in the substance which, in consequence, has assumed the shape of the particular man.

It is somewhere in this neighbourhood that I look for the connection between organic and inorganic.

The Universal Substance

i

We shall never get straight till we leave off trying to separate mind and matter. Mind is not a thing or, if it be, we know nothing about it; it is a function of matter. Matter is not a thing or, if it be, we know nothing about it; it is a function of mind.

We should see an omnipotent, universal substance, sometimes in a dynamical and sometimes in a statical condition and, in either condition, always retaining a little of its opposite; and we should see this substance as at once both material and mental, whether it be in the one condition or in the other. The statical condition represents content, the dynamical, discontent; and both content and discontent, each still retaining a little of its opposite, must be carried down to the lowest atom.

Action is the process whereby thought, which is mental, is materialised and whereby substance, which is material, is mentalised. It is like the present, which unites times past and future and which is the only time worth thinking of and yet is the only time which has no existence.

I do not say that thought actually passes into substance, or mind into matter, by way of action—I do not know what thought is—but every thought involves bodily change, i.e. action, and every action involves thought, conscious or unconscious. The action is the point of juncture between bodily change, visible and otherwise sensible, and mental change which is invisible except as revealed through action. So that action is the material symbol of certain states of mind. It translates the thought into a corresponding bodily change.

ii

When the universal substance is at rest, that is, not vibrating at all, it is absolutely imperceptible whether by itself or anything else. It is to all intents and purposes fast asleep or, rather, so completely non-existent that you can walk through it, or it through you, and it knows neither time nor space but presents all the appearance of perfect vacuum. It is in an absolutely statical state. But when it is not at rest, it becomes perceptible both to itself and others; that is to say, it assumes material guise such as makes it imperceptible both to itself and others. It is then tending towards rest, i.e. in a dynamical state. The not being at rest is the being in a vibratory condition. It is the disturbance of the repose of the universal, invisible and altogether imperceptible substance by way of vibration which constitutes matter at all; it is the character of the vibrations which constitutes the particular kind of matter. (May we imagine that some vibrations vibrate with a rhythm which has a tendency to recur like the figures in a recurring decimal, and that here we have the origin of the reproductive system?)

We should realise that all space is at all times full of a stuff endowed with a mind and that both stuff and mind are immaterial and imperceptible so long as they are undisturbed, but the moment they are disturbed the stuff becomes material and the mind perceptible. It is not easy to disturb them, for the atmosphere protects them. So long as they are undisturbed they transmit light, etc., just as though they were a rigid substance, for, not being disturbed, they detract nothing from any vibration which enters them.

What will cause a row will be the hitting upon some plan for waking up the ether. It is here that we must look for the extension of the world when it has become over-peopled or when, through its gradual cooling down, it becomes less suitable for a habitation. By and by we shall make new worlds.

Mental and Physical

A strong hope of £20,000 in the heart of a poor but capable man may effect a considerable redistribution of the forces of nature—may even remove mountains. The little, unseen impalpable hope sets up a vibrating movement in a messy substance shut in a dark warm place inside the man's skull. The vibrating substance undergoes a change that none can note, whereupon rings of rhythm circle outwards from it as from a stone thrown into a pond, so that the Alps are pierced in consequence.

Vibrations, Memory and Chemical Properties

The quality of every substance depends upon its vibrations, but so does the quality of all thought and action. Quality is only one mode of action; the action of developing, the desire to make this or that, and do this or that, and the stuff we make are alike due to the nature and characteristics of vibrations.

I want to connect the actual manufacture of the things a chicken makes inside an egg with the desire and memory of the chickens, so as to show that one and the same set of vibrations at once change the universal substratum into the particular phase of it required and awaken a consciousness of, and a memory of and a desire towards, this particular phase on the part of the molecules which are being vibrated into it. So, for example, that a set of vibrations shall at once turn plain white and yolk of egg into the feathers, blood and bones of a chicken and, at the same time, make the mind of the embryo to be such or such as it is.

Protoplasm and Reproduction

The reason why the offspring of protoplasm progressed, and the offspring of nothing else does so, is that the viscid nature of protoplasm allows vibrations to last a very long time, and so very old vibrations get carried into any fragment that is broken off; whereas in the case of air and water, vibrations get soon effaced and only very recent vibrations get carried into the young air and the young water which are, therefore, born fully grown; they cannot grow any more nor can they decay till they are killed outright by something decomposing them. If protoplasm was more viscid it would not vibrate easily enough; if less, it would run away into the surrounding water.

Germs within Germs

When we say that the germ within the hen's egg remembers having made itself into a chicken on past occasions, or that each one of 100,000 salmon germs remembers to have made itself into a salmon (male or female) in the persons of the single pair of salmon its parents, do we intend that each single one of these germs was a witness of, and a concurring agent in, the development of the parent forms from their respective germs, and that each one of them therefore, was shut up within the parent germ, like a small box inside a big one?

If so, then the parent germ with its millions of brothers and sisters was in like manner enclosed within a grand-parental germ, and so on till we are driven to admit, after even a very few generations, that each ancestor has contained more germs than could be expressed by a number written in small numerals, beginning at St. Paul's and ending at Charing Cross. Mr. Darwin's provisional theory of pangenesis comes to something very like this, so far as it can be understood at all.

Therefore it will save trouble (and we should observe no other consideration) to say that the germs that unite to form any given sexually produced individual were not present in the germs, or with the germs, from which the parents sprang, but that they came into the parents' bodies at some later period.

We may perhaps find it convenient to account for their intimate acquaintance with the past history of the body into which they have been introduced by supposing that in virtue of assimilation they have acquired certain periodical rhythms already pre-existing in the parental bodies, and that the communication of the characteristics of these rhythms determines at once the physical and psychical development of the individual in a course as nearly like that of the parents as changed surroundings will allow.

For, according to my *Life and Habit* theory, everything in connection with embryonic development is referred to memory, and this involves that the thing remembering should have been present and an actor in the development which it is supposed to remember; but we have just settled that the germs which unite to form any individual, and which when united proceed to develop according to what I suppose to be their memory of their previous developments, were not participators in any previous development and cannot therefore remember it. They cannot remember even a single development, much less can they remember that infinite series of developments the recollection and epitomisation of which is a *sine qua non* for the unconsciousness which we note in normal development. I see no way of getting out of this difficulty so convenient as to say that a memory is the reproduction and recurrence of a rhythm communicated directly or indirectly from one substance to another, and that where a certain rhythm exists there is a certain stock of memories, whether the actual matter in which the rhythm now subsists was present with the matter in which it arose or not.

There is another little difficulty in the question whether the matter that I suppose introduced into the parents' bodies during their life-histories, and that goes to form the germs that afterwards become their offspring, is living or non-living. If living, then it has its own memories and life-histories which must be cancelled and undone before the assimilation and the becoming imbued with new rhythms can be complete. That is to say it must become as near non-living as anything can become.

Sooner or later, then, we get this introduced matter to be non-living (as we may call it) and the puzzle is how to get it living again. For we strenuously deny equivocal generation. When matter is living we contend that it can only have been begotten of other like living matter; we deny that it can have become living from non-living. Here, however, within the bodies of animals and vegetables we find equivocal generation a necessity; nor do I see any way out of it except by maintaining that nothing is ever either quite dead or quite alive, but that a little leaven of the one is always left in the other. For it would be as difficult to get the thing dead if it is once all alive, as alive if once all dead.

According to this view to beget offspring is to communicate to two pieces of protoplasm (which afterwards combine) certain rhythmic vibrations which, though too feeble to generate visible action until they receive accession of fresh similar rhythms from exterior objects, yet on receipt of such accession set the game of development going and maintain it. It will be observed that the rhythms supposed to be communicated to any germs are such as have been already repeatedly refreshed by rhythms from exterior objects in preceding generations, so that a consonance is rehearsed and pre-arranged, as it were, between the rhythm in the germ and those that in the normal course of its ulterior existence are likely to flow into it. If there is too serious a discord between inner and outer rhythms the organism dies.

Atoms and Fixed Laws

When people talk of atoms obeying fixed laws, they are either ascribing some kind of intelligence and free will to atoms or they are talking nonsense. There is no obedience unless there is at any rate a potentiality of disobeying.

No objection can lie to our supposing potential or elementary volition and consciousness to exist in atoms, on the score that their action would be less regular or uniform if they had free will than if they had not. By giving them free will we do no more than those who make them bound to obey fixed laws. They will be as certain to use their freedom of will only in particular ways as to be driven into those ways by obedience to fixed laws.

The little element of individual caprice (supposing we start with free will), or (supposing we start with necessity) the little element of stiffneckedness, both of which elements we find everywhere in nature, these are the things that prevent even the most reliable things from being absolutely reliable. It is they that form the point of contact between this universe and something else quite different in which none of those fundamental ideas obtain without which we cannot think at all. So we say that nitrous acid is more reliable than nitric for etching.

Atoms have a mind as much smaller and less complex than ours as their bodies are smaller and less complex.

Complex mind involves complex matter and vice versa. On the whole I think it would be most convenient to endow all atoms with a something of consciousness and volition, and to hold them to be *pro tanto*, living. We must suppose them able to remember and forget, i.e. to retain certain vibrations that have been once established — gradually to lose them and to receive others instead. We must suppose some more intelligent, versatile and of greater associative power than others.

Thinking

All thinking is of disturbance, dynamical, a state of unrest tending towards equilibrium. It is all a mode of classifying and of criticising with a view of knowing whether it gives us, or is likely to give us, pleasure or no.

Equilibrium

In the highest consciousness there is still unconsciousness, in the lowest unconsciousness there is still consciousness. If there is no consciousness there is no thing, or nothing. To understand perfectly would be to cease to understand at all.

It is in the essence of heaven that we are not to be thwarted or irritated, this involves absolute equilibrium and absolute equilibrium involves absolute unconsciousness. Christ is equilibrium—the not wanting anything, either more or less. Death also is equilibrium. But Christ is a more living kind of death than death is.

VI
Mind and Matter

Motion

We cannot define either motion or matter, but we have certain rough and ready ideas concerning them which, right or wrong, we must make the best of without more words, for the chances are ten to one that attempted definition will fuzz more than it will clear.

Roughly, matter and motion are functions one of another, as are mind and matter; they are essentially concomitant with one another, and neither can vary but the other varies also. You cannot have a thing "matter" by itself which shall have no motion in it, nor yet a thing "motion" by itself which shall exist apart from matter; you must have both or neither. You can have matter moving much, or little, and in all conceivable ways; but you cannot have matter without any motion more than you can have motion without any matter that is moving.

Its states, its behaviour under varying circumstances, that is to say the characteristics of its motions, are all that we can cognise in respect of matter. We recognise certain varying states or conditions of matter and give one state one name, and another another, as though it were a man or a dog; but it is the state not the matter that we cognise, just as it is the man's moods and outward semblance that we alone note, while knowing nothing of the man. Of matter in its ultimate essence and apart from motion we know nothing whatever. As far as we are concerned there is no such thing: it has no existence: for *de non apparentibus et non existentibus eadem est ratio*.

It is a mistake, therefore, to speak about an "eternal unchangeable underlying substance" as I am afraid I did in the last pages of *Luck or Cunning*? but I am not going to be at the trouble of seeing. For, if the substance is eternal and unknowable and unchangeable, it is tantamount to nothing. Nothing can be nearer non-existence than eternal unknowableness and unchangeableness.

If, on the other hand, the substance changes, then it is not unknowable, or uncognisable, for by cognising its changes we cognise it. Changes are the only things that we can cognise. Besides, we cannot have substance changing without condition changing, and if we could we might as well ignore condition. Does it not seem as though, since the motions or states are all that we cognise, they should be all that we need take account of? Change of condition is change of substance. Then what do we want with substance? Why have two ideas when one will do?

I suppose it has all come about because there are so many tables and chairs and stones that appear not to be moving, and this gave us the idea of a solid substance without any motion in it.

How would it be to start with motion approximately patent, and motion approximately latent (absolute patency and absolute latency being unattainable), and lay down that motion latent as motion becomes patent as substance, or matter of chair-and-table order; and that when patent as motion it is latent as matter and substance?

I am only just recovering from severe influenza and have no doubt I have been writing nonsense.

Matter and Mind

i

People say we can conceive the existence of matter and the existence of mind. I doubt it. I doubt how far we have any definite conception of mind or of matter, pure and simple.

What is meant by conceiving a thing or understanding it? When we hear of a piece of matter instinct with mind, as protoplasm, for example, there certainly comes up before our closed eyes an idea, a picture which we imagine to bear some resemblance to the thing we are hearing of. But when we try to think of matter apart from every attribute of matter (and this I suspect comes ultimately to "apart from every attribute of mind") we get no image before our closed eyes—we realise nothing to ourselves. Perhaps we surreptitiously introduce some little attribute, and then we think we have conceived of matter pure and simple, but this I think is as far as we can go. The like holds good for mind: we must smuggle in a little matter before we get any definite idea at all.

ii

Matter and mind are as heat and cold, as life and death, certainty and uncertainty, union and separateness. There is no absolute heat, life, certainty, union, nor is there any absolute cold, death, uncertainty or separateness.

We can conceive of no ultimate limit beyond which a thing cannot become either hotter or colder, there is no limit; there are degrees of heat and cold, but there is no heat so great that we cannot fancy its becoming a little hotter, that is we cannot fancy its not having still a few degrees of cold in it which can be extracted. Heat and cold are always relative to one another, they are never absolute. So with life and death, there is neither perfect life nor perfect death, but in the highest life there is some death and in the lowest death there is still some life. The fraction is so small that in practice it may and must be neglected; it is neglected, however, not as of right but as of grace, and the right to insist on it is never finally and indefeasibly waived.

iii

An energy is a soul—a something working in us.

As we cannot imagine heat apart from something which is hot, nor motion without something that is moving, so we cannot imagine an energy, or working power, without matter through which it manifests itself.

On the other hand, we cannot imagine matter without thinking of it as capable of some kind of working power or energy — we cannot think of matter without thinking of it as in some way ensouled.

iv

Matter and mind form one another, i.e. they give to one another the form in which we see them. They are the helpmeets to one another that cross each other and undo each other and, in the undoing, do and, in the doing, undo, and so see-saw *ad infinitum*.

Organic and Inorganic

Animals and plants cannot understand our business, so we have denied that they can understand their own. What we call inorganic matter cannot understand the animals' and plants' business, we have therefore denied that it can understand anything whatever.

What we call inorganic is not so really, but the organisation is too subtle for our senses or for any of those appliances with which we assist them. It is deducible however as a necessity by an exercise of the reasoning faculties.

People looked at glaciers for thousands of years before they found out that ice was a fluid, so it has taken them and will continue to take them not less before they see that the inorganic is not wholly inorganic.

The Power to make Mistakes

This is one of the criteria of life as we commonly think of it. If oxygen could go wrong and mistake some other gas for hydrogen and thus learn not to mistake it any more, we should say oxygen was alive. The older life is, the more unerring it becomes in respect of things about which it is conversant—

the more like, in fact, it becomes to such a thing as the force of gravity, both as regards unerringness and unconsciousness.

Is life such a force as gravity in process of formation, and was gravity once — or rather, were things once liable to make mistakes on such a subject as gravity?

If any one will tell me what life is I will tell him whether the inorganic is alive or not.

The Omnipresence of Intelligence

A little while ago no one would admit that animals had intelligence. This is now conceded. At any rate, then, vegetables had no intelligence. This is being fast disputed. Even Darwin leans towards the view that they have intelligence. At any rate, then, the inorganic world has not got an intelligence. Even this is now being denied. Death is being defeated at all points. No sooner do we think we have got a *bona fide* barrier than it breaks down. The divisions between varieties, species, genus, all gone; between instinct and reason, gone; between animals and plants, gone; between man and the lower animals, gone; so, ere long, the division between organic and inorganic will go and will take with it the division between mind and matter.

The Super-Organic Kingdom

As the solid inorganic kingdom supervened upon the gaseous (vestiges of the old being, nevertheless, carried over into and still persisting in the new) and as the organic kingdom supervened upon the inorganic (vestiges of the old being, again, carried over into and still persisting in the new) so a third kingdom is now in process of development, the super-organic, of which we see the germs in the less practical and more emotional side of our nature.

Man, for example, is the only creature that interests himself in his own past, or forecasts his future to any considerable extent. This tendency I would see as the monad of a new regime — a regime that will be no more governed by the ideas and habits now prevailing among ourselves than we are by those still obtaining among stones or water. Nevertheless, if a man be shot out of a cannon, or fall from a great height, he is to all intents and purposes a mere stone. Place anything in circumstances entirely foreign to its immediate antecedents, and those antecedents become non-existent to it, it returns to what it was before they existed, to the last stage that it can recollect as at all analogous to its present.

Feeling

Man is a substance, he knows not what, feeling, he knows not how, a rest and unrest that he can only in part distinguish. He is a substance feeling equilibrium or want of equilibrium; that is to say, he is a substance in a statical or dynamical condition and feeling the passage from one state into the other.

Feeling is an art and, like any other art, can be acquired by taking pains. The analogy between feelings and words is very close. Both have their foundation in volition and deal largely in convention; as we should not be word-ridden so neither should we be feeling-ridden; feelings can deceive us; they can lie; they can be used in a non-natural, artificial sense; they can be forced; they can carry us away; they can be restrained.

When the surroundings are familiar, we know the right feeling and feel it accordingly, or if "we" (that is the central government of our personality) do not feel it, the subordinate departmental personality, whose business it is, feels it in the usual way and then goes on to something else. When the surroundings are less familiar and the departmental personality cannot deal with them, the position is reported through the nervous system to the central government which is frequently at a loss to know what feeling to apply. Sometimes it happens to discern the right feeling and apply it, sometimes it hits upon an inappropriate one and is thus induced to proceed from solecism to solecism till the consequences lead to a crisis from which we recover and which, then becoming a leading case, forms one of the decisions on which our future action is based. Sometimes it applies a feeling that is too inappropriate, as when the position is too horribly novel for us to have had any experience that can guide the central government in knowing how to feel about it, and this results in a cessation of the effort involved in trying to feel. Hence we may hope that the most horrible apparent suffering is not felt beyond a certain point, but is passed through unconsciously under a natural, automatic anæsthetic—the unconsciousness, in extreme cases, leading to death.

It is generally held that animals feel; it will soon be generally held that plants feel; after that it will be held that stones also can feel. For, as no matter is so organic that there is not some of the inorganic in it, so, also, no matter is so inorganic that there is not some of the organic in it. We know that we have nerves and that we feel, it does not follow that other things do not feel because they have no nerves—it only follows that they do not feel as we do. The difference between the organic and the inorganic kingdoms will some day be seen to lie in the greater power of discriminating its feelings which is possessed by the former. Both are made of the same universal substance but, in the case of the organic world, this substance is able to feel more fully and discreetly and to show us that it feels.

Animals and plants, as they advance in the scale of life differentiate their feelings more and more highly; they record them better and recognise them more readily. They get to know what they are doing and feeling, not step by step only, nor sentence by sentence, but in long flights, forming chapters and whole books of action and sensation. The difference as regards feeling between man and the lower animals is one of degree and not of kind. The inorganic is less expert in differentiating its feelings, therefore its memory of them must be less enduring; it cannot recognise what it could scarcely cognise. One might as well for some purposes, perhaps, say at once, as indeed people generally do for most purposes, that the inorganic does not feel; nevertheless the somewhat periphrastic way of putting it, by saying that the inorganic feels but does not know, or knows only very slightly, how to differentiate its feelings, has the advantage of expressing the fact that feeling depends upon differentiation and sense of relation *inter se* of the things differentiated — a fact which, if never expressed, is apt to be lost sight of.

As, therefore, human discrimination is to that of the lower animals, so the discrimination of the lower animals and plants is to that of inorganic things. In each case it is greater discriminating power (and this is mental power) that underlies the differentiation, but in no case can there be a denial of mental power altogether.

Opinion and Matter

Moral force and material force do pass into one another; a conflict of opinion often ends in a fight. Putting it the other way, there is no material conflict without attendant clash of opinion. Opinion and matter act and react as do all things else; they come up hand in hand out of something which is both and neither, but, so far as we can catch sight of either first on our mental horizon, it is opinion that is the prior of the two.

Moral Influence

The caracal lies on a shelf in its den in the Zoological Gardens quietly licking its fur. I go up and stand near it. It makes a face at me. I come a little nearer. It makes a worse face and raises itself up on its haunches. I stand and look. It jumps down from its shelf and makes as if it intended to go for me. I move back. The caracal has exerted a moral influence over me which I have been unable to resist.

Moral influence means persuading another that one can make that other more uncomfortable than that other can make oneself.

Mental and Physical Pabulum

When we go up to the shelves in the reading-room of the British Museum, how like it is to wasps flying up and down an apricot tree that is trained against a wall, or cattle coming down to drink at a pool!

Eating and Proselytising

All eating is a kind of proselytising — a kind of dogmatising — a maintaining that the eater's way of looking at things is better than the eatee's. We convert the food, or try to do so, to our own way of thinking, and, when it sticks to its own opinion and refuses to be converted, we say it disagrees with us. An animal that refuses to let another eat it has the courage of its convictions and, if it gets eaten, dies a martyr to them. So we can only proselytise fresh meat, the convictions of putrid meat begin to be too strong for us.

It is good for a man that he should not be thwarted — that he should have his own way as far, and with as little difficulty, as possible. Cooking is good because it makes matters easier by unsettling the meat's mind and preparing it for new ideas. All food must first be prepared for us by animals and plants, or we cannot assimilate it; and so thoughts are more easily assimilated that have been already digested by other minds. A man should avoid converse with things that have been stunted or starved, and should not eat such meat as has been overdriven or underfed or afflicted with disease, nor should he touch fruit or vegetables that have not been well grown.

Sitting quiet after eating is akin to sitting still during divine service so as not to disturb the congregation. We are catechising and converting our proselytes, and there should be no row. As we get older we must digest more quietly still, our appetite is less, our gastric juices are no longer so eloquent, they have lost that cogent fluency which carried away all that came in contact with it. They have become sluggish and unconciliatory. This is what happens to any man when he suffers from an attack of indigestion.

Sea-Sickness

Or, indeed, any other sickness is the inarticulate expression of the pain we feel on seeing a proselyte escape us just as we were on the point of converting it.

Indigestion

This, as I have said above, may be due to the naughtiness of the stiff-necked things that we have eaten, or to the poverty of our own arguments; but it may also arise from an attempt on the part of the stomach to be too damned clever, and to depart from precedent inconsiderately. The healthy stomach is nothing if not conservative. Few radicals have good digestions.

Assimilation and Persecution

We cannot get rid of persecution; if we feel at all we must persecute something; the mere acts of feeding and growing are acts of persecution. Our aim should be to persecute nothing but such things as are absolutely incapable of resisting us. Man is the only animal that can remain on friendly terms with the victims he intends to eat until he eats them.

Matter Infinitely Subdivisible

We must suppose it to be so, but it does not follow that we can know anything about it if it is divided into pieces smaller than a certain size; and, if we can know nothing about it when so divided, then, *qua* us, it has no existence and therefore matter, *qua* us, is not infinitely subdivisible.

Differences

We often say that things differ in degree but not in kind, as though there were a fixed line at which degree ends and kind begins. There is no such line. All differences resolve themselves into differences of degree. Everything can in the end be united with everything by easy stages if a way long enough and round-about enough be taken. Hence to the metaphysician everything will become one, being united with everything else by degrees so subtle that there is no escape from seeing the universe as a single whole. This in theory; but in practice it would get us into such a mess that we had better go on talking about differences of kind as well as of degree.

Union and Separation

In the closest union there is still some separate existence of component parts; in the most complete separation there is still a reminiscence of union. When they are most separate, the atoms seem to bear in mind that they may one day have to come together again; when most united, they still remember that they may come to fall out some day and do not give each other their full, unreserved confidence.

The difficulty is how to get unity and separateness at one and the same time. The two main ideas underlying all action are desire for closer unity and desire for more separateness. Nature is the puzzled sense of a vast number of things which feel they are in an illogical position and should be more either of one thing or the other than they are. So they will first be this and then that, and act and re-act and keep the balance as near equal as they can, yet they know all the time that it isn't right and, as they incline one way or the other, they will love or hate.

When we love, we draw what we love closer to us; when we hate a thing, we fling it away from us. All disruption and dissolution is a mode of hating; and all that we call affinity is a mode of loving.

The puzzle which puzzles every atom is the puzzle which puzzles ourselves — a conflict of duties — our duty towards ourselves, and our duty as members of a body politic. It is swayed by its sense of being a separate thing —

of having a life to itself which nothing can share; it is also swayed by the feeling that, in spite of this, it is only part of an individuality which is greater than itself and which absorbs it. Its action will vary with the predominance of either of these two states of opinion.

Unity and Multitude

We can no longer separate things as we once could: everything tends towards unity; one thing, one action, in one place, at one time. On the other hand, we can no longer unify things as we once could; we are driven to ultimate atoms, each one of which is an individuality. So that we have an infinite multitude of things doing an infinite multitude of actions in infinite time and space; and yet they are not many things, but one thing.

The Atom

The idea of an indivisible, ultimate atom is inconceivable by the lay mind. If we can conceive an idea of the atom at all, we can conceive it as capable of being cut in half indeed, we cannot conceive it at all unless we so conceive it. The only true atom, the only thing which we cannot subdivide and cut in half, is the universe. We cannot cut a bit off the universe and put it somewhere else. Therefore, the universe is a true atom and, indeed, is the smallest piece of indivisible matter which our minds can conceive; and they cannot conceive it any more than they can the indivisible, ultimate atom.

Our Cells

A string of young ducklings as they sidle along through grass beside a ditch—how like they are to a single serpent! I said in *Life and Habit* that a colossal being, looking at the earth through a microscope, would probably think the ants and flies of one year the same as those of the preceding year. I should have added:—So we think we are composed of the same cells from year to year, whereas in truth the cells are a succession of generations. The most continuous, homogeneous things we know are only like a lot of cowbells on an alpine pasture.

Nerves and Postmen

A letter, so long as it is connected with one set of nerves, is one thing; loose it from connection with those nerves—open your fingers and drop it in the opening of a pillar box—and it becomes part and parcel of another nervous system. Letters in transitu contain all manner of varied stimuli and shocks, yet to the postman, who is the nerve that conveys them, they are all alike, except as regards mere size and weight. I should think, therefore, that our nerves and ganglia really see no difference in the stimuli that they convey.

And yet the postman does see some difference: he knows a business letter from a valentine at a glance and practice teaches him to know much else which escapes ourselves. Who, then, shall say what the nerves and ganglia know and what they do not know? True, to us, as we think of a piece of brain inside our own heads, it seems as absurd to consider that it knows anything at all as it seems to consider that a hen's egg knows anything; but then if the brain could see us, perhaps the brain might say it was absurd to suppose that that thing could know this or that. Besides what is the self of which we say that we are self-conscious? No one can say what it is that we are conscious of. This is one of the things which lie altogether outside the sphere of words.

The postman can open a letter if he likes and know all about the message he is conveying, but, if he does this, he is diseased *qua* postman. So, maybe, a nerve might open a stimulus or a shock on the way sometimes, but it would not be a good nerve.

Night-Shirts and Babies

On Hindhead, last Easter, we saw a family wash hung out to dry. There were papa's two great night-shirts and mamma's two lesser night-gowns and then the children's smaller articles of clothing and mamma's drawers and the girls' drawers, all full swollen with a strong north-east wind. But mamma's night-gown was not so well pinned on and, instead of being full of steady wind like the others, kept blowing up and down as though she were preaching wildly. We stood and laughed for ten minutes. The housewife came to the window and wondered at us, but we could not resist the pleasure of watching the absurdly life-like gestures which the night-gowns made. I should like a *Santa Famiglia* with clothes drying in the background.

A love story might be told in a series of sketches of the clothes of two families hanging out to dry in adjacent gardens. Then a gentleman's night-shirt from one garden, and a lady's night-gown from the other should be shown hanging in a third garden by themselves. By and by there should be added a little night-shirt.

A philosopher might be tempted, on seeing the little night-shirt, to suppose that the big night-shirts had made it. What we do is much the same, for the body of a baby is not much more made by the two old babies, after whose pattern it has cut itself out, than the little night-shirt is made by the big ones. The thing that makes either the little night-shirt or the little baby is something about which we know nothing whatever at all.

Our Organism

Man is a walking tool-box, manufactory, workshop and bazaar worked from behind the scenes by someone or something that we never see. We are so used to never seeing more than the tools, and these work so smoothly, that we call them the workman himself, making much the same mistake as though we should call the saw the carpenter. The only workman of whom we know anything at all is the one that runs ourselves and even this is not perceivable by any of our gross palpable senses.

The senses seem to be the link between mind and matter—never forgetting that we can never have either mind or matter pure and without alloy of the other.

Beer and My Cat

Spilt beer or water seems sometimes almost human in its uncertainty whether or no it is worth while to get ever such a little nearer to the earth's centre by such and such a slight trickle forward.

I saw my cat undecided in his mind whether he should get up on the table and steal the remains of my dinner or not. The chair was some eighteen inches away with its back towards the table, so it was a little troublesome for him to get his feet first on the bar and then on the table. He was not at all hungry but he tried, saw it would not be quite easy and gave it up; then he thought better of it and tried again, and saw again that it was not all perfectly plain sailing; and so backwards and forwards with the first-he-would-and-then-he-wouldn'tism of a mind so nearly in equilibrium that a hair's weight would turn the scale one way or the other.

I thought how closely it resembled the action of beer trickling on a slightly sloping table.

The Union Bank

There is a settlement in the Union Bank building, Chancery Lane, which has made three large cracks in the main door steps. I remember these cracks more than twenty years ago, just after the bank was built, as mere thin lines and now they must be some half an inch wide and are still slowly widening. They have altered very gradually, but not an hour or a minute has passed without a groaning and travailing together on the part of every stone and piece of timber in the building to settle how a *modus vivendi* should be arrived at. This is why the crack is said to be caused by a settlement—some parts of the building willing this and some that, and the battle going on, as even the steadiest and most unbroken battles must go, by fits and starts which, though to us appearing as an even tenor, would, if we could see them under a microscope, prove to be a succession of bloody engagements between regiments that sometimes lost and sometimes won. Sometimes, doubtless, strained relations have got settled by peaceful arbitration and reference to the solicitors of the contending parts without open visible rupture; at other times, again, discontent has gathered on discontent as the snow upon a sub-alpine slope, flake by flake, till the last is one too many and the whole comes crashing down — whereon the cracks have opened some minute fraction of an inch wider.

Of this we see nothing. All we note is that a score of years have gone by and that the cracks are rather wider. So, doubtless, if the materials of which the bank is built could speak, they would say they knew nothing of the varied interests that sometimes coalesce and sometimes conflict within the building. The joys of the rich depositor, the anguish of the bankrupt are nothing to them; the stream of people coming in and going out is as steady, continuous a thing to them as a blowing wind or a running river to ourselves; all they know or care about is that they have a trifle more weight of books and clerks and bullion than they once had, and that this hinders them somewhat in their effort after a permanent settlement.

The Unity of Nature

I meet a melancholy old Savoyard playing on a hurdy-gurdy, grisly, dejected, dirty, with a look upon him as though the iron had long since entered into his soul. It is a frosty morning but he has very little clothing, and there is a dumb despairing look about him which is surely genuine. There passes him a young butcher boy with his tray of meat upon his shoulder. He is ruddy, lusty, full of life and health and spirits, and he vents these in a shrill whistle which eclipses the hurdy-gurdy of the Savoyard.

The like holds good with the horses and cats and dogs which I meet daily, with the flies in window panes and with plants, some are successful, other have now passed their prime. Look at the failures *per se* and they make one very unhappy, but it helps matters to look at them in their capacities as parts of a whole rather than as isolated.

I cannot see things round about me without feeling that they are all parts of one whole which is trying to do something; it has not perhaps a perfectly clear idea of what it is trying after, but it is doing its best. I see old age, decay and failure as the relaxation, after effort, of a muscle in the corporation of things, or as a tentative effort in a wrong direction, or as the dropping off of particles of skin from a healthy limb. This dropping off is the death of any given generation of our cells as they work their way nearer and nearer to our skins and then get rubbed off and go away. It is as though we sent people to live nearer and nearer the churchyard the older they grew. .As for the skin that is shed, in the first place it has had its turn, in the second it starts anew under fresh auspices, for it can at no time cease to be part of the universe, it must always live in one way or another.

Croesus and His Kitchen-Maid

I want people to see either their cells as less parts of themselves than they do, or their servants as more.

Croesus's kitchen-maid is part of him, bone of his bone and flesh of his flesh, for she eats what comes from his table and, being fed of one flesh, are they not brother and sister to one another in virtue of community of nutriment which is but a thinly veiled travesty of descent? When she eats peas with her knife, he does so too; there is not a bit of bread and butter she puts into her mouth, nor a lump of sugar she drops into her tea, but he knoweth it altogether, though he knows nothing whatever about it. She is en-Croesused and he enscullery-maided so long as she remains linked to him by the golden chain which passes from his pocket to hers, and which is greatest of all unifiers.

True, neither party is aware of the connection at all as long as things go smoothly. Croesus no more knows the name of, or feels the existence of, his kitchen-maid than a peasant in health knows about his liver; nevertheless he is awakened to a dim sense of an undefined something when he pays his grocer or his baker. She is more definitely aware of him than he of her, but it is by way of an overshadowing presence rather than a clear and intelligent comprehension. And though Croesus does not eat his kitchen-maid's meals otherwise than vicariously, still to eat vicariously is to eat: the meals so eaten by his kitchen-maid nourish the better ordering of the dinner which nourishes and engenders the better ordering of Croesus himself. He is fed therefore by the feeding of his kitchen-maid.

And so with sleep. When she goes to bed he, in part, does so too. When she gets up and lays the fire in the back-kitchen he, in part, does so. He lays it through her and in her, though knowing no more what he is doing than we know when we digest, but still doing it as by what we call a reflex action. *Qui facit per alium facit per se*, and when the back-kitchen fire is lighted on Croesus's behalf, it is Croesus who lights it, though he is all the time fast asleep in bed.

Sometimes things do not go smoothly. Suppose the kitchen-maid to be taken with fits just before dinner-time; there will be a reverberating echo of disturbance throughout the whole organisation of the palace. But the oftener she has fits, the more easily will the household know what it is all about when she is taken with them. On the first occasion Lady Croesus will send some one rushing down into the kitchen, there will, in fact, be a general flow of blood (i.e. household) to the part affected (that is to say, to the scullery-maid); the doctor will be sent for and all the rest of it. On each repetition of the fits the neighbouring organs, reverting to a more primary undifferentiated condition, will discharge duties for which they were not engaged, in a manner for which no one would have given them credit, and the disturbance will be less and less each time, till by and by, at the sound of the crockery smashing below, Lady Croesus will just look up to papa and say:

"My dear, I am afraid Sarah has got another fit."

And papa will say she will probably be better again soon, and will go on reading his newspaper.

In course of time the whole thing will come to be managed automatically downstairs without any reference either to papa, the cerebrum, or to mamma, the cerebellum, or even to the medulla oblongata, the housekeeper. A precedent or routine will be established, after which everything will work quite smoothly.

But though papa and mamma are unconscious of the reflex action which has been going on within their organisation, the kitchen-maid and the cells in her immediate vicinity (that is to say her fellow-servants) will know all about it. Perhaps the neighbours will think that nobody in the house knows, and that because the master and mistress show no sign of disturbance therefore there is no consciousness. They forget that the scullery-maid becomes more and more conscious of the fits if they grow upon her, as they probably will, and that Croesus and his lady do show more signs of consciousness, if they are watched closely, than can be detected on first inspection. There is not the same violent perturbation that there was on the previous occasions, but the tone of the palace is lowered. A dinner party has to be put off; the cooking is more homogeneous and uncertain, it is less highly differentiated than when the scullery-maid was well; and there is a grumble when the doctor has to be paid and also when the smashed crockery has to be replaced.

If Croesus discharges his kitchen-maid and gets another, it is as though he cut out a small piece of his finger and replaced it in due course by growth. But even the slightest cut may lead to blood-poisoning, and so even the dismissal of a kitchen-maid may be big with the fate of empires. Thus the cook, a valued servant, may take the kitchen-maid's part and go too. The next cook may spoil the dinner and upset Croesus's temper, and from this all manner of consequences may be evolved, even to the dethronement and death of the king himself. Nevertheless as a general rule an injury to such a low part of a great monarch's organism as a kitchen-maid has no important results. It is only when we are attacked in such vital organs as the solicitor or the banker that we need be uneasy. A wound in the solicitor is a very serious thing, and many a man has died from failure of his bank's action.

It is certain, as we have seen, that when the kitchen-maid lights the fire it is really Croesus who is lighting it, but it is less obvious that when Croesus goes to a ball the scullery-maid goes also. Still this should be held in the same way as it should be also held that she eats vicariously when Croesus dines. For he must return the balls and the dinner parties and this comes out in his requiring to keep a large establishment whereby the scullery-maid retains her place as part of his organism and is nourished and amused also.

On the other hand, when Croesus dies it does not follow that the scullery-maid should die at the same time. She may grow a new Croesus, as Croesus, if the maid dies, will probably grow a new kitchen-maid, Croesus's son or successor may take over the kingdom and palace, and the kitchen-maid, beyond having to wash up a few extra plates and dishes at Coronation time, will know little about the change. It is as though the establishment had had its hair cut and its beard trimmed; it is smartened up a little, but there is no other change. If, on the other hand, he goes bankrupt, or his kingdom is taken from him and his whole establishment is broken up and dissipated at the auction mart, then, even though not one of its component cells actually dies, the organism as a whole does so, and it is interesting to see that the lowest, least specialised and least highly differentiate parts of the organism, such as the scullery-maid and the stable-boys, most readily find an entry into the life of some new system, while the more specialised and highly differentiated parts, such as the steward, the old housekeeper and, still more so, the librarian or the chaplain may never be able to attach themselves to any new combination, and may die in consequence. I heard once of a large builder who retired unexpectedly from business and broke up his establishment to the actual death of several of his older employés. So a bit of flesh or even a finger may be taken from one body and grafted on to another, but a leg cannot be grafted; if a leg is cut off it must die. It may, however, be maintained that the owner dies too, even though he recovers, for a man who has lost a leg is not the man he was. [92]

VII
On the Making of Music, Pictures and Books

Thought and Word

i

Thought pure and simple is as near to God as we can get; it is through this that we are linked with God. The highest thought is ineffable; it must be felt from one person to another but cannot be articulated. All the most essential and thinking part of thought is done without words or consciousness. It is not till doubt and consciousness enter that words become possible.

The moment a thing is written, or even can be written, and reasoned about, it has changed its nature by becoming tangible, and hence finite, and hence it will have an end in disintegration. It has entered into death. And yet till it can be thought about and realised more or less definitely it has not entered into life. Both life and death are necessary factors of each other. But our profoundest and most important convictions are unspeakable.

So it is with unwritten and indefinable codes of honour, conventions, art-rules—things that can be felt but not explained—these are the most important, and the less we try to understand them, or even to think about them, the better.

ii

Words are organised thoughts, as living forms are organised actions. How a thought can find embodiment in words is nearly, though perhaps not quite, as mysterious as how an action can find embodiment in form, and appears to involve a somewhat analogous transformation and contradiction in terms.

There was a time when language was as rare an accomplishment as writing was in the days when it was first invented. Probably talking was originally confined to a few scholars, as writing was in the middle ages, and gradually became general. Even now speech is still growing; poor folks cannot understand the talk of educated people. Perhaps reading and writing will indeed one day come by nature. Analogy points in this direction, and though analogy is often misleading, it is the least misleading thing we have.

iii

Communications between God and man must always be either above words or below them; for with words come in translations, and all the interminable questions therewith connected.

iv

The mere fact that a thought or idea can be expressed articulately in words involves that it is still open to question; and the mere fact that a difficulty can be definitely conceived involves that it is open to solution.

v

We want words to do more than they can. We try to do with them what comes to very much like trying to mend a watch with a pickaxe or to paint a miniature with a mop; we expect them to help us to grip and dissect that which in ultimate essence is as ungrippable as shadow. Nevertheless there they are; we have got to live with them, and the wise course is to treat them as we do our neighbours, and make the best and not the worst of them. But they are parvenu people as compared with thought and action. What we should read is not the words but the man whom we feel to be behind the words.

vi

Words impede and either kill, or are killed by, perfect thought; but they are, as a scaffolding, useful, if not indispensable, for the building up of imperfect thought and helping to perfect it.

vii

All words are juggles. To call a thing a juggle of words is often a bigger juggle than the juggle it is intended to complain of. The question is whether it is a greater juggle than is generally considered fair trading.

viii

Words are like money; there is nothing so useless, unless when in actual use.

ix

Gold and silver coins are only the tokens, symbols, outward and visible signs and sacraments of money. When not in actual process of being applied in purchase they are no more money than words not in use are language. Books are like imprisoned souls until some one takes them down from a shelf and reads them. The coins are potential money as the words are potential language, it is the power and will to apply the counters that make them vibrate with life; when the power and the will are in abeyance the counters lie dead as a log.

The Law

The written law is binding, but the unwritten law is much more so. You may break the written law at a pinch and on the sly if you can, but the unwritten law — which often comprises the written — must not be broken. Not being written, it is not always easy to know what it is, but this has got to be done.

Ideas

They are like shadows — substantial enough until we try to grasp them.

Expression

The fact that every mental state is intensified by expression is of a piece with the fact that nothing has any existence at all save in its expression.

Development

All things are like exposed photographic plates that have no visible image on them till they have been developed.

Acquired Characteristics

If there is any truth in the theory that these are inherited — and who can doubt it? — the eye and the finger are but the aspiration, or word, made manifest in flesh.

Physical and Spiritual

The bodies of many abandoned undertakings lie rotting unburied up and down the country and their ghosts haunt the law-courts.

Trail and Writing

Before the invention of writing the range of one man's influence over another was limited to the range of sight, sound and scent; besides this there was trail, of many kinds. Trail unintentionally left is, as it were, hidden sight. Left intentionally, it is the unit of literature. It is the first mode of writing, from which grew that power of extending men's influence over one another by the help of written symbols of all kinds without which the development of modern civilisation would have been impossible.

Conveyancing and the Arts

In conveyancing the ultimately potent thing is not the deed but the invisible intention and desire of the parties to the deed; the written document itself is only evidence of this intention and desire. So it is with music, the written notes are not the main thing, nor is even the heard performance; these are only evidences of an internal invisible emotion that can be felt but never fully expressed. And so it is with the words of literature and with the forms and colours of painting.

The Rules for Making Literature, Music and Pictures

The arts of the musician, the painter and the writer are essentially the same. In composing a fugue, after you have exposed your subject, which must not be too unwieldly, you introduce an episode or episodes which must arise out of your subject. The great thing is that all shall be new, and yet nothing new, at the same time; the details must minister to the main effect and not obscure it; in other words, you must have a subject, develop it and not wander from it very far. This holds just as true for literature and painting and for art of all kinds.

No man should try even to allude to the greater part of what he sees in his subject, and there is hardly a limit to what he may omit. What is required is that he shall say what he elects to say discreetly; that he shall be quick to see the gist of a matter, and give it pithily without either prolixity or stint of words.

Relative Importances

It is the painter's business to help memory and imagination, not to supersede them. He cannot put the whole before the spectator, nothing can do this short of the thing itself; he should, therefore, not try to realise, and the less he looks as if he were trying to do so the more signs of judgment he will show. His business is to supply those details which will most readily bring the whole before the mind along with them. He must not give too few, but it is still more imperative on him not to give too many.

Seeing, thought and expression are rendered possible only by the fact that our minds are always ready to compromise and to take the part for the whole. We associate a number of ideas with any given object, and if a few of the most characteristic of these are put before us we take the rest as read, jump to a conclusion and realise the whole. If we did not conduct our thought on this principle—simplifying by suppression of detail and breadth of treatment—it would take us a twelvemonth to say that it was a fine morning and another for the hearer to apprehend our statement. Any other principle reduces thought to an absurdity.

All painting depends upon simplification. All simplification depends upon a perception of relative importances. All perception of relative importances depends upon a just appreciation of which letters in association's bond association will most readily dispense with. This depends upon the sympathy of the painter both with his subject and with him who is to look at the picture. And this depends upon a man's common sense.

He therefore tells best in painting, as in literature, who has best estimated the relative values or importances of the more special features characterising his subject: that is to say, who appreciates most accurately how much and how fast each one of them will carry, and is at most pains to give those only that will say most in the fewest words or touches. It is here that the most difficult, the most important, and the most generally neglected part of an artist's business will be found to lie.

The difficulties of doing are serious enough, nevertheless we can most of us overcome them with ordinary perseverance for they are small as compared with those of knowing what not to do—with those of learning to disregard the incessant importunity of small nobody-details that persist in trying to thrust themselves above their betters. It is less trouble to give in to these than to snub them duly and keep them in their proper places, yet it is precisely here that strength or weakness resides. It is success or failure in this respect that constitutes the difference between the artist who may claim to rank as a statesman and one who can rise no higher than a village vestryman.

It is here, moreover, that effort is most remunerative. For when we feel that a painter has made simplicity and subordination of importances his first aim, it is surprising how much shortcoming we will condone as regards actual execution. Whereas, let the execution be perfect, if the details given be ill-chosen in respect of relative importance the whole effect is lost—it becomes top-heavy, as it were, and collapses. As for the number of details given, this does not matter: a man may give as few or as many as he chooses; he may stop at outline, or he may go on to Jean Van Eyck; what is essential is that, no matter how far or how small a distance he may go, he should have begun with the most important point and added each subsequent feature in due order of importance, so that if he stopped at any moment there should be no detail ungiven more important than another which has been insisted on.

Supposing, by way of illustration, that the details are as grapes in a bunch, they should be eaten from the best grape to the next best, and so on downwards, never eating a worse grape while a better one remains uneaten.

Personally, I think that, as the painter cannot go the whole way, the sooner he makes it clear that he has no intention of trying to do so the better. When we look at a very highly finished picture (so called), unless we are in the hands of one who has attended successfully to the considerations insisted on above, we feel as though we were with a troublesome cicerone who will not let us look at things with our own eyes but keeps intruding himself at every touch and turn and trying to exercise that undue influence upon us which generally proves to have been the accompaniment of concealment and fraud. This is exactly what we feel with Van Mieris and, though in a less degree, with Gerard Dow; whereas with Jean Van Eyck and Metsu, no matter how far they may have gone, we find them essentially as impressionist as Rembrandt or Velasquez.

For impressionism only means that due attention has been paid to the relative importances of the impressions made by the various characteristics of a given subject, and that they have been presented to us in order of precedence.

Eating Grapes Downwards

Always eat grapes downwards—that is, always eat the best grape first; in this way there will be none better left on the bunch, and each grape will seem good down to the last. If you eat the other way, you will not have a good grape in the lot. Besides, you will be tempting Providence to kill you before you come to the best. This is why autumn seems better than spring: in the autumn we are eating our days downwards, in the spring each day still seems "Very bad." People should live on this principle more than they do, but they do live on it a good deal; from the age of, say, fifty we eat our days downwards.

In New Zealand for a long time I had to do the washing-up after each meal. I used to do the knives first, for it might please God to take me before I came to the forks, and then what a sell it would have been to have done the forks rather than the knives!

Terseness

Talking with Gogin last night, I said that in writing it took more time and trouble to get a thing short than long. He said it was the same in painting. It was harder not to paint a detail than to paint it, easier to put in all that one can see than to judge what may go without saying, omit it and range the irreducible minima in due order of precedence. Hence we all lean towards prolixity.

The difficulty lies in the nice appreciation of relative importances and in the giving each detail neither more nor less than its due. This is the difference between Gerard Dow and Metsu. Gerard Dow gives all he can, but unreflectingly; hence it does not reflect the subject effectively into the spectator. We see it, but it does not come home to us. Metsu on the other hand omits all he can, but omits intelligently, and his reflection excites responsive enthusiasm in ourselves. We are continually trying to see as much as we can, and to put it down. More wisely we should consider how much we can avoid seeing and dispense with.

So it is also in music. Cherubini says the number of things that can be done in fugue with a very simple subject is endless, but that the trouble lies in knowing which to choose from all these infinite possibilities.

As regards painting, any one can paint anything in the minute manner with a little practice, but it takes an exceedingly able man to paint so much as an egg broadly and simply. Bearing in mind the shortness of life and the complexity of affairs, it stands to reason that we owe most to him who packs our trunks for us, so to speak, most intelligently, neither omitting what we are likely to want, nor including what we can dispense with, and who, at the same time, arranges things so that they will travel most safely and be got at most conveniently. So we speak of composition and arrangement in all arts.

Making Notes

My notes always grow longer if I shorten them. I mean the process of compression makes them more pregnant and they breed new notes. I never try to lengthen them, so I do not know whether they would grow shorter if I did. Perhaps that might be a good way of getting them shorter.

Shortening

A young author is tempted to leave anything he has written through fear of not having enough to say if he goes cutting out too freely. But it is easier to be long than short. I have always found compressing, cutting out, and tersifying a passage suggests more than anything else does. Things pruned off in this way are like the heads of the hydra, two grow for every two that is lopped off.

Omission

If a writer will go on the principle of stopping everywhere and anywhere to put down his notes, as the true painter will stop anywhere and everywhere to sketch, he will be able to cut down his works liberally. He will become prodigal not of writing—any fool can be this—but of omission. You become brief because you have more things to say than time to say them in. One of the chief arts is that of knowing what to neglect and the more talk increases the more necessary does this art become.

Brevity

Handel's jig in the ninth *Suite de Pieces*, in G minor, is very fine but it is perhaps a little long. Probably Handel was in a hurry, for it takes much more time to get a thing short than to leave it a little long. Brevity is not only the soul of wit, but the soul of making oneself agreeable and of getting on with people, and, indeed, of everything that makes life worth living. So precious a thing, however, cannot be got without more expense and trouble than most of us have the moral wealth to lay out.

Diffuseness

This sometimes helps, as, for instance, when the subject is hard; words that may be, strictly speaking, unnecessary still may make things easier for the reader by giving him more time to master the thought while his eye is running over the verbiage. So, a little water may prevent a strong drink from burning throat and stomach. A style that is too terse is as fatiguing as one that is too diffuse. But when a passage is written a little long, with consciousness and compunction but still deliberately, as what will probably be most easy for the reader, it can hardly be called diffuse.

Difficulties in Art, Literature and Music

The difficult and the unintelligible are only conceivable at all in virtue of their catching on to something less difficult and less unintelligible and, through this, to things easily done and understood. It is at these joints in their armour that difficulties should be attacked.

Never tackle a serious difficulty as long as something which must be done, and about which you see your way fairly well, remains undone; the settling of this is sure to throw light upon the way in which the serious difficulty is to be resolved. It is doing the What-you-can that will best help you to do the What-you-cannot.

Arrears of small things to be attended to, if allowed to accumulate, worry and depress like unpaid debts. The main work should always stand aside for these, not these for the main work, as large debts should stand aside for small ones, or truth for common charity and good feeling. If we attend continually and promptly to the little that we can do, we shall ere long be surprised to find how little remains that we cannot do.

Knowledge is Power

Yes, but it must be practical knowledge. There is nothing less powerful than knowledge unattached, and incapable of application. That is why what little knowledge I have has done myself personally so much harm. I do not know much, but if I knew a good deal less than that little I should be far more powerful. The rule should be never to learn a thing till one is pretty sure one wants it, or that one will want it before long so badly as not to be able to get on without it. This is what sensible people do about money, and there is no reason why people should throw away their time and trouble more than their money. There are plenty of things that most boys would give their ears to know, these and these only are the proper things for them to sharpen their wits upon.

If a boy is idle and does not want to learn anything at all, the same principle should guide those who have the care of him—he should never be made to learn anything till it is pretty obvious that he cannot get on without it. This will save trouble both to boys and teachers, moreover it will be far more likely to increase a boy's desire to learn. I know in my own case no earthly power could make me learn till I had my head given me; and nothing has been able to stop me from incessant study from that day to this.

Academicism

Handicapped people sometimes owe their success to the misfortune which weights them. They seldom know beforehand how far they are going to reach, and this helps them; for if they knew the greatness of the task before them they would not attempt it. He who knows he is infirm, and would yet climb, does not think of the summit which he believes to be beyond his reach but climbs slowly onwards, taking very short steps, looking below as often as he likes but not above him, never trying his powers but seldom stopping, and then, sometimes, behold! he is on the top, which he would never have even aimed at could he have seen it from below. It is only in novels and sensational biographies that handicapped people, "fired by a knowledge of the difficulties that others have overcome, resolve to triumph over every obstacle by dint of sheer determination, and in the end carry everything before them." In real life the person who starts thus almost invariably fails. This is the worst kind of start.

The greatest secret of good work whether in music, literature or painting lies in not attempting too much; if it be asked, "What is too much?" the answer is, "Anything that we find difficult or unpleasant." We should not ask whether others find this same thing difficult or no. If we find the difficulty so great that the overcoming it is a labour and not a pleasure, we should either change our aim altogether, or aim, at any rate for a time, at some lower point. It must be remembered that no work is required to be more than right as far as it goes; the greatest work cannot get beyond this and the least comes strangely near the greatest if this can be said of it.

The more I see of academicism the more I distrust it. If I had approached painting as I have approached bookwriting and music, that is to say by beginning at once to do what I wanted, or as near as I could to what I could find out of this, and taking pains not by way of solving academic difficulties, in order to provide against practical ones, but by waiting till a difficulty arose in practice and then tackling it, thus making the arising of each difficulty be the occasion for learning what had to be learnt about it—if I had approached painting in this way I should have been all right. As it is I have been all wrong, and it was South Kensington and Heatherley's that set me wrong. I listened to the nonsense about how I ought to study before beginning to paint, and about never painting without nature, and the result was that I learned to study but not to paint. Now I have got too much to do and am too old to do what I might easily have done, and should have done, if I had found out earlier what writing *Life and Habit* was the chief thing to teach me.

So I painted study after study, as a priest reads his breviary, and at the end of ten years knew no more what the face of nature was like, unless I had it immediately before me, than I did at the beginning. I am free to confess that in respect of painting I am a failure. I have spent far more time on painting than I have on anything else, and have failed at it more than I have failed in any other respect almost solely for the reasons given above. I tried very hard, but I tried the wrong way.

Fortunately for me there are no academies for teaching people how to write books, or I should have fallen into them as I did into those for painting and, instead of writing, should have spent my time and money in being told that I was learning how to write. If I had one thing to say to students before I died (I mean, if I had got to die, but might tell students one thing first) I should say: —

"Don't learn to do, but learn in doing. Let your falls not be on a prepared ground, but let them be bona fide falls in the rough and tumble of the world; only, of course, let them be on a small scale in the first instance till you feel your feet safe under you. Act more and rehearse less."

A friend once asked me whether I liked writing books, composing music or painting pictures best. I said I did not know. I like them all; but I never find time to paint a picture now and only do small sketches and studies. I know in which I am strongest — writing; I know in which I am weakest — painting; I am weakest where I have taken most pains and studied most.

Agonising

In art, never try to find out anything, or try to learn anything until the not knowing it has come to be a nuisance to you for some time. Then you will remember it, but not otherwise. Let knowledge importune you before you will hear it. Our schools and universities go on the precisely opposite system.

Never consciously agonise; the race is not to the swift, nor the battle to the strong. Moments of extreme issue are unconscious and must be left to take care of themselves. During conscious moments take reasonable pains but no more and, above all, work so slowly as never to get out of breath. Take it easy, in fact, until forced not to do so.

There is no mystery about art. Do the things that you can see; they will show you those that you cannot see. By doing what you can you will gradually get to know what it is that you want to do and cannot do, and so to be able to do it.

The Choice of Subjects

Do not hunt for subjects, let them choose you, not you them. Only do that which insists upon being done and runs right up against you, hitting you in the eye until you do it. This calls you and you had better attend to it, and do it as well as you can. But till called in this way do nothing.

Imaginary Countries

Each man's mind is an unknown land to himself, so that we need not be at such pains to frame a mechanism of adventure for getting to undiscovered countries. We have not far to go before we reach them. They are, like the Kingdom of Heaven, within us.

My Books

I never make them: they grow; they come to me and insist on being written, and on being such and such. I did not want to write *Erewhon*, I wanted to go on painting and found it an abominable nuisance being dragged willy-nilly into writing it. So with all my books—the subjects were never of my own choosing; they pressed themselves upon me with more force than I could resist. If I had not liked the subjects I should have kicked, and nothing would have got me to do them at all. As I did like the subjects and the books came and said they were to be written, I grumbled a little and wrote them. [106]

Great Works

These have always something of the "de profundis" about them.

New Ideas

Every new idea has something of the pain and peril of childbirth about it; ideas are just as mortal and just as immortal as organised beings are.

Books and Children

If the literary offspring is not to die young, almost as much trouble must be taken with it as with the bringing up of a physical child. Still, the physical child is the harder work of the two.

The Life of Books

Some writers think about the life of books as some savages think about the life of men—that there are books which never die. They all die sooner or later; but that will not hinder an author from trying to give his book as long a life as he can get for it. The fact that it will have to die is no valid reason for letting it die sooner than can be helped.

Criticism

Critics generally come to be critics by reason not of their fitness for this but of their unfitness for anything else. Books should be tried by a judge and jury as though they were crimes, and counsel should be heard on both sides.

Le Style c'est l'Homme

It is with books, music, painting and all the arts as with children—only those live that have drained much of their author's own life into them. The personality of the author is what interests us more than his work. When we have once got well hold of the personality of the author we care comparatively little about the history of the work or what it means or even its technique; we enjoy the work without thinking of more than its beauty, and of how much we like the workman. "Le style c'est l'homme"—that style of which, if I may quote from memory, Buffon, again, says that it is like happiness, and "vient de la douceur de l'âme" [107]—and we care more about knowing what kind of person a man was than about knowing of his achievements, no matter how considerable they may have been. If he has made it clear that he was trying to do what we like, and meant what we should like him to have meant, it is enough; but if the work does not attract us to the workman, neither does it attract us to itself.

Portraits

A great portrait is always more a portrait of the painter than of the painted. When we look at a portrait by Holbein or Rembrandt it is of Holbein or Rembrandt that we think more than of the subject of their picture. Even a portrait of Shakespeare by Holbein or Rembrandt could tell us very little about Shakespeare. It would, however, tell us a great deal about Holbein or Rembrandt.

A Man's Style

A man's style in any art should be like his dress—it should attract as little attention as possible.

The Gauntlet of Youth

Everything that is to age well must have run the gauntlet of its youth. Hardly ever does a work of art hold its own against time if it was not treated somewhat savagely at first—I should say "artist" rather than "work of art."

Greatness in Art

If a work of art—music, literature or painting—is for all time, it must be independent of the conventions, dialects, costumes and fashions of any time; if not great without help from such unessential accessories, no help from them can greaten it. A man must wear the dress of his own time, but no dressing can make a strong man of a weak one.

Literary Power

They say the test of this is whether a man can write an inscription. I say "Can he name a kitten?" And by this test I am condemned, for I cannot.

Subject and Treatment

It is often said that treatment is more important than subject, but no treatment can make a repulsive subject not repulsive. It can make a trivial, or even a stupid, subject interesting, but a really bad flaw in a subject cannot be treated out. Happily the man who has sense enough to treat a subject well will generally have sense enough to choose a good one, so that the case of a really repulsive subject treated in a masterly manner does not often arise. It is often said to have arisen, but in nine cases out of ten the treatment will be found to have been overpraised.

Public Opinion

People say how strong it is; and indeed it is strong while it is in its prime. In its childhood and old age it is as weak as any other organism. I try to make my own work belong to the youth of a public opinion. The history of the world is the record of the weakness, frailty and death of public opinion, as geology is the record of the decay of those bodily organisms in which opinions have found material expression.

A Literary Man's Test

Molière's reading to his housemaid has, I think, been misunderstood as though he in some way wanted to see the effect upon the housemaid and make her a judge of his work. If she was an unusually clever, smart girl, this might be well enough, but the supposition commonly is that she was a typical housemaid and nothing more.

If Molière ever did read to her, it was because the mere act of reading aloud put his work before him in a new light and, by constraining his attention to every line, made him judge it more rigorously. I always intend to read, and generally do read, what I write aloud to some one; any one almost will do, but he should not be so clever that I am afraid of him. I feel weak places at once when I read aloud where I thought, as long as I read to myself only, that the passage was all right.

What Audience to Write for

People between the ages of twenty and thirty read a good deal, after thirty their reading drops off and by forty is confined to each person's special subject, newspapers and magazines; so that the most important part of one's audience, and that which should be mainly written for, consists of specialists and people between twenty and thirty.

Writing for a Hundred Years Hence

When a man is in doubt about this or that in his writing, it will often guide him if he asks himself how it will tell a hundred years hence.

VIII
Handel and Music

Handel and Beethoven

As a boy, from 12 years old or so, I always worshipped Handel. Beethoven was a *terra incognita* to me till I went up to Cambridge; I knew and liked a few of his waltzes but did not so much as know that he had written any sonatas or symphonies. At Cambridge Sykes tried to teach me Beethoven but I disliked his music and would go away as soon as Sykes began with any of his sonatas. After a long while I began to like some of the slow movements and then some entire sonatas, several of which I could play once fairly well without notes. I used also to play Bach and Mendelssohn's *Songs without Words* and thought them lovely, but I always liked Handel best. Little by little, however, I was talked over into placing Bach and Beethoven on a par as the greatest and I said I did not know which was the best man. I cannot tell now whether I really liked Beethoven or found myself carried away by the strength of the Beethoven current which surrounded me; at any rate I spent a great deal of time on him, for some ten or a dozen years.

One night, when I was about 30, I was at an evening party at Mrs. Longden's and met an old West End clergyman of the name of Smalley (Rector, I think, of Bayswater). I said I did not know which was greatest Handel, Bach or Beethoven.

He said: "I am surprised at that; I should have thought you would have known."

"Which," said I, "is the greatest?"

"Handel."

I knew he was right and have never wavered since. I suppose I was really of this opinion already, but it was not till I got a little touch from outside that I knew it. From that moment Beethoven began to go back, and now I feel towards him much as I did when I first heard his work, except, of course, that I see a gnosis in him of which as a young man I knew nothing. But I do not greatly care about gnosis, I want agape; and Beethoven's agape is not the healthy robust tenderness of Handel, it is a sickly maudlin thing in comparison. Anyhow I do not like him. I like Mozart and Haydn better, but not so much better as I should like to like them.

Handel and Domenico Scarlatti

Handel and Domenico Scarlatti were contemporaries almost to a year, both as regards birth and death. They knew each other very well in Italy and Scarlatti never mentioned Handel's name without crossing himself, but I have not heard that Handel crossed himself at the mention of Scarlatti's name. I know very little of Scarlatti's music and have not even that little well enough in my head to write about it; I retain only a residuary impression that it is often very charming and links Haydn with Bach, moreover that it is distinctly un-Handelian.

Handel must have known and comprehended Scarlatti's tendencies perfectly well: his rejection, therefore, of the principles that lead to them must have been deliberate. Scarlatti leads to Haydn, Haydn to Mozart and hence, through Beethoven, to modern music. That Handel foresaw this I do not doubt, nor yet that he felt, as I do myself, that modern music means something, I know not what, which is not what I mean by music. It is playing another game and has set itself aims which, no doubt, are excellent but which are not mine.

Of course I know that this may be all wrong: I know how very limited and superficial my own acquaintance with music is. Still I have a strong feeling as though from John Dunstable, or whoever it may have been, to Handel the tide of music was rising, intermittently no doubt but still rising, and that since Handel's time it has been falling. Or, rather perhaps I should say that music bifurcated with Handel and Bach—Handel dying musically as well as physically childless, while Bach was as prolific in respect of musical disciples as he was in that of children.

What, then, was it, supposing I am right at all, that Handel distrusted in the principles of Scarlatti as deduced from those of Bach? I imagine that he distrusted chiefly the abuse of the appoggiatura, the abuse of the unlimited power of modulation which equal temperament placed at the musician's disposition and departure from well-marked rhythm, beat or measured tread. At any rate I believe the music I like best myself to be sparing of the appoggiatura, to keep pretty close to tonic and dominant and to have a well-marked beat, measure and rhythm.

Handel and Homer

Handel was a greater man than Homer (I mean the author of the *Iliad*); but the very people who are most angry with me for (as they incorrectly suppose) sneering at Homer are generally the ones who never miss an opportunity of cheapening and belittling Handel, and, which is very painful to myself, they say I was laughing at him in *Narcissus*. Perhaps — but surely one can laugh at a person and adore him at the same time.

Handel and Bach

i

If you tie Handel's hands by debarring him from the rendering of human emotion, and if you set Bach's free by giving him no human emotion to render — if, in fact, you rob Handel of his opportunities and Bach of his difficulties — the two men can fight after a fashion, but Handel will even so come off victorious. Otherwise it is absurd to let Bach compete at all. Nevertheless the cultured vulgar have at all times preferred gymnastics and display to reticence and the healthy, graceful, normal movements of a man of birth and education, and Bach is esteemed a more profound musician than Handel in virtue of his frequent and more involved complexity of construction. In reality Handel was profound enough to eschew such wildernesses of counterpoint as Bach instinctively resorted to, but he knew also that public opinion would be sure to place Bach on a level with himself, if not above him, and this probably made him look askance at Bach. At any rate he twice went to Germany without being at any pains to meet him, and once, if not twice, refused Bach's invitation.

ii

Rockstro says that Handel keeps much more closely to the old Palestrina rules of counterpoint than Bach does, and that when Handel takes a licence it is a good bold one taken rarely, whereas Bach is niggling away with small licences from first to last.

Handel and the British Public

People say the generous British public supported Handel. It did nothing of the kind. On the contrary, for some 30 years it did its best to ruin him, twice drove him to bankruptcy, badgered him till in 1737 he had a paralytic seizure which was as near as might be the death of him and, if he had died then, we should have no *Israel*, nor *Messiah*, nor *Samson*, nor any of his greatest oratorios. The British public only relented when he had become old and presently blind. Handel, by the way, is a rare instance of a man doing his greatest work subsequently to an attack of paralysis. What kept Handel up was not the public but the court. It was the pensions given him by George I and George II that enabled him to carry on at all. So that, in point of fact, it is to these two very prosaic kings that we owe the finest musical poems the world knows anything about.

Handel and Madame Patey

Rockstro told me that Sir Michael Costa, after his severe paralytic stroke, had to conduct at some great performance—I cannot be sure, but I think he said a Birmingham Festival—at any rate he came in looking very white and feeble and sat down in front of the orchestra to conduct a morning rehearsal. Madame Patey was there, went up to the poor old gentleman and kissed his forehead.

It is a curious thing about this great singer that not only should she have been (as she has always seemed to me) strikingly like Handel in the face, and not only should she have been such an incomparable renderer of Handel's music—I cannot think that I shall ever again hear any one who seemed to have the spirit of Handel's music so thoroughly penetrating his or her whole being—but that she should have been struck with paralysis at, so far as I can remember, the same age that Handel was. Handel was struck in 1737 when he was 53 years old, but happily recovered. I forget Madame Patey's exact age, but it was somewhere about this.

Handel and Shakespeare

Jones and I had been listening to Gaetano Meo's girls playing Handel and were talking about him and Shakespeare, and how those two men can alike stir us more than any one else can. Neither were self-conscious in production, but when the thing had come out Shakespeare looks at it and wonders, whereas Handel takes it as a matter of course.

A Yankee Handelian

I only ever met one American who seemed to like and understand Handel. How far he did so in reality I do not know, but *inter alia* he said that Handel "struck ile with the *Messiah*," and that "it panned out well, the *Messiah* did."

Waste

Handel and Shakespeare have left us the best that any have left us; yet, in spite of this, how much of their lives was wasted. Fancy Handel expending himself upon the Moabites and Ammonites, or even the Jews themselves, year after year, as he did in the fulness of his power; and fancy what we might have had from Shakespeare if he had gossipped to us about himself and his times and the people he met in London and at Stratford-on-Avon instead of writing some of what he did write. Nevertheless we have the men, seen through their work notwithstanding their subjects, who stand and live to us. It is the figure of Handel as a man, and of Shakespeare as a man, which we value even more than their work. I feel the presence of Handel behind every note of his music.

Handel a Conservative

He left no school because he was a protest. There were men in his time, whose music he perfectly well knew, who are far more modern than Handel. He was opposed to the musically radical tendencies of his age and, as a musician, was a decided conservative in all essential respects — though ready, of course, to go any length in any direction if he had a fancy at the moment for doing so.

Handel and Ernest Pontifex

It cost me a great deal to make Ernest [in *The Way of All Flesh*] play Beethoven and Mendelssohn; I did it simply *ad captandum*. As a matter of fact he played only the music of Handel and of the early Italian and old English composers — but Handel most of all.

Handel's Commonplaces

It takes as great a composer as Handel — or rather it would take as great a composer if he could be found — to be able to be as easily and triumphantly commonplace as Handel often is, just as it takes — or rather would take — as great a composer as Handel to write another *Hallelujah* chorus. It is only the man who can do the latter who can do the former as Handel has done it. Handel is so great and so simple that no one but a professional musician is unable to understand him.

Handel and Dr. Morell

After all, Dr. Morell suited Handel exactly well — far better than Tennyson would have done. I don't believe even Handel could have set Tennyson to music comfortably. What a mercy it is that he did not live in Handel's time! Even though Handel had set him ever so well he would have spoiled the music, and this Dr. Morell does not in the least do.

Wordsworth

And I have been as far as Hull to see
What clothes he left or other property.

I am told that these lines occur in a poem by Wordsworth. (Think of the expense!) How thankful we ought to be that Wordsworth was only a poet and not a musician. Fancy a symphony by Wordsworth! Fancy having to sit it out! And fancy what it would have been if he had written fugues!

Sleeping Beauties

There are plenty of them. Take Handel; look at such an air as "Loathsome urns, disclose your treasure" or "Come, O Time, and thy broad wings displaying," both in *The Triumph of Time and Truth,* or at "Convey me to some peaceful shore," in *Alexander Balus,* especially when he comes to "Forgetting and forgot the will of fate." Who know these? And yet, can human genius do more?

"And the Glory of the Lord"

It would be hard to find a more satisfactory chorus even in the *Messiah,* but I do not think the music was originally intended for these words:

And the glo - ry, the glo - ry of the Lord.

If Handel had approached these words without having in his head a subject the spirit of which would do, and which he thought the words with a little management might be made to fit, he would not, I think, have repeated "the glory" at all, or at any rate not here. If these words had been measured, as it were, for a new suit instead of being, as I suppose, furnished with a good second-hand one, the word "the" would not have been tacked on to the "glory" which precedes it and made to belong to it rather than to the "glory" which follows. It does not matter one straw, and if Handel had asked me whether I minded his forcing the words a little, I should have said, "Certainly not, nor more than a little, if you like." Nevertheless I think as a matter of fact that there is a little forcing. I remember that as a boy this always struck me as a strange arrangement of the words, but it was not until I came to write a chorus myself that I saw how it came about. I do not suspect any forcing when it comes to "And all flesh shall see it together."

Handel and the Speaking Voice

The former of these two extracts is from the chorus "Venus laughing from the skies" in *Theodora*; the other is from the air "Wise men flattering" in *Judas Maccabæus*. I know no better examples of the way Handel sometimes derives his melody from the natural intonation of the speaking voice. The "pleasure" (in bar four of the chorus) suggests a man saying "with pleasure" when accepting an invitation to dinner. Of course one can say, "with pleasure" in a variety of tones, but a sudden exaltation on the second syllable is very common.

In the other example, the first bar of the accompaniment puts the argument in a most persuasive manner; the second simply re-states it; the third is the clincher, I cannot understand any man's holding out against bar three. The fourth bar re-states the clincher, but at a lower pitch, as by one who is quite satisfied that he has convinced his adversary.

Handel and the Wetterhorn

When last I saw the Wetterhorn I caught myself involuntarily humming: —

And the go-vernment shall be up-on his shoul - - - - - - der.

The big shoulder of the Wetterhorn seemed to fall just like the run on "shoulder."

"Tyrants now no more shall Dread"

The music to this chorus in *Hercules* is written from the tyrant's point of view. This is plain from the jubilant defiance with which the chorus opens, and becomes still plainer when the magnificent strain to which he has set the words "All fear of punishment, all fear is o'er" bursts upon us. Here he flings aside all considerations save that of the gospel of doing whatever we please without having to pay for it. He has, however, remembered himself and become almost puritanical over "The world's avenger is no more." Here he is quite proper.

From a dramatic point of view Handel's treatment of these words must be condemned for reasons in respect of which Handel was very rarely at fault. It puzzles the listener who expects the words to be treated from the point of view of the vanquished slaves and not from that of the tyrants. There is no pretence that these particular tyrants are not so bad as ordinary tyrants, nor these particular vanquished slaves not so good as ordinary vanquished slaves, and, unless this has been made clear in some way, it is dramatically *de rigueur* that the tyrants should come to grief, or be about to come to grief. The hearer should know which way his sympathies are expected to go, and here we have the music dragging us one way and the words another.

Nevertheless, we pardon the departure from the strict rules of the game, partly because of the welcome nature of good tidings so exultantly announced to us about all fear of punishment being o'er, and partly because the music is, throughout, so much stronger than the words that we lose sight of them almost entirely. Handel probably wrote as he did from a profound, though perhaps unconscious, perception of the fact that even in his day there was a great deal of humanitarian nonsense talked and that, after all, the tyrants were generally quite as good sort of people as the vanquished slaves. Having begun on this tack, it was easy to throw morality to the winds when he came to the words about all fear of punishment being over.

Handel and Marriage

> To man God's universal law
> Gave power to keep the wife in awe

sings Handel in a comically dogmatic little chorus in *Samson*. But the universality of the law must be held to have failed in the case of Mr. and Mrs. M'Culloch.

Handel and a Letter to a Solicitor

Jones showed me a letter that had been received by the solicitor in whose office he was working:

"Dear Sir; I enclose the name of the lawyer of the lady I am engaged to and her name and address are Miss B. Richmond. His address is W. W. Esq. Manchester.

"I remain, Yours truly W. D. C."

I said it reminded me of the opening bars of "Welcome, welcome, Mighty King" in *Saul*:

Handel's Shower of Rain

The falling shower in the air "As cheers the sun" in *Joshua* is, I think, the finest description of a warm sunny refreshing rain that I have ever come across and one of the most wonderfully descriptive pieces of music that even Handel ever did.

Theodora and Susanna

In my preface to *Evolution Old and New* I imply a certain dissatisfaction with *Theodora* and *Susanna*, and imply also that Handel himself was so far dissatisfied that in his next work, *Jephtha* (which I see I inadvertently called his last), he returned to his earlier manner. It is true that these works are not in Handel's usual manner; they are more difficult and more in the style of Bach. I am glad that Handel gave us these two examples of a slightly (for it is not much) varied manner and I am interested to observe that he did not adhere to that manner in *Jephtha*, but I should be sorry to convey an impression that I think *Theodora* and *Susanna* are in any way unworthy of Handel. I prefer both to *Judas Maccabæus* which, in spite of the many fine things it contains, I like perhaps the least of all his oratorios. I have played *Theodora* and *Susanna* all through, and most parts (except the recitatives) many times over, Jones and I have gone through them again and again; I have heard *Susanna* performed once, and *Theodora* twice, and I find no single piece in either work which I do not admire, while many are as good as anything which it is in my power to conceive. I like the chorus "He saw the lovely youth" the least of anything in *Theodora* so far as I remember at this moment, but knowing it to have been a favourite with Handel himself I am sure that I must have missed understanding it.

How comes it, I wonder, that the chorale-like air "Blessing, Honour, Adoration" is omitted in Novello's edition? It is given in Clarke's edition and is very beautiful.

Jones says of "With darkness deep", that in the accompaniment to this air the monotony of dazed grief is just varied now and again with a little writhing passage. Whether Handel meant this or no, the interpretation put upon the passage fits the feeling of the air.

John Sebastian Bach

It is imputed to him for righteousness that he goes over the heads of the general public and appeals mainly to musicians. But the greatest men do not go over the heads of the masses, they take them rather by the hand. The true musician would not snub so much as a musical critic. His instinct is towards the man in the street rather than the Academy. Perhaps I say this as being myself a man in the street musically. I do not know, but I know that Bach does not appeal to me and that I do appeal from Bach to the man in the street and not to the Academy, because I believe the first of these to be the sounder.

Still, I own Bach does appeal to me sometimes. In my own poor music I have taken passages from him before now, and have my eye on others which I have no doubt will suit me somewhere. Whether Bach would know them again when I have worked my will on them, and much more whether he would own them, I neither know nor care. I take or leave as I choose, and alter or leave untouched as I choose. I prefer my music to be an outgrowth from a germ whose source I know, rather than a waif and stray which I fancy to be my own child when it was all the time begotten of a barrel organ. It is a wise tune that knows its own father and I like my music to be the legitimate offspring of respectable parents. Roughly, however, as I have said over and over again, if I think something that I know and greatly like in music, no matter whose, is appropriate, I appropriate it. I should say I was under most obligations to Handel, Purcell and Beethoven.

For example, any one who looked at my song "Man in Vain" in *Ulysses* might think it was taken from "Batti, batti." I should like to say it was taken from, or suggested by, a few bars in the opening of Beethoven's pianoforte sonata o, and a few bars in the accompaniment to the duet "Hark how the Songsters" in Purcell's *Timon of Athens*. I am not aware of having borrowed more in the song than what follows as natural development of these two passages which run thus:

From the pianoforte arrangement in The Beauties of Purcell by John Clarke, Mus. Doc.

Honesty

Honesty consists not in never stealing but in knowing where to stop in stealing, and how to make good use of what one does steal. It is only great proprietors who can steal well and wisely. A good stealer, a good user of what he takes, is *ipso facto* a good inventor. Two men can invent after a fashion to one who knows how to make the best use of what has been done already.

Musical Criticism

I went to the Bach Choir concert and heard Mozart's *Requiem*. I did not rise warmly to it. Then I heard an extract from *Parsifal* which I disliked very much. If Bach wriggles, Wagner writhes. Yet next morning in the *Times* I saw this able, heartless failure, compact of gnosis as much as any one pleases but without one spark of either true pathos or true humour, called "the crowning achievement of dramatic music." The writer continues: "To the unintelligent, music of this order does not appeal"; which only means "I am intelligent and you had better think as I tell you." I am glad that such people should call Handel a thieving plagiarist.

On Borrowing in Music

In books it is easy to make mention of the forgotten dead to whom we are indebted, and to acknowledge an obligation at the same time and place that we incur it. The more original a writer is, the more pleasure will he take in calling attention to the forgotten work of those who have gone before him. The conventions of painting and music, on the other hand, while they admit of borrowing no less freely than literature does, do not admit of acknowledgement; it is impossible to interrupt a piece of music, or paint some words upon a picture to explain that the composer or painter was at such and such a point indebted to such and such a source for his inspiration, but it is not less impossible to avoid occasionally borrowing, or rather taking, for there is no need of euphemism, from earlier work. Where, then, is the line to be drawn between lawful and unlawful adoption of what has been done by others? This question is such a nice one that there are almost as many opinions upon it as there are painters and musicians.

To leave painting on one side, if a musician wants some forgotten passage in an earlier writer, is he, knowing where this sleeping beauty lies, to let it sleep on unknown and unenjoyed, or shall he not rather wake it and take it—as likely enough the earlier master did before him—with, or without modification? It may be said this should be done by republishing the original work with its composer's name, giving him his due laurels. So it should, if the work will bear it; but more commonly times will have so changed that it will not. A composer may want a bar, or bar and a half, out of, say, a dozen pages—he may not want even this much without more or less modification— is he to be told that he must republish the ten or dozen original pages within which the passage he wants lies buried, as the only righteous way of giving it new life? No one should be allowed such dog-in-the-manger-like ownership in beauty that because it has once been revealed to him therefore none for ever after shall enjoy it unless he be their cicerone. If this rule were sanctioned, he who first produced anything beautiful would sign its death warrant for an earlier or later date, or at best would tether that which should forthwith begin putting girdles round the world.

Beauty lives not for the self-glorification of the priests of any art, but for the enjoyment of priests and laity alike. He is the best art-priest who brings most beauty most home to the hearts of most men. If any one tells an artist that part of what he has brought home is not his but another's, "Yea, let him take all," should be his answer. He should know no self in the matter. He is a fisher of men's hearts from love of winning them, and baits his hook with what will best take them without much heed where he gets it from. He can gain nothing by offering people what they know or ought to know already, he will not therefore take from the living or lately dead; for the same reason he will instinctively avoid anything with which his hearers will be familiar, except as recognised common form, but beyond these limits he should take freely even as he hopes to be one day taken from.

True, there is a hidden mocking spirit in things which ensures that he alone can take well who can also make well, but it is no less true that he alone makes well who takes well. A man must command all the resources of his art, and of these none is greater than knowledge of what has been done by predecessors. What, I wonder, may he take from these—how may he build himself upon them and grow out of them—if he is to make it his chief business to steer clear of them? A safer canon is that the development of a musician should be like that of a fugue or first movement, in which, the subject having been enounced, it is essential that thenceforward everything shall be both new and old at one and the same time—new, but not too new—old, but not too old.

Indeed no musician can be original in respect of any large percentage of his work. For independently of his turning to his own use the past labour involved in musical notation, which he makes his own as of right without more thanks to those who thought it out than we give to him who invented wheels when we hire a cab, independently of this, it is surprising how large a part even of the most original music consists of common form scale passages, and closes. *Mutatis mutandis*, the same holds good with even the most original book or picture; these passages or forms are as light and air, common to all of us; but the principle having been once admitted that some parts of a man's work cannot be original—not, that is to say, if he has descended with only a reasonable amount of modification—where is the line to be drawn? Where does common form begin and end?

The answer is that it is not mere familiarity that should forbid borrowing, but familiarity with a passage as associated with special surroundings. If certain musical progressions are already associated with many different sets of antecedents and consequents, they have no special association, except in so far as they may be connected with a school or epoch; no one, therefore, is offended at finding them associated with one set the more. Familiarity beyond a certain point ceases to be familiarity, or at any rate ceases to be open to the objections that lie against that which, though familiar, is still not familiar as common form. Those on the other hand who hold that a musician should never knowingly borrow will doubtless say that common form passages are an obvious and notorious exception to their rule, and the one the limits of which are easily recognised in practice however hard it may be to define them neatly on paper.

It is not suggested that when a musician wants to compose an air or chorus he is to cast about for some little-known similar piece and lay it under contribution. This is not to spring from the loins of living ancestors but to batten on dead men's bones. He who takes thus will ere long lose even what little power to take he may have ever had. On the other hand there is no enjoyable work in any art which is not easily recognised as the affiliated outcome of something that has gone before it. This is more especially true of music, whose grammar and stock in trade are so much simpler than those of any other art. He who loves music will know what the best men have done, and hence will have numberless passages from older writers floating at all times in his mind, like germs in the air, ready to hook themselves on to anything of an associated character. Some of these he will reject at once, as already too strongly wedded to associations of their own; some are tried and found not so suitable as was thought; some one, however, will probably soon assert itself as either suitable, or easily altered so as to become exactly what is wanted; if, indeed, it is the right passage in the right man's mind, it will have modified itself unbidden already. How, then, let me ask again, is the musician to comport himself towards those uninvited guests of his thoughts? Is he to give them shelter, cherish them, and be thankful? or is he to shake them rudely off, bid them begone, and go out of his way so as not to fall in with them again?

Can there be a doubt what the answer to this question should be? As it is fatal deliberately to steer on to the work of other composers, so it is no less fatal deliberately to steer clear of it; music to be of any value must be a man's freest and most instinctive expression. Instinct in the case of all the greatest artists, whatever their art may be, bids them attach themselves to, and grow out of those predecessors who are most congenial to them. Beethoven grew out of Mozart and Haydn, adding a leaven which in the end leavened the whole lump, but in the outset adding little; Mozart grew out of Haydn, in the outset adding little; Haydn grew out of Domenico Scarlatti and Emmanuel Bach, adding, in the outset, little. These men grew out of John Sebastian Bach, for much as both of them admired Handel I cannot see that they allowed his music to influence theirs. Handel even in his own lifetime was more or less of a survival and protest; he saw the rocks on to which music was drifting and steered his own good ship wide of them; as for his musical parentage, he grew out of the early Italians and out of Purcell.

The more original a composer is the more certain is he to have made himself a strong base of operations in the works of earlier men, striking his roots deep into them, so that he, as it were, gets inside them and lives in them, they in him, and he in them; then, this firm foothold having been obtained, he sallies forth as opportunity directs, with the result that his works will reflect at once the experiences of his own musical life and of those musical progenitors to whom a loving instinct has more particularly attached him. The fact that his work is deeply imbued with their ideas and little ways, is not due to his deliberately taking from them. He makes their ways his own as children model themselves upon those older persons who are kind to them. He loves them because he feels they felt as he does, and looked on men and things much as he looks upon them himself; he is an outgrowth in the same direction as that in which they grew; he is their son, bound by every law of heredity to be no less them than himself; the manner, therefore, which came most naturally to them will be the one which comes also most naturally to him as being their descendant. Nevertheless no matter how strong a family likeness may be, (and it is sometimes, as between Handel and his forerunners, startlingly close) two men of different generations will never be so much alike that the work of each will not have a character of its own—unless indeed the one is masquerading as the other, which is not tolerable except on rare occasions and on a very small scale. No matter how like his father a man may be we can always tell the two apart; but this once given, so that he has a clear life of his own, then a strong family likeness to some one else is no more to be regretted or concealed if it exists than to be affected if it does not.

It is on these terms alone that attractive music can be written, and it is a musician's business to write attractive music. He is, as it were, tenant for life of the estate of and trustee for that school to which he belongs. Normally, that school will be the one which has obtained the firmest hold upon his own countrymen. An Englishman cannot successfully write like a German or a Hungarian, nor is it desirable that he should try. If, by way of variety, we want German or Hungarian music we shall get a more genuine article by going direct to German or Hungarian composers. For the most part, however, the soundest Englishmen will be stay-at-homes, in spite of their being much given to summer flings upon the continent. Whether as writers, therefore, or as listeners, Englishmen should stick chiefly to Purcell, Handel, and Sir Arthur Sullivan. True, Handel was not an Englishman by birth, but no one was ever more thoroughly English in respect of all the best and most distinguishing features of Englishmen. As a young man, though Italy and Germany were open to him, he adopted the country of Purcell, feeling it, doubtless, to be, as far as he was concerned, more Saxon than Saxony itself. He chose England; nor can there be a doubt that he chose it because he believed it to be the country in which his music had the best chance of being appreciated. And what does this involve, if not that England, take it all round, is the most musically minded country in the world? That this is so, that it has produced the finest music the world has known, and is therefore the finest school of music in the world, cannot be reasonably disputed.

To the born musician, it is hardly necessary to say, neither the foregoing remarks nor any others about music, except those that may be found in every text book, can be of the smallest use. Handel knew this and no man ever said less about his art—or did more in it. There are some semi-apocryphal [128] rules for tuning the harpsichord that pretend, with what truth I know not, to hail from him, but here his theoretical contributions to music begin and end. The rules begin "In this chord" (the tonic major triad) "tune the fifth pretty flat, and the third considerably too sharp." There is an absence of fuss about these words which suggests Handel himself.

The written and spoken words of great painters or musicians who can talk or write is seldom lasting—artists are a dumb inarticulate folk, whose speech is in their hands not in their tongues. They look at us like seals, but cannot talk to us. To the musician, therefore, what has been said above is useless, if not worse; its object will have been attained if it aids the uncreative reader to criticise what he hears with more intelligence.

Music

So far as I can see, this is the least stable of the arts. From the earliest records we learn that there were musicians, and people seem to have been just as fond of music as we are ourselves, but, whereas we find the old sculpture, painting (what there is of it) and literature to have been in all essentials like our own, and not only this but whereas we find them essentially the same in existing nations in Europe, Asia, Africa and America, this is not so as regards music either looking to antiquity or to the various existing nations. I believe we should find old Greek and Roman music as hideous as we do Persian and Japanese, or as Persians and Japanese find our own.

I believe therefore that the charm of music rests on a more unreasoning basis, and is more dependent on what we are accustomed to, than the pleasure given by the other arts. We now find all the ecclesiastical modes, except the Ionian and the Æolian, unsatisfactory, indeed almost intolerable, but I question whether, if we were as much in the habit of using the Dorian, Phrygian, Lydian and Mixo-Lydian modes as we are of using the later Æolian mode (the minor scale), we should not find these just as satisfactory. Is it not possible that our indisputable preference for the Ionian mode (the major scale) is simply the result of its being the one to which we are most accustomed? If another mode were to become habitual, might not this scale or mode become first a kind of supplementary moon-like mode (as the Æolian now is) and finally might it not become intolerable to us? Happily it will last my time as it is.

Discords

Formerly all discords were prepared, and Monteverde's innovation of taking the dominant seventh unprepared was held to be cataclysmic, but in modern music almost any conceivable discord may be taken unprepared. We have grown so used to this now that we think nothing of it, still, whenever it can be done without sacrificing something more important, I think even a dominant seventh is better prepared.

It is only the preparation, however, of discords which is now less rigorously insisted on; their resolution — generally by the climbing down of the offending note — is as necessary as ever if the music is to flow on smoothly.

This holds good exactly in our daily life. If a discord has to be introduced, it is better to prepare it as a concord, take it on a strong beat, and resolve it downwards on a weak one. The preparation being often difficult or impossible may be dispensed with, but the resolution is still de rigueur.

Anachronism

It has been said "Thou shalt not masquerade in costumes not of thine own period," but the history of art is the history of revivals. Musical criticism, so far as I can see, is the least intelligent of the criticisms on this score. Unless a man writes in the exotic style of Brahms, Wagner, Dvořák and I know not what other Slav, Czech, Teuton or Hebrew, the critics are sure to accuse him of being an anachronism. The only man in England who is permitted to write in a style which is in the main of home growth is the Irish Jew, Sir Arthur Sullivan. If we may go to a foreign style why may we not go to one of an earlier period? But surely we may do whatever we like, and the better we like it the better we shall do it. The great thing is to make sure that we like the style we choose better than we like any other, that we engraft on it whatever we hear that we think will be a good addition, and depart from it wherever we dislike it. If a man does this he may write in the style of the year one and he will be no anachronism; the musical critics may call him one but they cannot make him one.

Chapters in Music

The analogy between literature, painting and music, so close in so many respects, suggests that the modern custom of making a whole scene, act or even drama into a single, unbroken movement without subdivision is like making a book without chapters, or a picture, like Bernardino Luini's great Lugano fresco in which a long subject is treated within the compass of a single piece. Better advised, as it seems to me, Gaudenzio Ferrari broke up a space of the same shape and size at Varallo into many compartments, each more or less complete in itself, grouped round a central scene. The subdivision of books into chapters, each with a more or less emphatic full close in its own key, is found to be a help as giving the attention halting places by the way. Everything that is worth attending to fatigues as well as delights, much as the climbing of a mountain does so. Chapters and short pieces give rests during which the attention gathers renewed strength and attacks with fresh ardour a new stretch of the ascent. Each bar is, as it were, a step cut in ice and one does not see, if set pieces are objected to, why phrases and bars should not be attacked next.

At the Opera

Jones and I went last Friday to *Don Giovanni*, Mr. Kemp [131] putting us in free. It bored us both, and we like *Narcissus* better. We admit the beauty of many of the beginnings of the airs, but this beauty is not maintained, in every case the air tails off into something that is much too near being tiresome. The plot, of course, is stupid to a degree, but plot has very little to do with it; what can be more uninteresting than the plot of many of Handel's oratorios? We both believe the scheme of Italian opera to be a bad one; we think that music should never be combined with acting to a greater extent than is done, we will say, in the *Mikado*; that the oratorio form is far more satisfactory than opera; and we agreed that we had neither of us ever yet been to an opera (I mean a Grand Opera) without being bored by it. I am not sorry to remember that Handel never abandoned oratorio after he had once fairly taken to it.

At a Philharmonic Concert

We went last night to the Philharmonic and sat in the shilling orchestra, just behind the drums, so that we could see and hear what each instrument was doing. The concert began with Mozart's G Minor Symphony. We liked this fairly well, especially the last movement, but we found all the movements too long and, speaking for myself, if I had a tame orchestra for which I might write programmes, I should probably put it down once or twice again, not from any spontaneous wish to hear more of it but as a matter of duty that I might judge it with fuller comprehension—still, if each movement had been half as long I should probably have felt cordially enough towards it, except of course in so far as that the spirit of the music is alien to that of the early Italian school with which alone I am in genuine sympathy and of which Handel is the climax.

Then came a terribly long-winded recitative by Beethoven and an air with a good deal of "Che farò" in it. I do not mind this, and if it had been "Che farò" absolutely I should, I daresay, have liked it better. I never want to hear it again and my orchestra should never play it.

Beethoven's Concerto for violin and orchestra (op. 61) which followed was longer and more tedious still. I have not a single good word for it. If the subject of the last movement was the tune of one of Arthur Robert's comic songs, or of any music-hall song, it would do very nicely and I daresay we should often hum it. I do not mean at the opening of the movement but about half way through, where the character is just that of a common music-hall song and, so far, good.

Part II opened with a suite in F Major for orchestra (op. 39) by Moszkowski. This was much more clear and, in every way, interesting than the Beethoven; every now and then there were passages that were pleasing, not to say more. Jones liked it better than I did; still, one could not feel that any of the movements were the mere drivelling show stuff of which the concerto had been full. But it, like everything else done at these concerts, is too long, cut down one-half it would have been all right and we should have liked to hear it twice. As it was, all we could say was that it was much better than we had expected. I did not like the look of the young man who wrote it and who also conducted. He had long yellowish hair and kept tossing his head to fling it back on to his shoulders, instead of keeping it short as Jones and I keep ours.

Then came Schubert's "Erl König," which, I daresay, is very fine but with which I have absolutely nothing in common.

And finally there was a tiresome characteristic overture by Berlioz, which, if Jones could by any possibility have written anything so dreary, I should certainly have begged him not to publish.

The general impression left upon me by the concert is that all the movements were too long, and that, no matter how clever the development may be, it spoils even the most pleasing and interesting subject if there is too much of it. Handel knew when to stop and, when he meant stopping, he stopped much as a horse stops, with little, if any, peroration. Who can doubt that he kept his movements short because he knew that the worst music within a reasonable compass is better than the best which is made tiresome by being spun out unduly? I only know one concerted piece of Handel's which I think too long, I mean the overture to *Saul*, but I have no doubt that if I were to try to cut it down I should find some excellent reason that had made Handel decide on keeping it as it is.

At the Wind Concerts

There have been some interesting wind concerts lately; I say interesting, because they brought home to us the unsatisfactory character of wind unsupported by strings. I rather pleased Jones by saying that the hautbois was the clarionet with a cold in its head, and the bassoon the same with a cold on its chest.

At a Handel Festival

i

The large sweeps of sound floated over the orchestra like the wind playing upon a hill-side covered with young heather, and I sat and wondered which of the Alpine passes Handel crossed when he went into Italy. What time of the year was it? What kind of weather did he have? Were the spring flowers out? Did he walk the greater part of the way as we do now? And what did he hear? For he must sometimes have heard music inside him—and that, too, as much above what he has written down as what he has written down is above all other music. No man can catch all, or always the best, of what is put for a moment or two within his reach. Handel took as much and as near the best, doubtless, as mortal man can take; but he must have had moments and glimpses which were given to him alone and which he could tell no man.

ii

I saw the world a great orchestra filled with angels whose instruments were of gold. And I saw the organ on the top of the axis round which all should turn, but nothing turned and nothing moved and the angels stirred not and all was as still as a stone, and I was myself also, like the rest, as still as a stone.

Then I saw some huge, cloud-like forms nearing, and behold! it was the Lord bringing two of his children by the hand.

"O Papa!" said one, "isn't it pretty?"

"Yes, my dear," said the Lord, "and if you drop a penny into the box the figures will work."

Then I saw that what I had taken for the keyboard of the organ was no keyboard but only a slit, and one of the little Lords dropped a plaque of metal into it. And then the angels played and the world turned round and the organ made a noise and the people began killing one another and the two little Lords clapped their hands and were delighted.

Handel and Dickens

They buried Dickens in the very next grave, cheek by jowl with Handel. It does not matter, but it pained me to think that people who could do this could become Deans of Westminster.

IX
A Painter's Views on Painting

The Old Masters and Their Pupils

The old masters taught, not because they liked teaching, nor yet from any idea of serving the cause of art, nor yet because they were paid to teach by the parents of their pupils. The parents probably paid no money at first. The masters took pupils and taught them because they had more work to do than they could get through and wanted some one to help them. They sold the pupil's work as their own, just as people do now who take apprentices. When people can sell a pupil's work, they will teach the pupil all they know and will see he learns it. This is the secret of the whole matter.

The modern schoolmaster does not aim at learning from his pupils, he hardly can, but the old masters did. See how Giovanni Bellini learned from Titian and Giorgione who both came to him in the same year, as boys, when Bellini was 63 years old. What a day for painting was that! All Bellini's best work was done thenceforward. I know nothing in the history of art so touching as this. [1883.]

P.S. I have changed my mind about Titian. I don't like him. [1897.]

The Academic System and Repentance

The academic system goes almost on the principle of offering places for repentance, and letting people fall soft, by assuming that they should be taught how to do things before they do them, and not by the doing of them. Good economy requires that there should be little place for repentance, and that when people fall they should fall hard enough to remember it.

The Jubilee Sixpence

We have spent hundreds of thousands, or more probably of millions, on national art collections, schools of art, preliminary training and academicism, without wanting anything in particular, but when the nation did at last try all it knew to design a sixpence, it failed. [136] The other coins are all very well in their way, and so are the stamps — the letters get carried, and the money passes; but both stamps and coins would have been just as good, and very likely better, if there had not been an art-school in the country. [1888.]

Studying from Nature

When is a man studying from nature, and when is he only flattering himself that he is doing so because he is painting with a model or lay-figure before him? A man may be working his eight or nine hours a day from the model and yet not be studying from nature. He is painting but not studying. He is like the man in the Bible who looks at himself in a glass and goeth away forgetting what manner of man he was. He will know no more about nature at the end of twenty years than a priest who has been reading his breviary day after day without committing it to memory will know of its contents. Unless he gets what he has seen well into his memory, so as to have it at his fingers' ends as familiarly as the characters with which he writes a letter, he can be no more held to be familiar with, and to have command over, nature than a man who only copies his signature from a copy kept in his pocket, as I have known French Canadians do, can be said to be able to write. It is painting without nature that will give a man this, and not painting directly from her. He must do both the one and the other, and the one as much as the other.

The Model and the Lay-Figure

It may be doubted whether they have not done more harm than good. They are an attempt to get a bit of stuffed nature and to study from that instead of studying from the thing itself. Indeed, the man who never has a model but studies the faces of people as they sit opposite him in an omnibus, and goes straight home and puts down what little he can of what he has seen, dragging it out piecemeal from his memory, and going into another omnibus to look again for what he has forgotten as near as he can find it—that man is studying from nature as much as he who has a model four or five hours daily—and probably more. For you may be painting from nature as much without nature actually before you as with; and you may have nature before you all the while you are painting and yet not be painting from her.

Sketching from Nature

Is very like trying to put a pinch of salt on her tail. And yet many manage to do it very nicely.

Great Art and Sham Art

Art has no end in view save the emphasising and recording in the most effective way some strongly felt interest or affection. Where there is neither interest nor desire to record with good effect, there is but sham art, or none at all: where both these are fully present, no matter how rudely and inarticulately, there is great art. Art is at best a dress, important, yet still nothing in comparison with the wearer, and, as a general rule, the less it attracts attention the better.

Inarticulate Touches

An artist's touches are sometimes no more articulate than the barking of a dog who would call attention to something without exactly knowing what. This is as it should be, and he is a great artist who can be depended on not to bark at nothing.

Detail

One reason why it is as well not to give very much detail is that, no matter how much is given, the eye will always want more; it will know very well that it is not being paid in full. On the other hand, no matter how little one gives, the eye will generally compromise by wanting only a little more. In either case the eye will want more, so one may as well stop sooner or later. Sensible painting, like sensible law, sensible writing, or sensible anything else, consists as much in knowing what to omit as what to insist upon. It consists in the tact that tells the painter where to stop.

Painting and Association

Painting is only possible by reason of association's not sticking to the letter of its bond, so that we jump to conclusions.

The Credulous Eye

Painters should remember that the eye, as a general rule, is a good, simple, credulous organ—very ready to take things on trust if it be told them with any confidence of assertion.

Truths from Nature

We must take as many as we can, but the difficulty is that it is often so hard to know what the truths of nature are.

Accuracy

After having spent years striving to be accurate, we must spend as many more in discovering when and how to be inaccurate.

Herbert Spencer

He is like nature to Fuseli—he puts me out.

Shade Colour and Reputation

When a thing is near and in light, colour and form are important; when far and in shadow, they are unimportant. Form and colour are like reputations which when they become shady are much of a muchness.

Money and Technique

Money is very like technique (or vice versa). We see that both musicians or painters with great command of technique seldom know what to do with it, while those who have little often know how to use what they have.

Action and Study

These things are antagonistic. The composer is seldom a great theorist; the theorist is never a great composer. Each is equally fatal to and essential in the other.

Sacred and Profane Statues

I have never seen statues of Jove, Neptune, Apollo or any of the pagan gods that are not as great failures as the statues of Christ and the Apostles.

Seeing

If a man has not studied painting, or at any rate black and white drawing, his eyes are wild; learning to draw tames them. The first step towards taming the eyes is to teach them not to see too much.

Quickness in seeing as in everything else comes from long sustained effort after rightness and comes unsought. It never comes from effort after quickness.

Improvement in Art

Painting depends upon seeing; seeing depends upon looking for this or that, at least in great part it does so.

Think of and look at your work as though it were done by your enemy. If you look at it to admire it you are lost.

Any man, as old Heatherley used to say, will go on improving as long as he is bona fide dissatisfied with his work.

Improvement in one's painting depends upon how we look at our work. If we look at it to see where it is wrong, we shall see this and make it righter. If we look at it to see where it is right, we shall see this and shall not make it righter. We cannot see it both wrong and right at the same time.

Light and Shade

Tell the young artist that he wants a black piece here or there, when he sees no such black piece in nature, and that he must continue this or that shadow thus, and break this light into this or that other, when in nature he sees none of these things, and you will puzzle him very much. He is trying to put down what he sees; he does not care two straws about composition or light and shade; if he sees two tones of such and such relative intensity in nature, he will give them as near as he can the same relative intensity in his picture, and to tell him that he is perhaps exactly to reverse the natural order in deference to some canon of the academicians, and that at the same time he is drawing from nature, is what he cannot understand.

I am very doubtful how far people do not arrange their light and shade too much with the result with which we are familiar in drawing-masters' copies; it may be right or it may not, I don't know—I am afraid I ought to know, but I don't; but I do know that those pictures please me best which were painted without the slightest regard to any of these rules.

I suppose the justification of those who talk as above lies in the fact that, as we cannot give all nature, we lie by *suppressio veri* whether we like it or no, and that you sometimes lie less by putting in something which does not exist at the moment, but which easily might exist and which gives a lot of facts which you otherwise could not give at all, than by giving so much as you can alone give if you adhere rigidly to the facts. If this is so the young painter would understand the matter, if it were thus explained to him, better than he is likely to do if he is merely given it as a canon.

At the same time, I admit it to be true that one never sees light but it has got dark in it, nor vice versa, and that this comes to saying that if you are to be true to nature you must break your lights into your shadows and vice versa; and so usual is this that, if there happens here or there to be an exception, the painter had better say nothing about it, for it is more true to nature's general practice not to have it so than to have it.

Certainly as regards colour, I never remember to have seen a piece of one colour without finding a bit of a very similar colour not far off, but having no connection with it. This holds good in such an extraordinary way that if it happens to fail the matter should be passed over in silence.

Colour

The expression "seeing colour" used to puzzle me. I was aware that some painters made their pictures more pleasing in colour than others and more like the colour of the actual thing as a whole, still there were any number of bits of brilliant colour in their work which for the life of me I could not see in nature. I used to hear people say of a man who got pleasing and natural colour, "Does he not see colour well?" and I used to say he did, but, as far as I was concerned, it would have been more true to say that he put down colour which he did not see well, or at any rate that he put down colour which I could not see myself.

In course of time I got to understand that seeing colour does not mean inventing colour, or exaggerating it, but being on the look out for it, thus seeing it where another will not see it, and giving it the preference as among things to be preserved and rendered amid the wholesale slaughter of innocents which is inevitable in any painting. Painting is only possible as a quasi-hieroglyphic epitomising of nature; this means that the half goes for the whole, whereon the question arises which half is to be taken and which made to go? The colourist will insist by preference on the coloured half, the man who has no liking for colour, however much else he may sacrifice, will not be careful to preserve this and, as a natural consequence, he will not preserve it.

Good, that is to say, pleasing, beautiful, or even pretty colour cannot be got by putting patches of pleasing, beautiful or pretty colour upon one's canvas and, which is a harder matter, leaving them when they have been put. It is said of money that it is more easily made than kept and this is true of many things, such as friendship; and even life itself is more easily got than kept. The same holds good of colour. It is also true that, as with money, more is made by saving than in any other way, and the surest way to lose colour is to play with it inconsiderately, not knowing how to leave well alone. A touch of pleasing colour should on no account be stirred without consideration.

That we can see in a natural object more colour than strikes us at a glance, if we look for it attentively, will not be denied by any who have tried to look for it. Thus, take a dull, dead, level, grimy old London wall: at a first glance we can see no colour in it, nothing but a more or less purplish mass, got, perhaps as nearly as in any other way, by a tint mixed with black, Indian red and white. If, however, we look for colour in this, we shall find here and there a broken brick with a small surface of brilliant crimson, hard by there will be another with a warm orange hue perceivable through the grime by one who is on the look out for it, but by no one else. Then there may be bits of old advertisement of which here and there a gaily coloured fragment may remain, or a rusty iron hook or a bit of bright green moss; few indeed are the old walls, even in the grimiest parts of London, on which no redeeming bits of colour can be found by those who are practised in looking for them. To like colour, to wish to find it, and thus to have got naturally into a habit of looking for it, this alone will enable a man to see colour and to make a note of it when he has seen it, and this alone will lead him towards a pleasing and natural scheme of colour in his work.

Good colour can never be got by putting down colour which is not seen; at any rate only a master who has long served accuracy can venture on occasional inaccuracy — telling a lie, knowing it to be a lie, and as, *se non vera, ben trovata*. The grown man in his art may do this, and indeed is not a man at all unless he knows how to do it daily and hourly without departure from the truth even in his boldest lie; but the child in art must stick to what he sees. If he looks harder he will see more, and may put more, but till he sees it without being in any doubt about it, he must not put it. There is no such sure way of corrupting one's colour sense as the habitual practice of putting down colour which one does not see; this and the neglecting to look for it are equal faults. The first error leads to melodramatic vulgarity, the other to torpid dullness, and it is hard to say which is worse.

It may be said that the preservation of all the little episodes of colour which can be discovered in an object whose general effect is dingy and the suppression of nothing but the uninteresting colourless details amount to what is really a forcing and exaggeration of nature, differing but little from downright fraud, so far as its effect goes, since it gives an undue preference to the colour side of the matter. In equity, if the exigencies of the convention under which we are working require a sacrifice of a hundred details, the majority of which are uncoloured, while in the minority colour can be found if looked for, the sacrifice should be made *pro rata* from coloured and uncoloured alike. If the facts of nature are a hundred, of which ninety are dull in colour and ten interesting, and the painter can only give ten, he must not give the ten interesting bits of colour and neglect the ninety soberly coloured details. Strictly, he should sacrifice eighty-one sober details and nine coloured ones; he will thus at any rate preserve the balance and relation which obtain in nature between coloured and uncoloured.

This, no doubt, is what he ought to do if he leaves the creative, poetic and more properly artistic aspect of his own function out of the question; if he is making himself a mere transcriber, holding the mirror up to nature with such entire forgetfulness of self as to be rather looking-glass than man, this is what he must do. But the moment he approaches nature in this spirit he ceases to be an artist, and the better he succeeds as painter of something that might pass for a coloured photograph, the more inevitably must he fail to satisfy, or indeed to appeal to us at all as poet — as one whose sympathies with nature extend beyond her superficial aspect, or as one who is so much at home with her as to be able readily to dissociate the permanent and essential from the accidental which may be here to-day and gone to-morrow. If he is to come before us as an artist, he must do so as a poet or creator of that which is not, as well as a mirror of that which is. True, experience in all kinds of poetical work shows that the less a man creates the better, that the more, in fact, he makes, the less is he of a maker; but experience also shows that the course of true nature, like that of true love, never does run smooth, and that occasional, judicious, slight departures from the actual facts, by one who knows the value of a lie too well to waste it, bring nature more vividly and admirably before us than any amount of adherence to the letter of strict accuracy. It is the old story, the letter killeth but the spirit giveth life.

With colour, then, he who does not look for it will begin by not seeing it unless it is so obtrusive that there is no escaping it; he will therefore, in his rendering of the hundred facts of nature above referred to, not see the ten coloured bits at all, supposing them to be, even at their brightest, somewhat sober, and his work will be colourless or disagreeable in colour. The faithful copyist, who is still a mere copyist, will give nine details of dull uninteresting colour and one of interesting. The artist or poet will find some reason for slightly emphasising the coloured details and will scatter here and there a few slight, hardly perceptible, allusions to more coloured details than come within the letter of his bond, but will be careful not to overdo it. The vulgar sensational painter will force in his colour everywhere, and of all colourists he must be pronounced the worst.

Briefly then, to see colour is simply to have got into a habit of not overlooking the patches of colour which are seldom far to seek or hard to see by those who look for them. It is not the making one's self believe that one sees all manner of colours which are not there, it is only the getting oneself into a mental habit of looking out for episodes of colour, and of giving them a somewhat undue preference in the struggle for rendering, wherever anything like a reasonable pretext can be found for doing so. For if a picture is to be pleasing in colour, pleasing colours must be put upon the canvas, and reasons have got to be found for putting them there. [1886.]

P.S. — The foregoing note wants a great deal of reconsideration for which I cannot find time just now. Jan. 31, 1898.

Words and Colour

A man cannot be a great colourist unless he is a great deal more. A great colourist is no better than a great wordist unless the colour is well applied to a subject which at any rate is not repellent.

Amateurs and Professionals

There is no excuse for amateur work being bad. Amateurs often excuse their shortcomings on the ground that they are not professionals, the professional could plead with greater justice that he is not an amateur. The professional has not, he might well say, the leisure and freedom from money anxieties which will let him devote himself to his art in singleness of heart, telling of things as he sees them without fear of what man shall say unto him; he must think not of what appears to him right and loveable but of what his patrons will think and of what the critics will tell his patrons to say they think; he has got to square everyone all round and will assuredly fail to make his way unless he does this; if, then, he betrays his trust he does so under temptation. Whereas the amateur who works with no higher aim than that of immediate recognition betrays it from the vanity and wantonness of his spirit. The one is naughty because he is needy, the other from natural depravity. Besides, the amateur can keep his work to himself, whereas the professional man must exhibit or starve.

The question is what is the amateur an amateur of? What is he really in love with? Is he in love with other people, thinking he sees something which he would like to show them, which he feels sure they would enjoy if they could only see it as he does, which he is therefore trying as best he can to put before the few nice people whom he knows? If this is his position he can do no wrong, the spirit in which he works will ensure that his defects will be only as bad spelling or bad grammar in some pretty saying of a child. If, on the other hand, he is playing for social success and to get a reputation for being clever, then no matter how dexterous his work may be, it is but another mode of the speaking with the tongues of men and angels without charity; it is as sounding brass or a tinkling cymbal, full of sound and fury signifying nothing.

The Ansidei Raffaelle

This picture is inspired by no deeper feeling than a determination to adhere to the conventions of the time. These conventions ensure an effect of more or less devotional character, and this, coupled with our reverence for the name of Raffaelle, the sentiments arising from antiquity and foreignness, and the inability of most people to judge of the work on technical grounds, because they can neither paint nor draw, prevents us from seeing what a mere business picture it is and how poor the painting is throughout. A master in any art should be first man, then poet, then craftsman; this picture must have been painted by one who was first worldling, then religious-property-manufacturer, then painter with brains not more than average and no heart.

The Madonna's head has indeed a certain prettiness of a not very uncommon kind; the paint has been sweetened with a soft brush and licked smooth till all texture as of flesh is gone and the head is wooden and tight; I can see no expression in it; the hand upon the open book is as badly drawn as the hand of S. Catharine (also by Raffaelle) in our gallery, or even worse; so is the part of the other hand which can be seen; they are better drawn than the hands in the *Ecce homo* of Correggio in our gallery, for the fingers appear to have the right number of joints, which none of those in the Correggio have, but this is as much as can be said.

The dress is poorly painted, the gold thread work being of the cheapest, commonest kind, both as regards pattern and the quantity allowed; especially note the meagre allowance and poor pattern of the embroidery on the virgin's bosom; it is done as by one who knew she ought to have, and must have, a little gold work, but was determined she should have no more than he could help. This is so wherever there is gold thread work in the picture. It is so on S. Nicholas's cloak where a larger space is covered, but the pattern is dull and the smallest quantity of gold is made to go the longest way. The gold cording which binds this is more particularly badly done. Compare the embroidery and gold thread work in "The Virgin adoring the Infant Christ," ascribed to Andrea Verrocchio, No. 296, Room V; "The Annunciation" by Carlo Crivelli, No. 739, Room VIII; in "The Angel Raphael accompanies Tobias on his Journey into Media" attributed to Botticini, No. 781, Room V; in "Portrait of a Lady," school of Pollaiuolo, No. 585, Room V; in "A Canon of the Church with his Patron Saints" by Gheeraert David, No. 1045, Room XI; or indeed the general run of the gold embroidery of the period as shown in our gallery. [147]

So with the jewels; there are examples of jewels in most of the pictures named above, none of them, perhaps, very first-rate, but all of them painted with more care and serious aim than the eighteen-penny trinket which serves S. Nicholas for a brooch. The jewels in the mitre are rather better than this, but much depends upon the kind of day on which the picture is seen; on a clear bright day they, and indeed every part of the picture, look much worse than on a dull one because the badness can be more clearly seen. As for the mitre itself, it is made of the same hard unyielding material as the portico behind the saint, whatever this may be, presumably wood.

Observe also the crozier which S. Nicholas is holding; observe the cheap streak of high light exactly the same thickness all the way and only broken in one place; so with the folds in the draperies; all is monotonous, unobservant, unimaginative — the work of a feeble man whose pains will never extend much beyond those necessary to make him pass as stronger than he is; especially the folds in the white linen over S. Nicholas's throat, and about his girdle — weaker drapery can hardly be than this, unless, perhaps, that from under which S. Nicholas's hands come. There is not only no art here to conceal, but there is not even pains to conceal the want of art. As for the hands themselves, and indeed all the hands and feet throughout the picture, there is not one which is even tolerably drawn if judged by the standard which Royal Academicians apply to Royal Academy students now.

Granted that this is an early work, nevertheless I submit that the drawing here is not that of one who is going to do better by and by, it is that of one who is essentially insincere and who will never aim higher than immediate success. Those who grow to the best work almost always begin by laying great stress on details which are all they as yet have strength for; they cannot do much, but the little they can do they do and never tire of doing; they grow by getting juster notions of proportion and subordination of parts to the whole rather than by any greater amount of care and patience bestowed upon details. Here there are no bits of detail worked out as by one who was interested in them and enjoyed them. Wherever a thing can be scamped it is scamped. As the whole is, so are the details, and as the details are, so is the whole; all is tainted with eye-service and with a vulgarity not the less profound for being veiled by a due observance of conventionality.

I shall be told that Raffaelle did come to draw and paint much better than he has done here. I demur to this. He did a little better; he just took so much pains as to prevent him from going down-hill headlong, and, with practice, he gained facility, but he was never very good, either as a draughtsman or as a painter. His reputation, indeed, rests mainly on his supposed exquisitely pure and tender feeling. His colour is admittedly inferior, his handling is not highly praised by any one, his drawing has been much praised, but it is of a penmanship freehand kind which is particularly apt to take people in. Of course he could draw in some ways, no one giving all his time to art and living in Raffaelle's surroundings could, with even ordinary pains, help becoming a facile draughtsman, but it is the expression and sentiment of his pictures which are supposed to be so ineffable and to make him the prince of painters.

I do not think this reputation will be maintained much longer. I can see no ineffable expression in the Ansidei Madonna's head, nor yet in that of the Garvagh Madonna in our gallery, nor in the S. Catharine. He has the saint-touch, as some painters have the tree-touch and others the water-touch. I remember the time when I used to think I saw religious feeling in these last two pictures, but each time I see them I wonder more and more how I can have been taken in by them. I hear people admire the head of S. Nicholas in the Ansidei picture. I can see nothing in it beyond the power of a very ordinary painter, and nothing that a painter of more than very ordinary power would be satisfied with. When I look at the head of Bellini's Doge, Loredano Loredani, I can see defects, as every one can see defects in every picture, but the more I see it the more I marvel at it, and the more profoundly I respect the painter. With Raffaelle I find exactly the reverse; I am carried away at first, as I was when a young man by Mendelssohn's *Songs Without Words*, only to be very angry with myself presently on finding that I could have believed even for a short time in something that has no real hold upon me. I know the S. Catharine in our gallery has been said by some not to be by Raffaelle. No one will doubt its genuineness who compares the drawing, painting and feeling of S. Catharine's eyes and nose with those of the S. John in the Ansidei picture. The doubts have only been raised owing to the fact that the picture, being hung on a level with the eye, is so easily seen to be bad that people think Raffaelle cannot have painted it.

Returning to the S. Nicholas; apart from the expression, or as it seems to me want of expression, the modelling of the head is not only poor but very poor. The forehead is formless and boneless, the nose is entirely wanting in that play of line and surface which an old man's nose affords; no one ever yet drew or painted a nose absolutely as nature has made it, but he who compares carefully drawn noses, as that in Rembrandt's younger portrait of himself, in his old woman, in the three Van Eycks, in the Andrea Solario, in the Loredano Loredani by Bellini, all in our gallery, with the nose of Raffaelle's S. Nicholas will not be long in finding out how slovenly Raffaelle's treatment in reality is. Eyes, eyebrows, mouth, cheeks and chin are treated with the same weakness, and this not the weakness of a child who is taking much pains to do something beyond his strength, and whose intention can be felt through and above the imperfections of his performance (as in the case of the two Apostles' heads by Giotto in our gallery), but of one who is not even conscious of weakness save by way of impatience that his work should cost him time and trouble at all, and who is satisfied if he can turn it out well enough to take in patrons who have themselves never either drawn or painted.

Finally, let the spectator turn to the sky and landscape. It is the cheapest kind of sky with no clouds and going down as low as possible, so as to save doing more country details than could be helped. As for the little landscape there is, let the reader compare it with any of the examples by Bellini, Basaiti, or even Cima da Conegliano, which may be found in the same or the adjoining rooms.

How, then, did Raffaelle get his reputation? It may be answered, How did Virgil get his? or Dante? or Bacon? or Plato? or Mendelssohn? or a score of others who not only get the public ear but keep it sometimes for centuries? How did Guido, Guercino and Domenichino get their reputations? A hundred years ago these men were held as hardly inferior to Raffaelle himself. They had a couple of hundred years or so of triumph—why so much? And if so much, why not more? If we begin asking questions, we may ask why anything at all? *Populus vult decipi* is the only answer, and nine men out of ten will follow on with *et decipiatur*. The immediate question, however, is not how Raffaelle came by his reputation but whether, having got it, he will continue to hold it now that we have a fair amount of his work at the National Gallery.

I grant that the general effect of the picture if looked at as a mere piece of decoration is agreeable, but I have seen many a picture which though not bearing consideration as a serious work yet looked well from a purely decorative standpoint. I believe, however, that at least half of those who sit gazing before this Ansidei Raffaelle by the half-hour at a time do so rather that they may be seen than see; half, again, of the remaining half come because they are made to do so, the rest see rather what they bring with them and put into the picture than what the picture puts into them.

And then there is the charm of mere age. Any Italian picture of the early part of the sixteenth century, even though by a worse painter than Raffaelle, can hardly fail to call up in us a solemn, old-world feeling, as though we had stumbled unexpectedly on some holy, peaceful survivors of an age long gone by, when the struggle was not so fierce and the world was a sweeter, happier place than we now find it, when men and women were comelier, and we should like to have lived among them, to have been golden-hued as they, to have done as they did; we dream of what might have been if our lines had been cast in more pleasant places—and so on, all of it rubbish, but still not wholly unpleasant rubbish so long as it is not dwelt upon.

Bearing in mind the natural tendency to accept anything which gives us a peep as it were into a golden age, real or imaginary, bearing in mind also the way in which this particular picture has been written up by critics, and the prestige of Raffaelle's name, the wonder is not that so many let themselves be taken in and carried away with it but that there should not be a greater gathering before it than there generally is.

Buying a Rembrandt

As an example of the evenness of the balance of advantages between the principles of staying still and taking what comes, and going about to look for things, [151] I might mention my small Rembrandt, "The Robing of Joseph before Pharaoh." I have wanted a Rembrandt all my life, and I have wanted not to give more than a few shillings for it. I might have travelled all Europe over for no one can say how many years, looking for a good, well-preserved, forty-shilling Rembrandt (and this was what I wanted), but on two occasions of my life cheap Rembrandts have run right up against me. The first was a head cut out of a ruined picture that had only in part escaped destruction when Belvoir Castle was burned down at the beginning of this century. I did not see the head but have little doubt it was genuine. It was offered me for a pound; I was not equal to the occasion and did not at once go to see it as I ought, and when I attended to it some months later the thing had gone. My only excuse must be that I was very young.

I never got another chance till a few weeks ago when I saw what I took, and take, to be an early, but very interesting, work by Rembrandt in the window of a pawnbroker opposite St. Clement Danes Church in the Strand. I very nearly let this slip too. I saw it and was very much struck with it, but, knowing that I am a little apt to be too sanguine, distrusted my judgment; in the evening I mentioned the picture to Gogin who went and looked at it; finding him not less impressed than I had been with the idea that the work was an early one by Rembrandt, I bought it, and the more I look at it the more satisfied I am that we are right.

People talk as though the making the best of what comes was such an easy matter, whereas nothing in reality requires more experience and good sense. It is only those who know how not to let the luck that runs against them slip, who will be able to find things, no matter how long and how far they go in search of them. [1887.]

Trying to Buy a Bellini

Flushed with triumph in the matter of Rembrandt, a fortnight or so afterwards I was at Christie's and saw two pictures that fired me. One was a Madonna and Child by Giovanni Bellini, I do not doubt genuine, not in a very good state, but still not repainted. The Madonna was lovely, the Child very good, the landscape sweet and Belliniesque. I was much smitten and determined to bid up to a hundred pounds; I knew this would be dirt cheap and was not going to buy at all unless I could get good value. I bid up to a hundred guineas, but there was someone else bent on having it and when he bid 105 guineas I let him have it, not without regret. I saw in the *Times* that the purchaser's name was Lesser.

The other picture I tried to get at the same sale (this day week); it was a small sketch numbered 72 (I think) and purporting to be by Giorgione but, I fully believe, by Titian. I bid up to £10 and then let it go. It went for £28, and I should say would have been well bought at £40. [1887.]

Watts

I was telling Gogin how I had seen at Christie's some pictures by Watts and how much I had disliked them. He said some of them had been exhibited in Paris a few years ago and a friend of his led him up to one of them and said in a serious, puzzled, injured tone:

"Mon cher ami, racontez-moi donc ceci, s'il vous plait," as though their appearance in such a place at all were something that must have an explanation not obvious upon the face of it.

Lombard Portals

The crouching beasts, on whose backs the pillars stand, generally have a little one beneath them or some animal which they have killed, or something, in fact, to give them occupation; it was felt that, though an animal by itself was well, an animal doing something was much better. The mere fact of companionship and silent sympathy is enough to interest, but without this, sculptured animals are stupid, as our lions in Trafalgar Square — which, among other faults, have that of being much too well done.

So Jones's cat, Prince, picked up a little waif in the court and brought it home, and the two lay together and were much lovelier than Prince was by himself. [153]

Holbein at Basle

How well he has done Night in his "Crucifixion"! Also he has tried to do the Alps, putting them as background to the city, but he has not done them as we should do them now. I think the tower on the hill behind the city is the tower which we see on leaving Basle on the road for Lucerne, I mean I think Holbein had this tower in his head.

Van Eyck

Van Eyck is delightful rather in spite of his high finish than because of it. De Hooghe finishes as highly as any one need do. Van Eyck's finish is saved because up to the last he is essentially impressionist, that is, he keeps a just account of relative importances and keeps them in their true subordination one to another. The only difference between him and Rembrandt or Velasquez is that these, as a general rule, stay their hand at an earlier stage of impressionism.

Giotto

There are few modern painters who are not greater technically than Giotto, but I cannot call to mind a single one whose work impresses me as profoundly as his does. How is it that our so greatly better should be so greatly worse — that the farther we go beyond him the higher he stands above us? Time no doubt has much to do with it, for, great as Giotto was, there are painters of to-day not less so, if they only dared express themselves as frankly and unaffectedly as he did.

Early Art

The youth of an art is, like the youth of anything else, its most interesting period. When it has come to the knowledge of good and evil it is stronger, but we care less about it.

Sincerity

It is not enough that the painter should make the spectator feel what he meant him to feel; he must also make him feel that this feeling was shared by the painter himself *bona fide* and without affectation. Of all the lies a painter can tell the worst is saying that he likes what he does not like. But the poor wretch seldom knows himself; for the art of knowing what gives him pleasure has been so neglected that it has been lost to all but a very few. The old Italians knew well enough what they liked and were as children in saying it.

X
The Position of a Homo Unius Libri

Trübner and Myself

When I went back to Trübner, after Bogue had failed, I had a talk with him and his partner. I could see they had lost all faith in my literary prospects. Trübner told me I was a *homo unius libri*, meaning *Erewhon*. He said I was in a very solitary position. I replied that I knew I was, but it suited me. I said:

"I pay my way; when I was with you before, I never owed you money; you find me now not owing my publisher money, but my publisher in debt to me; I never owe so much as a tailor's bill; beyond secured debts, I do not owe £5 in the world and never have" (which is quite true). "I get my summer's holiday in Italy every year; I live very quietly and cheaply, but it suits my health and tastes, and I have no acquaintances but those I value. My friends stick by me. If I was to get in with these literary and scientific people I should hate them and they me. I should fritter away my time and my freedom without getting a *quid pro quo*: as it is, I am free and I give the swells every now and then such a facer as they get from no one else. Of course I don't expect to get on in a commercial sense at present, I do not go the right way to work for this; but I am going the right way to secure a lasting reputation and this is what I do care for. A man cannot have both, he must make up his mind which he means going in for. I have gone in for posthumous fame and I see no step in my literary career which I do not think calculated to promote my being held in esteem when the heat of passion has subsided."

Trübner shrugged his shoulders. He plainly does not believe that I shall succeed in getting a hearing; he thinks the combination of the religious and cultured world too strong for me to stand against.

If he means that the reviewers will burke me as far as they can, no doubt he is right; but when I am dead there will be other reviewers and I have already done enough to secure that they shall from time to time look me up. They won't bore me then but they will be just like the present ones. [1882.]

Capping a Success

When I had written *Erewhon* people wanted me at once to set to work and write another book like it. How could I? I cannot think how I escaped plunging into writing some laboured stupid book. I am very glad I did escape. Nothing is so cruel as to try and force a man beyond his natural pace. If he has got more stuff in him it will come out in its own time and its own way: if he has not—let the poor wretch alone; to have done one decent book should be enough; the very worst way to get another out of him is to press him. The more promise a young writer has given, the more his friends should urge him not to over-tax himself.

A Lady Critic

A lady, whom I meet frequently in the British Museum reading-room and elsewhere, said to me the other day:

"Why don't you write another *Erewhon*?"

"Why, my dear lady," I replied, "*Life and Habit* was another *Erewhon*."

They say these things to me continually to plague me and make out that I could do one good book but never any more. She is the sort of person who if she had known Shakespeare would have said to him, when he wrote *Henry the IVth*:

"Ah, Mr. Shakespeare, why don't you write us another *Titus Andronicus*? Now that was a sweet play, that was."

And when he had done *Antony and Cleopatra* she would have told him that her favourite plays were the three parts of *King Henry VI*.

Compensation

If I die prematurely, at any rate I shall be saved from being bored by my own success.

Hudibras and Erewhon

I was completing the purchase of some small houses at Lewisham and had to sign my name. The vendor, merely seeing the name and knowing none of my books, said to me, rather rudely, but without meaning any mischief:

"Have you written any books like *Hudibras*?"

I said promptly: "Certainly; *Erewhon* is quite as good a book as *Hudibras*."

This was coming it too strong for him, so he thought I had not heard and repeated his question. I said again as before, and he shut up. I sent him a copy of *Erewhon* immediately after we had completed. It was rather tall talk on my part, I admit, but he should not have challenged me unprovoked.

Life and Habit and Myself

At the Century Club I was talking with a man who asked me why I did not publish the substance of what I had been saying. I believed he knew me and said:

"Well, you knŏw, there's *Life and Habit*."

He did not seem to rise at all, so I asked him if he had seen the book.

"Seen it?" he answered. "Why, I should think every one has seen *Life and Habit*: but what's that got to do with it?"

I said it had taken me so much time lately that I had had none to spare for anything else. Again he did not seem to see the force of the remark and a friend, who was close by, said:

"You know, Butler wrote *Life and Habit*."

He would not believe it, and it was only after repeated assurance that he accepted it. It was plain he thought a great deal of *Life and Habit* and had idealised its author, whom he was disappointed to find so very commonplace a person. Exactly the same thing happened to me with *Erewhon*. I was glad to find that *Life and Habit* had made so deep an impression at any rate upon one person.

A Disappointing Person

I suspect I am rather a disappointing person, for every now and then there is a fuss and I am to meet some one who would very much like to make my acquaintance, or some one writes me a letter and says he has long admired my books, and may he, etc.? Of course I say "Yes," but experience has taught me that it always ends in turning some one who was more or less inclined to run me into one who considers he has a grievance against me for not being a very different kind of person from what I am. These people however (and this happens on an average once or twice a year) do not come solely to see me, they generally tell me all about themselves and the impression is left upon me that they have really come in order to be praised. I am as civil to them as I know how to be but enthusiastic I never am, for they have never any of them been nice people, and it is my want of enthusiasm for themselves as much as anything else which disappoints them. They seldom come again. Mr. Alfred Tylor was the only acquaintance I have ever made through being sent for to be looked at, or letting some one come to look at me, who turned out a valuable ally; but then he sent for me through mutual friends in the usual way.

Entertaining Angels

I doubt whether any angel would find me very entertaining. As for myself, if ever I do entertain one it will have to be unawares. When people entertain others without an introduction they generally turn out more like devils than angels.

Myself and My Books

The balance against them is now over £350. How completely they must have been squashed unless I had had a little money of my own. Is it not likely that many a better writer than I am is squashed through want of money? Whatever I do I must not die poor; these examples of ill-requited labour are immoral, they discourage the effort of those who could and would do good things if they did not know that it would ruin themselves and their families; moreover, they set people on to pamper a dozen fools for each neglected man of merit, out of compunction. Genius, they say, always wears an invisible cloak; these men wear invisible cloaks—therefore they are geniuses; and it flatters them to think that they can see more than their neighbours. The neglect of one such man as the author of *Hudibras* is compensated for by the petting of a dozen others who would be the first to jump upon the author of *Hudibras* if he were to come back to life.

Heaven forbid that I should compare myself to the author of *Hudibras*, but still, if my books succeed after my death—which they may or may not, I know nothing about it—any way, if they do succeed, let it be understood that they failed during my life for a few very obvious reasons of which I was quite aware, for the effect of which I was prepared before I wrote my books, and which on consideration I found insufficient to deter me. I attacked people who were at once unscrupulous and powerful, and I made no alliances. I did this because I did not want to be bored and have my time wasted and my pleasures curtailed. I had money enough to live on, and preferred addressing myself to posterity rather than to any except a very few of my own contemporaries. Those few I have always kept well in mind. I think of them continually when in doubt about any passage, but beyond those few I will not go. Posterity will give a man a fair hearing; his own times will not do so if he is attacking vested interests, and I have attacked two powerful sets of vested interests at once. [The Church and Science.] What is the good of addressing people who will not listen? I have addressed the next generation and have therefore said many things which want time before they become palatable. Any man who wishes his work to stand will sacrifice a good deal of his immediate audience for the sake of being attractive to a much larger number of people later on. He cannot gain this later audience unless he has been fearless and thorough-going, and if he is this he is sure to have to tread on the corns of a great many of those who live at the same time with him, however little he may wish to do so. He must not expect these people to help him on, nor wonder if, for a time, they succeed in snuffing him out. It is part of the swim that it should be so. Only, as one who believes himself to have practised what he preaches, let me assure any one who has money of his own that to write fearlessly for posterity and not get paid for it is much better fun than I can imagine its being to write like, we will say, George Eliot and make a lot of money by it. [1883.]

Dragons

People say that there are neither dragons to be killed nor distressed maidens to be rescued nowadays. I do not know, but I think I have dropped across one or two, nor do I feel sure whether the most mortal wounds have been inflicted by the dragons or by myself.

Trying to Know

There are some things which it is madness not to try to know but which it is almost as much madness to try to know. Sometimes publishers, hoping to buy the Holy Ghost with a price, fee a man to read for them and advise them. This is but as the vain tossing of insomnia. God will not have any human being know what will sell, nor when any one is going to die, nor anything about the ultimate, or even the deeper, springs of growth and action, nor yet such a little thing as whether it is going to rain to-morrow. I do not say that the impossibility of being certain about these and similar matters was designed, but it is as complete as though it had been not only designed but designed exceedingly well.

Squaring Accounts

We owe past generations not only for the master discoveries of music, science, literature and art—few of which brought profit to those to whom they were revealed—but also for our organism itself which is an inheritance gathered and garnered by those who have gone before us. What money have we paid not for Handel and Shakespeare only but for our eyes and ears?

And so with regard to our contemporaries. A man is sometimes tempted to exclaim that he does not fare well at the hands of his own generation; that, although he may play pretty assiduously, he is received with more hisses than applause; that the public is hard to please, slow to praise, and bent on driving as hard a bargain as it can. This, however, is only what he should expect. No sensible man will suppose himself to be of so much importance that his contemporaries should be at much pains to get at the truth concerning him.

As for my own position, if I say the things I want to say without troubling myself about the public, why should I grumble at the public for not troubling about me? Besides, not being paid myself, I can in better conscience use the works of others, as I daily do, without paying for them and without being at the trouble of praising or thanking them more than I have a mind to. And, after all, how can I say I am not paid? In addition to all that I inherit from past generations I receive from my own everything that makes life worth living—London, with its infinite sources of pleasure and amusement, good theatres, concerts, picture galleries, the British Museum Reading-Room, newspapers, a comfortable dwelling, railways and, above all, the society of the friends I value.

Charles Darwin on what Sells a Book

I remember when I was at Down we were talking of what it is that sells a book. Mr. Darwin said he did not believe it was reviews or advertisements, but simply "being talked about" that sold a book.

I believe he is quite right here, but surely a good flaming review helps to get a book talked about. I have often inquired at my publishers' after a review and I never found one that made any perceptible increase or decrease of sale, and the same with advertisements. I think, however, that the review of *Erewhon* in the *Spectator* did sell a few copies of *Erewhon*, but then it was such a very strong one and the anonymousness of the book stimulated curiosity. A perception of the value of a review, whether friendly or hostile, is as old as St. Paul's Epistle to the Philippians. [162]

Hoodwinking the Public

Sincerity or honesty is a low and very rudimentary form of virtue that is only to be found to any considerable extent among the protozoa. Compare, for example, the integrity, sincerity and absolute refusal either to deceive or be deceived that exists in the germ-cells of any individual, with the instinctive aptitude for lying that is to be observed in the full-grown man. The full-grown man is compacted of lies and shams which are to him as the breath of his nostrils. Whereas the germ-cells will not be humbugged; they will tell the truth as near as they can. They know their ancestors meant well and will tend to become even more sincere themselves.

Thus, if a painter has not tried hard to paint well and has tried hard to hoodwink the public, his offspring is not likely to show hereditary aptitude for painting, but is likely to have an improved power of hoodwinking the public. So it is with music, literature, science or anything else. The only thing the public can do against this is to try hard to develop a hereditary power of not being hoodwinked. From the small success it has met with hitherto we may think that the effort on its part can have been neither severe nor long sustained. Indeed, all ages seem to have held that "the pleasure is as great of being cheated as to cheat."

The Public Ear

Those who have squatted upon it may be trusted to keep off other squatters if they can. The public ear is like the land which looks infinite but is all parcelled out into fields and private ownerships—barring, of course, highways and commons. So the universe, which looks so big, may be supposed as really all parcelled out among the stars that stud it.

Or the public ear is like a common; there is not much to be got off it, but that little is for the most part grazed down by geese and donkeys.

Those who wish to gain the public ear should bear in mind that people do not generally want to be made less foolish or less wicked. What they want is to be told that they are not foolish and not wicked. Now it is only a fool or a liar or both who can tell them this; the masses therefore cannot be expected to like any but fools or liars or both. So when a lady gets photographed, what she wants is not to be made beautiful but to be told that she is beautiful.

H2Secular Thinking

The ages do their thinking much as the individual does. When considering a difficult question, we think alternately for several seconds together of details, even the minutest seeming important, and then of broad general principles, whereupon even large details become unimportant; again we have bouts during which rules, logic and technicalities engross us, followed by others in which the unwritten and unwritable common sense of grace defies and over-rides the law. That is to say, we have our inductive fits and our deductive fits, our arrangements according to the letter and according to the spirit, our conclusions drawn from logic *secundum artem* and from absurdity and the character of the arguer. This heterogeneous mass of considerations forms the mental pabulum with which we feed our minds. How that pabulum becomes amalgamated, reduced to uniformity and turned into the growth of complete opinion we can no more tell than we can say when, how and where food becomes flesh and blood. All we can say is that the miracle, stupendous as it is and involving the stultification of every intelligible principle on which thought and action are based, is nevertheless worked a thousand times an hour by every one of us.

The formation of public opinion is as mysterious as that of individual, but, so far as we can form any opinion about that which forms our opinions in such large measure, the processes appear to resemble one another much as rain drops resemble one another. There is essential agreement in spite of essential difference. So that here, as everywhere else, we no sooner scratch the soil than we come upon the granite of contradiction in terms and can scratch no further.

As for ourselves, we are passing through an inductive, technical, speculative period and have gone such lengths in this direction that a reaction, during which we shall pass to the other extreme, may be confidently predicted.

The Art of Propagating Opinion

He who would propagate an opinion must begin by making sure of his ground and holding it firmly. There is as little use in trying to breed from weak opinion as from other weak stock, animal or vegetable.

The more securely a man holds an opinion, the more temperate he can afford to be, and the more temperate he is, the more weight he will carry with those who are in the long run weightiest. Ideas and opinions, like living organisms, have a normal rate of growth which cannot be either checked or forced beyond a certain point. They can be held in check more safely than they can be hurried. They can also be killed; and one of the surest ways to kill them is to try to hurry them.

The more unpopular an opinion is, the more necessary is it that the holder should be somewhat punctilious in his observance of conventionalities generally, and that, if possible, he should get the reputation of being well-to-do in the world.

Arguments are not so good as assertion. Arguments are like fire-arms which a man may keep at home but should not carry about with him. Indirect assertion, leaving the hearer to point the inference, is, as a rule, to be preferred. The one great argument with most people is that another should think this or that. The reasons of the belief are details and, in nine cases out of ten, best omitted as confusing and weakening the general impression.

Many, if not most, good ideas die young—mainly from neglect on the part of the parents, but sometimes from over-fondness. Once well started, an opinion had better be left to shift for itself.

Insist as far as possible on the insignificance of the points of difference as compared with the resemblances to opinions generally accepted.

Gladstone as a Financier

I said to my tobacconist that Gladstone was not a financier because he bought a lot of china at high prices and it fetched very little when it was sold at Christie's.

"Did he give high prices?" said the tobacconist.

"Enormous prices," said I emphatically.

Now, to tell the truth, I did not know whether Mr. Gladstone had ever bought the china at all, much less what he gave for it, if he did; he may have had it all left him for aught I knew. But I was going to appeal to my tobacconist by arguments that he could understand, and I could see he was much impressed.

Argument

Argument is generally waste of time and trouble. It is better to present one's opinion and leave it to stick or no as it may happen. If sound, it will probably in the end stick, and the sticking is the main thing.

Humour

What a frightful thing it would be if true humour were more common or, rather, more easy to see, for it is more common than those are who can see it. It would block the way of everything. Perhaps this is what people rather feel. It would be like Music in the *Ode for St. Cecilia's Day*, it would "untune the sky."

I do not know quite what is meant by untuning the sky and, if I did, I cannot think that there is anything to be particularly gained by having the sky untuned; still, if it has got to be untuned at all, I am sure music is the only thing that can untune it. Rapson, however, whom I used to see in the coin room at the British Museum, told me it should be "entune the sky" and it sounds as though he were right.

Myself and "Unconscious Humour"

The phrase "unconscious humour" is the one contribution I have made to the current literature of the day. I am continually seeing unconscious humour (without quotation marks) alluded to in *Times* articles and other like places, but I never remember to have come across it as a synonym for dullness till I wrote *Life and Habit*.

My Humour

The thing to say about me just now is that my humour is forced. This began to reach me in connection with my article "Quis Desiderio . . .?" [*Universal Review*, 1888] and is now, [1889] I understand, pretty generally perceived even by those who had not found it out for themselves.

I am not aware of forcing myself to say anything which has not amused me, which is not apposite and which I do not believe will amuse a neutral reader, but I may very well do so without knowing it. As for my humour, I am like my father and grandfather, both of whom liked a good thing heartily enough if it was told them, but I do not often say a good thing myself. Very likely my humour, what little there is of it, is forced enough. I do not care so long as it amuses me and, such as it is, I shall vent it in my own way and at my own time.

Myself and My Publishers

I see my publishers are bringing out a new magazine with all the usual contributors. Of course they don't ask me to write and this shows that they do not think my name would help their magazine. This, I imagine, means that Andrew Lang has told them that my humour is forced. I should not myself say that Andrew Lang's humour would lose by a little forcing.

I have seen enough of my publishers to know that they have no ideas of their own about literature save what they can clutch at as believing it to be a straight tip from a business point of view. Heaven forbid that I should blame them for doing exactly what I should do myself in their place, but, things being as they are, they are no use to me. They have no confidence in me and they must have this or they will do nothing for me beyond keeping my books on their shelves.

Perhaps it is better that I should not have a chance of becoming a hack-writer, for I should grasp it at once if it were offered me.

XI
Cash and Credit

The Unseen World

I believe there is an unseen world about which we know nothing as firmly as any one can believe it. I see things coming up from it into the visible world and going down again from the seen world to the unseen. But my unseen world is to be bona fide unseen and, in so far as I say I know anything about it, I stultify myself. It should no more be described than God should be represented in painting or sculpture. It is as the other side of the moon; we know it must be there but we know also that, in the nature of things, we can never see it. Sometimes, some trifle of it may sway into sight and out again, but it is so little that it is not worth counting as having been seen.

The Kingdom of Heaven

The world admits that there is another world, that there is a kingdom, veritable and worth having, which, nevertheless, is invisible and has nothing to do with any kingdom such as we now see. It agrees that the wisdom of this other kingdom is foolishness here on earth, while the wisdom of the world is foolishness in the Kingdom of Heaven. In our hearts we know that the Kingdom of Heaven is the higher of the two and the better worth living and dying for, and that, if it is to be won, it must be sought steadfastly and in singleness of heart by those who put all else on one side and, shrinking from no sacrifice, are ready to face shame, poverty and torture here rather than abandon the hope of the prize of their high calling. Nobody who doubts any of this is worth talking with.

The question is, where is this Heavenly Kingdom, and what way are we to take to find it? Happily the answer is easy, for we are not likely to go wrong if in all simplicity, humility and good faith we heartily desire to find it and follow the dictates of ordinary common-sense.

The Philosopher

He should have made many mistakes and been saved often by the skin of his teeth, for the skin of one's teeth is the most teaching thing about one.

He should have been, or at any rate believed himself, a great fool and a great criminal. He should have cut himself adrift from society, and yet not be without society. He should have given up all, even Christ himself, for Christ's sake. He should be above fear or love or hate, and yet know them extremely well. He should have lost all save a small competence and know what a vantage ground it is to be an outcast. Destruction and Death say they have heard the fame of Wisdom with their ears, and the philosopher must have been close up to these if he too would hear it.

The Artist and the Shopkeeper

Most artists, whether in religion, music, literature, painting, or what not, are shopkeepers in disguise. They hide their shop as much as they can, and keep pretending that it does not exist, but they are essentially shopkeepers and nothing else. Why do I try to sell my books and feel regret at never seeing them pay their expenses if I am not a shopkeeper? Of course I am, only I keep a bad shop—a shop that does not pay.

In like manner, the professed shopkeeper has generally a taint of the artist somewhere about him which he tries to conceal as much as the professed artist tries to conceal his shopkeeping.

The business man and the artist are like matter and mind. We can never get either pure and without some alloy of the other.

Art and Trade

People confound literature and article-dealing because the plant in both cases is similar, but no two things can be more distinct. Neither the question of money nor that of friend or foe can enter into literature proper. Here, right feeling—or good taste, if this expression be preferred—is alone considered. If a bona fide writer thinks a thing wants saying, he will say it as tersely, clearly and elegantly as he can. The question whether it will do him personally good or harm, or how it will affect this or that friend, never enters his head, or, if it does, it is instantly ordered out again. The only personal gratifications allowed him (apart, of course, from such as are conceded to every one, writer or no) are those of keeping his good name spotless among those whose opinion is alone worth having and of maintaining the highest traditions of a noble calling. If a man lives in fear and trembling lest he should fail in these respects, if he finds these considerations alone weigh with him, if he never writes without thinking how he shall best serve good causes and damage bad ones, then he is a genuine man of letters. If in addition to this he succeeds in making his manner attractive, he will become a classic. He knows this. He knows, although the Greeks in their mythology forgot to say so, that Conceit was saved to mankind as well as Hope when Pandora clapped the lid on to her box.

With the article-dealer, on the other hand, money is, and ought to be, the first consideration. Literature is an art; article-writing, when a man is paid for it, is a trade and none the worse for that; but pot-boilers are one thing and genuine pictures are another. People have indeed been paid for some of the most genuine pictures ever painted, and so with music, and so with literature itself—hard-and-fast lines ever cut the fingers of those who draw them—but, as a general rule, most lasting art has been poorly paid, so far as money goes, till the artist was near the end of his time, and, whether money passed or no, we may be sure that it was not thought of. Such work is done as a bird sings—for the love of the thing; it is persevered in as long as body and soul can be kept together, whether there be pay or no, and perhaps better if there be no pay.

Nevertheless, though art disregards money and trade disregards art, the artist may stand not a little trade-alloy and be even toughened by it, and the tradesmen may be more than half an artist. Art is in the world but not of it; it lives in a kingdom of its own, governed by laws that none but artists can understand. This, at least, is the ideal towards which an artist tends, though we all very well know we none of us reach it. With the trade it is exactly the reverse; this world is, and ought to be, everything, and the invisible world is as little to the trade as this visible world is to the artist.

When I say the artist tends towards such a world, I mean not that he tends consciously and reasoningly but that his instinct to take this direction will be too strong to let him take any other. He is incapable of reasoning on the subject; if he could reason he would be lost *qua* artist; for, by every test that reason can apply, those who sell themselves for a price are in the right. The artist is guided by a faith that for him transcends all reason. Granted that this faith has been in great measure founded on reason, that it has grown up along with reason, that if it lose touch with reason it is no longer faith but madness; granted, again, that reason is in great measure founded on faith, that it has grown up along with faith, that if it lose touch with faith it is no longer reason but mechanism; granted, therefore, that faith grows with reason as will with power, as demand with supply, as mind with body, each stimulating and augmenting the other until an invisible, minute nucleus attains colossal growth—nevertheless the difference between the man of the world and the man who lives by faith is that the first is drawn towards the one and the second towards the other of two principles which, so far as we can see, are co-extensive and co-equal in importance.

Money

It is curious that money, which is the most valuable thing in life, *exceptis excipiendis*, should be the most fatal corrupter of music, literature, painting and all the arts. As soon as any art is pursued with a view to money, then farewell, in ninety-nine cases out of a hundred, all hope of genuine good work. If a man has money at his back, he may touch these things and do something which will live a long while, and he may be very happy in doing it; if he has no money, he may do good work, but the chances are he will be killed in doing it and for having done it; or he may make himself happy by doing bad work and getting money out of it, and there is no great harm in this, provided he knows his work is done in this spirit and rates it for its commercial value only. Still, as a rule, a man should not touch any of the arts as a creator unless be has a *discreta posizionina* behind him.

Modern Simony

It is not the dealing in livings but the thinking they can buy the Holy Ghost for money which vulgar rich people indulge in when they dabble in literature, music and painting.

Nevertheless, on reflection it must be admitted that the Holy Ghost is very hard to come by without money. For the Holy Ghost is only another term for the Fear of the Lord, which is Wisdom. And though Wisdom cannot be gotten for gold, still less can it be gotten without it. Gold, or the value that is equivalent to gold, lies at the root of Wisdom, and enters so largely into the very essence of the Holy Ghost that "No gold, no Holy Ghost" may pass as an axiom. This is perhaps why it is not easy to buy Wisdom by whatever name it be called—I mean, because it is almost impossible to sell it. It is a very unmarketable commodity, as those who have received it truly know to their own great bane and boon.

My Grandfather and Myself

My grandfather worked very hard all his life, and was making money all the time until he became a bishop. I have worked very hard all my life, but have never been able to earn money. As usefulness is generally counted, no one can be more useless. This I believe to be largely due to the public-school and university teaching through which my grandfather made his money. Yes, but then if he is largely responsible for that which has made me useless, has he not also left me the hardly-won money which makes my uselessness sufficiently agreeable to myself? And would not the poor old gentleman gladly change lots with me, if he could?

I do not know; but I should be sorry to change lots with him or with any one else, so I need not grumble. I said in *Luck or Cunning*? that the only way (at least I think I said so) in which a teacher can thoroughly imbue an unwilling learner with his own opinions is for the teacher to eat the pupil up and thus assimilate him—if he can, for it is possible that the pupil may continue to disagree with the teacher. And as a matter of fact, school-masters do live upon their pupils, and I, as my grandfather's grandson, continue to batten upon old pupil.

Art and Usefulness

Tedder, the Librarian of the Athenæum, said to me when I told him (I have only seen him twice) what poor success my books had met with:

"Yes, but you have made the great mistake of being useful."

This, for the moment, displeased me, for I know that I have always tried to make my work useful and should not care about doing it at all unless I believed it to subserve use more or less directly. Yet when I look at those works which we all hold to be the crowning glories of the world as, for example, the *Iliad*, the *Odyssey, Hamlet*, the *Messiah*, Rembrandt's portraits, or Holbein's, or Giovanni Bellini's, the connection between them and use is, to say the least of it, far from obvious. Music, indeed, can hardly be tortured into being useful at all, unless to drown the cries of the wounded in battle, or to enable people to talk more freely at evening parties. The uses, again, of painting in its highest forms are very doubtful—I mean in any material sense; in its lower forms, when it becomes more diagrammatic, it is materially useful. Literature may be useful from its lowest forms to nearly its highest, but the highest cannot be put in harness to any but spiritual uses; and the fact remains that the "Hallelujah Chorus," the speech of Hamlet to the players, Bellini's "Doge" have their only uses in a spiritual world whereto the word "uses" is as alien as bodily flesh is to a choir of angels. As it is fatal to the highest art that it should have been done for money, so it seems hardly less fatal that it should be done with a view to those uses that tend towards money.

And yet, was not the *Iliad* written mainly with a view to money? Did not Shakespeare make money by his plays, Handel by his music, and the noblest painters by their art? True; but in all these cases, I take it, love of fame and that most potent and, at the same time, unpractical form of it, the lust after fame beyond the grave, was the mainspring of the action, the money being but a concomitant accident. Money is like the wind that bloweth whithersoever it listeth, sometimes it chooses to attach itself to high feats of literature and art and music, but more commonly it prefers lower company . . .

I can continue this note no further, for there is no end to it. Briefly, the world resolves itself into two great classes—those who hold that honour after death is better worth having than any honour a man can get and know anything about, and those who doubt this; to my mind, those who hold it, and hold it firmly, are the only people worth thinking about. They will also hold that, important as the physical world obviously is, the spiritual world, of which we know little beyond its bare existence, is more important still.

Genius

i

Genius is akin both to madness and inspiration and, as every one is both more or less inspired and more or less mad, every one has more or less genius. When, therefore, we speak of genius we do not mean an absolute thing which some men have and others have not, but a small scale-turning overweight of a something which we all have but which we cannot either define or apprehend—the quantum which we all have being allowed to go without saying.

This small excess weight has been defined as a supreme capacity for taking trouble, but he who thus defined it can hardly claim genius in respect of his own definition—his capacity for taking trouble does not seem to have been abnormal. It might be more fitly described as a supreme capacity for getting its possessors into trouble of all kinds and keeping them therein so long as the genius remains. People who are credited with genius have, indeed, been sometimes very painstaking, but they would often show more signs of genius if they had taken less. "You have taken too much trouble with your opera," said Handel to Gluck. It is not likely that the "Hailstone Chorus" or Mrs. Quickly cost their creators much pains, indeed, we commonly feel the ease with which a difficult feat has been performed to be a more distinctive mark of genius than the fact that the performer took great pains before he could achieve it. Pains can serve genius, or even mar it, but they cannot make it.

We can rarely, however, say what pains have or have not been taken in any particular case, for, over and above the spent pains of a man's early efforts, the force of which may carry him far beyond all trace of themselves, there are the still more remote and invisible ancestral pains, repeated we know not how often or in what fortunate correlation with pains taken in some other and unseen direction. This points to the conclusion that, though it is wrong to suppose the essence of genius to lie in a capacity for taking pains, it is right to hold that it must have been rooted in pains and that it cannot have grown up without them.

Genius, again, might, perhaps almost as well, be defined as a supreme capacity for saving other people from having to take pains, if the highest flights of genius did not seem to know nothing about pains one way or the other. What trouble can *Hamlet* or the *Iliad* save to any one? Genius can, and does, save it sometimes; the genius of Newton may have saved a good deal of trouble one way or another, but it has probably engendered as much new as it has saved old.

This, however, is all a matter of chance, for genius never seems to care whether it makes the burden or bears it. The only certain thing is that there will be a burden, for the Holy Ghost has ever tended towards a breach of the peace, and the New Jerusalem, when it comes, will probably be found so far to resemble the old as to stone its prophets freely. The world thy world is a jealous world, and thou shalt have none other worlds but it. Genius points to change, and change is a hankering after another world, so the old world suspects it. Genius disturbs order, it unsettles *mores* and hence it is immoral. On a small scale it is intolerable, but genius will have no small scales; it is even more immoral for a man to be too far in front than to lag too far behind. The only absolute morality is absolute stagnation, but this is unpractical, so a peck of change is permitted to every one, but it must be a peck only, whereas genius would have ever so many sacks full. There is a myth among some Eastern nation that at the birth of Genius an unkind fairy marred all the good gifts of the other fairies by depriving it of the power of knowing where to stop.

Nor does genius care more about money than about trouble. It is no respecter of time, trouble, money or persons, the four things round which human affairs turn most persistently. It will not go a hair's breadth from its way either to embrace fortune or to avoid her. It is, like Love, "too young to know the worth of gold." [176] It knows, indeed, both love and hate, but not as we know them, for it will fly for help to its bitterest foe, or attack its dearest friend in the interests of the art it serves.

Yet this genius, which so despises the world, is the only thing of which the world is permanently enamoured, and the more it flouts the world, the more the world worships it, when it has once well killed it in the flesh. Who can understand this eternal crossing in love and contradiction in terms which warps the woof of actions and things from the atom to the universe? The more a man despises time, trouble, money, persons, place and everything on which the world insists as most essential to salvation, the more pious will this same world hold him to have been. What a fund of universal unconscious scepticism must underlie the world's opinions! For we are all alike in our worship of genius that has passed through the fire. Nor can this universal instinctive consent be explained otherwise than as the welling up of a spring whose sources lie deep in the conviction that great as this world is, it masks a greater wherein its wisdom is folly and which we know as blind men know where the sun is shining, certainly, but not distinctly.

This should in itself be enough to prove that such a world exists, but there is still another proof in the fact that so many come among us showing instinctive and ineradicable familiarity with a state of things which has no counterpart here, and cannot, therefore, have been acquired here. From such a world we come, every one of us, but some seem to have a more living recollection of it than others. Perfect recollection of it no man can have, for to put on flesh is to have all one's other memories jarred beyond power of conscious recognition. And genius must put on flesh, for it is only by the hook and crook of taint and flesh that tainted beings like ourselves can apprehend it, only in and through flesh can it be made manifest to us at all. The flesh and the shop will return no matter with how many pitchforks we expel them, for we cannot conceivably expel them thoroughly; therefore it is better not to be too hard upon them. And yet this same flesh cloaks genius at the very time that it reveals it. It seems as though the flesh must have been on and must have gone clean off before genius can be discerned, and also that we must stand a long way from it, for the world grows more and more myopic as it grows older. And this brings another trouble, for by the time the flesh has gone off it enough, and it is far enough away for us to see it without glasses, the chances are we shall have forgotten its very existence and lose the wish to see at the very moment of becoming able to do so. Hence there appears to be no remedy for the oft-repeated complaint that the world knows nothing of its greatest men. How can it be expected to do so? And how can its greatest men be expected to know more than a very little of the world? At any rate, they seldom do, and it is just because they cannot and do not that, if they ever happen to be found out at all, they are recognised as the greatest and the world weeps and wrings its hands that it cannot know more about them.

Lastly, if genius cannot be bought with money, still less can it sell what it produces. The only price that can be paid for genius is suffering, and this is the only wages it can receive. The only work that has any considerable permanence is written, more or less consciously, in the blood of the writer, or in that of his or her forefathers. Genius is like money, or, again, like crime, every one has a little, if it be only a half-penny, and he can beg or steal this much if he has not got it; but those who have little are rarely very fond of millionaires. People generally like and understand best those who are of much about the same social standing and money status as their own; and so it is for the most part as between those who have only the average amount of genius and the Homers, Shakespeares and Handels of the race.

And yet, so paradoxical is everything connected with genius, that it almost seems as though the nearer people stood to one another in respect either of money or genius, the more jealous they become of one another. I have read somewhere that Thackeray was one day flattening his nose against a grocer's window and saw two bags of sugar, one marked tenpence halfpenny and the other elevenpence (for sugar has come down since Thackeray's time). As he left the window he was heard to say, "How they must hate one another!" So it is in the animal and vegetable worlds. The war of extermination is generally fiercest between the most nearly allied species, for these stand most in one another's light. So here again the same old paradox and contradiction in terms meets us, like a stone wall, in the fact that we love best those who are in the main like ourselves, but when they get too like, we hate them, and, at the same time, we hate most those who are unlike ourselves, but if they become unlike enough, we may often be very fond of them.

Genius must make those that have it think apart, and to think apart is to take one's view of things instead of being, like Poins, a blessed fellow to think as every man thinks. A man who thinks for himself knows what others do not, but does not know what others know. Hence the *belli causa*, for he cannot serve two masters, the God of his own inward light and the Mammon of common sense, at one and the same time. How can a man think apart and not apart? But if he is a genius this is the riddle he must solve. The uncommon sense of genius and the common sense of the rest of the world are thus as husband and wife to one another; they are always quarrelling, and common sense, who must be taken to be the husband, always fancies himself the master—nevertheless genius is generally admitted to be the better half.

He who would know more of genius must turn to what he can find in the poets, or to whatever other sources he may discover, for I can help him no further.

ii

The destruction of great works of literature and art is as necessary for the continued development of either one or the other as death is for that of organic life. We fight against it as long as we can, and often stave it off successfully both for ourselves and others, but there is nothing so great—not Homer, Shakespeare, Handel, Rembrandt, Giovanni Bellini, De Hooghe, Velasquez and the goodly company of other great men for whose lives we would gladly give our own—but it has got to go sooner or later and leave no visible traces, though the invisible ones endure from everlasting to everlasting. It is idle to regret this for ourselves or others, our effort should tend towards enjoying and being enjoyed as highly and for as long time as we can, and then chancing the rest.

iii

Inspiration is never genuine if it is known as inspiration at the time. True inspiration always steals on a person; its importance not being fully recognised for some time. So men of genius always escape their own immediate belongings, and indeed generally their own age.

iv

Dullness is so much stronger than genius because there is so much more of it, and it is better organised and more naturally cohesive *inter se*. So the arctic volcano can do no thing against arctic ice.

v

America will have her geniuses, as every other country has, in fact she has already had one in Walt Whitman, but I do not think America is a good place in which to be a genius. A genius can never expect to have a good time anywhere, if he is a genuine article, but America is about the last place in which life will be endurable at all for an inspired writer of any kind.

Great Things

All men can do great things, if they know what great things are. So hard is this last that even where it exists the knowledge is as much unknown as known to them that have it and is more a leaning upon the Lord than a willing of one that willeth. And yet all the leaning on the Lord in Christendom fails if there be not a will of him that willeth to back it up. God and the man are powerless without one another.

Genius and Providence

Among all the evidences for the existence of an overruling Providence that I can discover, I see none more convincing than the elaborate and for the most part effectual provision that has been made for the suppression of genius. The more I see of the world, the more necessary I see it to be that by far the greater part of what is written or done should be of so fleeting a character as to take itself away quickly. That is the advantage in the fact that so much of our literature is journalism.

Schools and colleges are not intended to foster genius and to bring it out. Genius is a nuisance, and it is the duty of schools and colleges to abate it by setting genius-traps in its way. They are as the artificial obstructions in a hurdle race — tests of skill and endurance, but in themselves useless. Still, so necessary is it that genius and originality should be abated that, did not academies exist, we should have had to invent them.

The Art of Covery

This is as important and interesting as Dis-covery. Surely the glory of finally getting rid of and burying a long and troublesome matter should be as great as that of making an important discovery. The trouble is that the coverer is like Samson who perished in the wreck of what he had destroyed; if he gets rid of a thing effectually he gets rid of himself too.

Wanted

We want a Society for the Suppression of Erudite Research and the Decent Burial of the Past. The ghosts of the dead past want quite as much laying as raising.

Ephemeral and Permanent Success

The supposition that the world is ever in league to put a man down is childish. Hardly less childish is it for an author to lay the blame on reviewers. A good sturdy author is a match for a hundred reviewers. He, I grant, knows nothing of either literature or science who does not know that a *mot d'ordre* given by a few wire-pullers can, for a time, make or mar any man's success. People neither know what it is they like nor do they want to find out, all they care about is the being supposed to derive their likings from the best West-end magazines, so they look to the shop with the largest plate-glass windows and take what the shop-man gives them. But no amount of plate-glass can carry off more than a certain amount of false pretences, and there is no *mot d'ordre* that can keep a man permanently down if he is as intent on winning lasting good name as I have been. If I had played for immediate popularity I think I could have won it. Having played for lasting credit I doubt not that it will in the end be given me. A man should not be held to be ill-used for not getting what he has not played for. I am not saying that it is better or more honourable to play for lasting than for immediate success. I know which I myself find pleasanter, but that has nothing to do with it.

It is a nice question whether the light or the heavy armed soldier of literature and art is the more useful. I joined the plodders and have aimed at permanent good name rather than brilliancy. I have no doubt I did this because instinct told me (for I never thought about it) that this would be the easier and less thorny path. I have more of perseverance than of those, perhaps, even more valuable gifts — facility and readiness of resource. I hate being hurried. Moreover I am too fond of independence to get on with the leaders of literature and science. Independence is essential for permanent but fatal to immediate success. Besides, luck enters much more into ephemeral than into permanent success and I have always distrusted luck. Those who play a waiting game have matters more in their own hands, time gives them double chances; whereas if success does not come at once to the ephemerid he misses it altogether.

I know that the ordinary reviewer who either snarls at my work or misrepresents it or ignores it or, again, who pats it sub-contemptuously on the back is as honourably and usefully employed as I am. In the kingdom of literature (as I have just been saying in the *Universal Review* about Science) there are many mansions and what is intolerable in one is common form in another. It is a case of the division of labour and a man will gravitate towards one class of workers or another according as he is built. There is neither higher nor lower about it.

I should like to put it on record that I understand it and am not inclined to regret the arrangements that have made me possible.

My Birthright

I had to steal my own birthright. I stole it and was bitterly punished. But I saved my soul alive.

XII
The Enfant Terrible of Literature

Myself

I am the *enfant terrible* of literature and science. If I cannot, and I know I cannot, get the literary and scientific big-wigs to give me a shilling, I can, and I know I can, heave bricks into the middle of them.

Blake, Dante, Virgil and Tennyson

Talking it over, we agreed that Blake was no good because he learnt Italian at 60 in order to study Dante, and we knew Dante was no good because he was so fond of Virgil, and Virgil was no good because Tennyson ran him, and as for Tennyson — well, Tennyson goes without saying.

My Father and Shakespeare

My father is one of the few men I know who say they do not like Shakespeare. I could forgive my father for not liking Shakespeare if it was only because Shakespeare wrote poetry; but this is not the reason. He dislikes Shakespeare because he finds him so very coarse. He also says he likes Tennyson and this seriously aggravates his offence.

Tennyson

We were saying what a delightful dispensation of providence it was that prosperous people will write their memoirs. We hoped Tennyson was writing his. [1890.]

P.S. — We think his son has done nearly as well. [1898.]

Walter Pater and Matthew Arnold

Mr. Walter Pater's style is, to me, like the face of some old woman who has been to Madame Rachel and had herself enamelled. The bloom is nothing but powder and paint and the odour is cherry-blossom. Mr. Matthew Arnold's odour is as the faint sickliness of hawthorn.

My Random Passages

At the Century Club a friend very kindly and hesitatingly ventured to suggest to me that I should get some one to go over my MS. before printing; a judicious editor, he said, would have prevented me from printing many a bit which, it seemed to him, was written too recklessly and offhand. The fact is that the more reckless and random a passage appears to be, the more carefully it has been submitted to friends and considered and re-considered; without the support of friends I should never have dared to print one half of what I have printed.

I am not one of those who can repeat the General Confession unreservedly. I should say rather:

"I have left unsaid much that I am sorry I did not say, but I have said little that I am sorry for having said, and I am pretty well on the whole, thank you."

Moral Try-Your-Strengths

There are people who, if they only had a slot, might turn a pretty penny as moral try-your-strengths, like those we see in railway-stations for telling people their physical strength when they have dropped a penny in the slot. In a way they have a slot, which is their mouths, and people drop pennies in by asking them to dinner, and then they try their strength against them and get snubbed; but this way is roundabout and expensive. We want a good automatic asinometer by which we can tell at a moderate cost how great or how little of a fool we are.

Populus Vult

If people like being deceived—and this can hardly be doubted—there can rarely have been a time during which they can have had more of the wish than now. The literary, scientific and religious worlds vie with one another in trying to gratify the public.

Men and Monkeys

In his latest article (Feb. 1892) Prof. Garner says that the chatter of monkeys is not meaningless, but that they are conveying ideas to one another. This seems to me hazardous. The monkeys might with equal justice conclude that in our magazine articles, or literary and artistic criticisms, we are not chattering idly but are conveying ideas to one another.

"One Touch of Nature"

"One touch of nature makes the whole world kin." Should it not be "marks," not "makes"? There is one touch of nature, or natural feature, which marks all mankind as of one family.

P.S. — Surely it should be "of ill-nature." "One touch of ill-nature marks —
or several touches of ill-nature mark the whole world kin."

Genuine Feeling

In the *Times* of to-day, June 4, 1887, there is an obituary notice of a Rev.
Mr. Knight who wrote about 200 songs, among others "She wore a wreath of
roses." The *Times* says that, though these songs have no artistic merit, they
are full of genuine feeling, or words to this effect; as though a song which was
full of genuine feeling could by any possibility be without artistic merit.

George Meredith

The *Times* in a leading article says (Jany. 3, 1899) "a talker," as Mr. George
Meredith has somewhere said, "involves the existence of a talkee," or words
to this effect.

I said what comes to the same thing as this in *Life and Habit* in 1877, and I
repeated it in the preface to my translation of the *Iliad* in 1898. I do not believe
George Meredith has said anything to the same effect, but I have read so very
little of that writer, and have so utterly rejected what I did read, that he may
well have done so without my knowing it. He damned *Erewhon*, as Chapman
and Hall's reader, in 1871, and, as I am still raw about this after 28 years,
(I am afraid unless I say something more I shall be taken as writing these
words seriously) I prefer to assert that the *Times* writer was quoting from my
preface to the *Iliad*, published a few weeks earlier, and fathering the remark
on George Meredith. By the way the *Times* did not give so much as a line to
my translation in its "Books of the Week," though it was duly sent to them.

Froude and Freeman

I think it was last Saturday (A) (at any rate it was a day just thereabouts)
the *Times* had a leader on Froude's appointment as Reg. Prof. of Mod. Hist.
at Oxford. It said Froude was perhaps our greatest living master of style, or
words to that effect, only that, like Freeman, he was too long: i.e. only he is an
habitual offender against the most fundamental principles of his art. If then
Froude is our greatest master of style, what are the rest of us?

There was a much better article yesterday on Marbot, on which my
namesake A. J. Butler got a dressing for talking rubbish about style. [1892.]

Style

In this day's *Sunday Times* there is an article on Mrs. Browning's letters
which begins with some remarks about style. "It is recorded," says the writer,
"of Plato, that in a rough draft of one of his Dialogues, found after his death,
the first paragraph was written in seventy different forms. Wordsworth

spared no pains to sharpen and polish to the utmost the gifts with which nature had endowed him; and Cardinal Newman, one of the greatest masters of English style, has related in an amusing essay the pains he took to acquire his style."

I never knew a writer yet who took the smallest pains with his style and was at the same time readable. Plato's having had seventy shies at one sentence is quite enough to explain to me why I dislike him. A man may, and ought to take a great deal of pains to write clearly, tersely and euphemistically: he will write many a sentence three or four times over—to do much more than this is worse than not rewriting at all: he will be at great pains to see that he does not repeat himself, to arrange his matter in the way that shall best enable the reader to master it, to cut out superfluous words and, even more, to eschew irrelevant matter: but in each case he will be thinking not of his own style but of his reader's convenience.

Men like Newman and R. L. Stevenson seem to have taken pains to acquire what they called a style as a preliminary measure—as something that they had to form before their writings could be of any value. I should like to put it on record that I never took the smallest pains with my style, have never thought about it, and do not know or want to know whether it is a style at all or whether it is not, as I believe and hope, just common, simple straightforwardness. I cannot conceive how any man can take thought for his style without loss to himself and his readers.

I have, however, taken all the pains that I had patience to endure in the improvement of my handwriting (which, by the way, has a constant tendency to resume feral characteristics) and also with my MS. generally to keep it clean and legible. I am having a great tidying just now, in the course of which the MS. of *Erewhon* turned up, and I was struck with the great difference between it and the MS. of *The Authoress of the Odyssey*. I have also taken great pains, with what success I know not, to correct impatience, irritability and other like faults in my own character—and this not because I care two straws about my own character, but because I find the correction of such faults as I have been able to correct makes life easier and saves me from getting into scrapes, and attaches nice people to me more readily. But I suppose this really is attending to style after all. [1897.]

Diderot on Criticism

"Il est si difficile de produire une chose même médiocre; il est si facile de sentir la médiocrité."

I have lately seen this quoted as having been said by Diderot. It is easy to say we feel the mediocrity when we have heard a good many people say that the work is mediocre, but, unless in matters about which he has been long conversant, no man can easily form an independent judgment as to whether or not a work is mediocre. I know that in the matter of books, painting and music I constantly find myself unable to form a settled opinion till I have heard what many men of varied tastes have to say, and have also made myself acquainted with details about a man's antecedents and ways of life which are generally held to be irrelevant.

Often, of course, this is unnecessary; a man's character, if he has left much work behind him, or if he is not coming before us for the first time, is generally easily discovered without extraneous aid. We want no one to give us any clues to the nature of such men as Giovanni Bellini, or De Hooghe. Hogarth's character is written upon his work so plainly that he who runs may read it, so is Handel's upon his, so is Purcell's, so is Corelli's, so, indeed, are the characters of most men; but often where only little work has been left, or where a work is by a new hand, it is exceedingly difficult "sentir la médiocrité" and, it might be added, "ou même sentir du tout."

How many years, I wonder, was it before I learned to dislike Thackeray and Tennyson as cordially as I now do? For how many years did I not almost worship them?

Bunyan and Others

I have been reading *The Pilgrim's Progress* again — the third part and all — and wish that some one would tell one what to think about it.

The English is racy, vigorous and often very beautiful; but the language of any book is nothing except in so far as it reveals the writer. The words in which a man clothes his thoughts are like all other clothes — the cut raises presumptions about his thoughts, and these generally turn out to be just, but the words are no more the thoughts than a man's coat is himself. I am not sure, however, that in Bunyan's case the dress in which he has clothed his ideas does not reveal him more justly than the ideas do.

The Pilgrim's Progress consists mainly of a series of infamous libels upon life and things; it is a blasphemy against certain fundamental ideas of right and wrong which our consciences most instinctively approve; its notion of heaven is hardly higher than a transformation scene at Drury Lane; it is essentially infidel. "Hold out to me the chance of a golden crown and harp with freedom from all further worries, give me angels to flatter me and fetch and carry for me, and I shall think the game worth playing, notwithstanding the great and horrible risk of failure; but no crown, no cross for me. Pay me well and I will wait for payment, but if I have to give credit I shall expect to be paid better in the end."

There is no conception of the faith that a man should do his duty cheerfully with all his might though, as far as he can see, he will never be paid directly or indirectly either here or hereafter. Still less is there any conception that unless a man has this faith he is not worth thinking about. There is no sense that as we have received freely so we should give freely and be only too thankful that we have anything to give at all. Furthermore there does not appear to be even the remotest conception that this honourable, comfortable and sustaining faith is, like all other high faiths, to be brushed aside very peremptorily at the bidding of common-sense.

What a pity it is that Christian never met Mr. Common-Sense with his daughter, Good-Humour, and her affianced husband, Mr. Hate-Cant; but if he ever saw them in the distance he steered clear of them, probably as feeling that they would be more dangerous than Giant Despair, Vanity Fair and Apollyon all together—for they would have stuck to him if he had let them get in with him. Among other things they would have told him that, if there was any truth in his opinions, neither man nor woman ought to become a father or mother at all, inasmuch as their doing so would probably entail eternity of torture on the wretched creature whom they were launching into the world. Life in this world is risk enough to inflict on another person who has not been consulted in the matter, but death will give quittance in full. To weaken our faith in this sure and certain hope of peace eternal (except so far as we have so lived as to win life in others after we are gone) would be a cruel thing, even though the evidence against it were overwhelming, but to rob us of it on no evidence worth a moment's consideration and, apparently, from no other motive than the pecuniary advantage of the robbers themselves is infamy. For the Churches are but institutions for the saving of men's souls from hell.

This is true enough. Nevertheless it is untrue that in practice any Christian minister, knowing what he preaches to be both very false and very cruel, yet insists on it because it is to the advantage of his own order. In a way the preachers believe what they preach, but it is as men who have taken a bad £10 note and refuse to look at the evidence that makes for its badness, though, if the note were not theirs, they would see at a glance that it was not a good one. For the man in the street it is enough that what the priests teach in respect of a future state is palpably both cruel and absurd while, at the same time, they make their living by teaching it and thus prey upon other men's fears of the unknown. If the Churches do not wish to be misunderstood they should not allow themselves to remain in such an equivocal position.

But let this pass. Bunyan, we may be sure, took all that he preached in its most literal interpretation; he could never have made his book so interesting had he not done so. The interest of it depends almost entirely on the unquestionable good faith of the writer and the strength of the impulse that compelled him to speak that which was within him. He was not writing a book which he might sell, he was speaking what was borne in upon him from heaven. The message he uttered was, to my thinking, both low and false, but it was truth of truths to Bunyan.

No. This will not do. The Epistles of St. Paul were truth of truths to Paul, but they do not attract us to the man who wrote them, and, except here and there, they are very uninteresting. Mere strength of conviction on a writer's part is not enough to make his work take permanent rank. Yet I know that I could read the whole of *The Pilgrim's Progress* (except occasional episodical sermons) without being at all bored by it, whereas, having spent a penny upon Mr. Stead's abridgement of *Joseph Andrews*, I had to give it up as putting me out of all patience. I then spent another penny on an abridgement of *Gulliver's Travels*, and was enchanted by it. What is it that makes one book so readable and another so unreadable? Swift, from all I can make out, was a far more human and genuine person than he is generally represented, but I do not think I should have liked him, whereas Fielding, I am sure, must have been delightful. Why do the faults of his work overweigh its many great excellences, while the less great excellences of the *Voyage to Lilliput* outweigh its more serious defects?

I suppose it is the prolixity of Fielding that fatigues me. Swift is terse, he gets through what he has to say on any matter as quickly as he can and takes the reader on to the next, whereas Fielding is not only long, but his length is made still longer by the disconnectedness of the episodes that appear to have been padded into the books—episodes that do not help one forward, and are generally so exaggerated, and often so full of horse-play as to put one out of conceit with the parts that are really excellent.

Whatever else Bunyan is he is never long; he takes you quickly on from incident to incident and, however little his incidents may appeal to us, we feel that he is never giving us one that is not *bona fide* so far as he is concerned. His episodes and incidents are introduced not because he wants to make his book longer but because he cannot be satisfied without these particular ones, even though he may feel that his book is getting longer than he likes.

. . .

And here I must break away from this problem, leaving it unsolved. [1897.]

Bunyan and the *Odyssey*

Anything worse than *The Pilgrim's Progress* in the matter of defiance of literary canons can hardly be conceived. The allegory halts continually; it professes to be spiritual, but nothing can be more carnal than the golden splendour of the eternal city; the view of life and the world generally is flat blasphemy against the order of things with which we are surrounded. Yet, like the *Odyssey*, which flatly defies sense and criticism (no, it doesn't; still, it defies them a good deal), no one can doubt that it must rank among the very greatest books that have ever been written. How Odyssean it is in its sincerity and downrightness, as well as in the marvellous beauty of its language, its freedom from all taint of the schools and, not least, in complete victory of genuine internal zeal over a scheme initially so faulty as to appear hopeless.

I read that part where Christian passes the lions which he thought were free but which were really chained and it occurred to me that all lions are chained until they actually eat us and that, the moment they do this, they chain themselves up again automatically, as far as we are concerned. If one dissects this passage it fares as many a passage in the *Odyssey* does when we dissect it. Christian did not, after all, venture to pass the lions till he was assured that they were chained. And really it is more excusable to refuse point-blank to pass a couple of lions till one knows whether they are chained or not—and the poor wicked people seem to have done nothing more than this,—than it would be to pass them. Besides, by being told, Christian fights, as it were, with loaded dice.

Poetry

The greatest poets never write poetry. The Homers and Shakespeares are not the greatest—they are only the greatest that we can know. And so with Handel among musicians. For the highest poetry, whether in music or literature, is ineffable—it must be felt from one person to another, it cannot be articulated.

Verse

Versifying is the lowest form of poetry; and the last thing a great poet will do in these days is to write verses.

I have been trying to read *Venus and Adonis* and the *Rape of Lucrece* but cannot get on with them. They teem with fine things, but they are got-up fine things. I do not know whether this is quite what I mean but, come what may, I find the poems bore me. Were I a schoolmaster I should think I was setting a boy a very severe punishment if I told him to read *Venus and Adonis* through in three sittings. If, then, the magic of Shakespeare's name, let alone the great beauty of occasional passages, cannot reconcile us (for I find most people of the same mind) to verse, and especially rhymed verse as a medium of sustained expression, what chance has any one else? It seems to me that a sonnet is the utmost length to which a rhymed poem should extend.

Verse, Poetry and Prose

The preface to Bunyan's *Pilgrim's Progress* is verse, but it is not poetry. The body of the work is poetry, but it is not verse.

Ancient Work

If a person would understand either the *Odyssey* or any other ancient work, he must never look at the dead without seeing the living in them, nor at the living without thinking of the dead. We are too fond of seeing the ancients as one thing and the moderns as another.

Nausicaa and Myself

I am elderly, grey-bearded and, according to my clerk, Alfred, disgustingly fat; I wear spectacles and get more and more bronchitic as I grow older. Still no young prince in a fairy story ever found an invisible princess more effectually hidden behind a hedge of dullness or more fast asleep than Nausicaa was when I woke her and hailed her as Authoress of the *Odyssey*. And there was no difficulty about it either — all one had to do was to go up to the front door and ring the bell.

Telemachus and Nicholas Nickleby

The virtuous young man defending a virtuous mother against a number of powerful enemies is one of the *ignes fatui* of literature. The scheme ought to be very interesting, and often is so, but it always fails as regards the hero who, from Telemachus to Nicholas Nickleby, is always too much of the good young man to please.

Gadshill and Trapani

While getting our lunch one Sunday at the east end of the long room in the Sir John Falstaff Inn, Gadshill, we overheard some waterside-looking dwellers in the neighbourhood talking among themselves. I wrote down the following: —

Bill: Oh, yes. I've got a mate that works in my shop; he's chucked the Dining Room because they give him too much to eat. He found another place where they gave him four pennyworth of meat and two vegetables and it was quite as much as he could put up with.

George: You can't kid me, Bill, that they give you too much to eat, but I'll believe it to oblige you, Bill. Shall I see you to-night?

Bill: No, I must go to church.

George: Well, so must I; I've got to go.

So at Trapani, I heard two small boys one night on the quay (I am sure I have written this down somewhere, but it is less trouble to write it again than to hunt for it) singing with all their might, with their arms round one another's necks. I should say they were about ten years old, not more.

I asked Ignazio Giacalone: "What are they singing?"

He replied that it was a favourite song among the popolino of Trapani about a girl who did not want to be seen going about with a man. "The people in this place," says the song, "are very ill-natured, and if they see you and me together, they will talk," &c.

I do not say that there was any descent here from Nausicaa's speech to Ulysses, but I felt as though that speech was still in the air. [*Od. VI.* 273.]

I reckon Gadshill and Trapani as perhaps the two most classic grounds that I frequent familiarly, and at each I have seemed to hear echoes of the scenes that have made them famous. Not that what I heard at Gadshill is like any particular passage in Shakespeare.

Waiting to be Hired

At Castelvetrano (about thirty miles from Trapani) I had to start the next morning at 4 a.m. to see the ruins of Selinunte, and slept lightly with my window open. About two o'clock I began to hear a buzz of conversation in the piazza outside and it kept me awake, so I got up to shut the window and see what it was. I found it came from a long knot of men standing about, two deep, but not strictly marshalled. When I got up at half-past three, it was still dark and the men were still there, though perhaps not so many. I enquired and found they were standing to be hired for the day, any one wanting labourers would come there, engage as many as he wanted and go off with them, others would come up, and so on till about four o'clock, after which no one would hire, the day being regarded as short in weight after that hour. Being so collected the men gossip over their own and other people's affairs—wonder who was that fine-looking stranger going about yesterday with Nausicaa, and so on. [*Od. VI.* 273.] This, in fact, is their club and the place where the public opinion of the district is formed.

Ilium and Padua

The story of the Trojan horse is more nearly within possibility than we should readily suppose. In 1848, during the rebellion of the North Italians against the Austrians, eight or nine young men, for whom the authorities were hunting, hid themselves inside Donatello's wooden horse in the Salone at Padua and lay there for five days, being fed through the trap door on the back of the horse with the connivance of the custode of the Salone. No doubt they were let out for a time at night. When pursuit had become less hot, their friends smuggled them away. One of those who had been shut up was still living in 1898 and, on the occasion of the jubilee festivities, was carried round the town in triumph.

Eumaeus and Lord Burleigh

The inference which Arthur Platt (*Journal of Philology*, Vol. 24, No. 47) wishes to draw from Eumaeus being told to bring Ulysses' bow ν δώματα (*Od.* XXI. 234) suggests to met to me the difference which some people in future ages may wish to draw between the character of Lord Burleigh's steps in Tennyson's poem, according as he was walking up or pacing down. Wherefrom also the critic will argue that the scene of Lord Burleigh's weeping *must* have been on an inclined plane.

> Weeping, weeping late and early,
>   Walking up and pacing down,
> Deeply mourned the Lord of Burleigh,
>   Burleigh-house by Stamford-town.

My Reviewers' Sense of Need

My reviewers felt no sense of need to understand me — if they had they would have developed the mental organism which would have enabled them to do so. When the time comes that they want to do so they will throw out a little mental pseudopodium without much difficulty. They threw it out when they wanted to misunderstand me — with a good deal of the pseudo in it, too.

The Authoress of the Odyssey

The amount of pains which my reviewers have taken to understand this book is not so great as to encourage the belief that they would understand the *Odyssey*, however much they studied it. Again, the people who could read the *Odyssey* without coming to much the same conclusions as mine are not likely to admit that they ought to have done so.

If a man tells me that a house in which I have long lived is inconvenient, not to say unwholesome, and that I have been very stupid in not finding this out for myself, I should be apt in the first instance to tell him that he knew nothing about it, and that I was quite comfortable; by and by, I should begin to be aware that I was not so comfortable as I thought I was, and in the end I should probably make the suggested alterations in my house if, on reflection, I found them sensibly conceived. But I should kick hard at first.

Homer and his Commentators

Homeric commentators have been blind so long that nothing will do for them but Homer must be blind too. They have transferred their own blindness to the poet.

The Iliad

In the *Iliad*, civilisation bursts upon us as a strong stream out of a rock. We know that the water has gathered from many a distant vein underground, but we do not see these. Or it is like the drawing up the curtain on the opening of a play — the scene is then first revealed.

Glacial Periods of Folly

The moraines left by secular glacial periods of folly stretch out over many a plain of our civilisation. So in the *Odyssey*, especially in the second twelve books, whenever any one eats meat it is called "sacrificing" it, as though we were descended from a race that did not eat meat. Then it was said that meat might be eaten if one did not eat the life. What was the life? Clearly the blood, for when you stick a pig it lives till the blood is gone. You must sacrifice the blood, therefore, to the gods, but so long as you abstain from things strangled and from blood, and so long as you call it sacrificing, you may eat as much meat as you please.

What a mountain of lies — what a huge geological formation of falsehood, with displacement of all kinds, and strata twisted every conceivable way, must have accreted before the *Odyssey* was possible!

Translations from Verse into Prose

Whenever this is attempted, great licence must be allowed to the translator in getting rid of all those poetical common forms which are foreign to the genius of prose. If the work is to be translated into prose, let it be into such prose as we write and speak among ourselves. A volume of poetical prose, i.e. affected prose, had better be in verse outright at once. Poetical prose is never tolerable for more than a very short bit at a time. And it may be questioned whether poetry itself is not better kept short in ninety-nine cases out of a hundred.

Translating the *Odyssey*

If you wish to preserve the spirit of a dead author, you must not skin him, stuff him, and set him up in a case. You must eat him, digest him and let him live in you, with such life as you have, for better or worse. The difference between the Andrew Lang manner of translating the *Odyssey* and mine is that between making a mummy and a baby. He tries to preserve a corpse (for the *Odyssey* is a corpse to all who need Lang's translation), whereas I try to originate a new life and one that is instinct (as far as I can effect this) with the spirit though not the form of the original.

They say no woman could possibly have written the *Odyssey*. To me, on the other hand, it seems even less possible that a man could have done so. As for its being by a practised and elderly writer, nothing but youth and inexperience could produce anything so naïve and so lovely. That is where the work will suffer by my translation. I am male, practised and elderly, and the trail of sex, age and experience is certain to be over my translation. If the poem is ever to be well translated, it must be by some high-spirited English girl who has been brought up at Athens and who, therefore, has not been jaded by academic study of the language.

A translation is at best a dislocation, a translation from verse to prose is a double dislocation and corresponding further dislocations are necessary if an effect of deformity is to be avoided.

The people who, when they read "Athene" translated by "Minerva," cannot bear in mind that every Athene varies more or less with, and takes colour from, the country and temperament of the writer who is being translated, will not be greatly helped by translating "Athene" and not "Minerva." Besides many readers would pronounce the word as a dissyllable or an anapæst.

The *Odyssey* and a Tomb at Carcassonne

There is a tomb at some place in France, I think at Carcassonne, on which there is some sculpture representing the friends and relations of the deceased in paroxysms of grief with their cheeks all cracked, and crying like Gaudenzio's angels on the Sacro Monte at Varallo-Sesia. Round the corner, however, just out of sight till one searches, there is a man holding both his sides and splitting with laughter. In some parts of the *Odyssey*, especially about Ulysses and Penelope, I fancy that laughing man as being round the corner. [Oct. 1891.]

Getting it Wrong

Zeffirino Carestia, a sculptor, told me we had a great sculptor in England named Simpson. I demurred, and asked about his work. It seemed he had made a monument to Nelson in Westminster Abbey. Of course I saw he meant Stevens, who had made a monument to Wellington in St. Paul's. I cross-questioned him and found I was right.

Suppose that in some ancient writer I had come upon a similar error about which I felt no less certain than I did here, ought I to be debarred from my conclusion merely by the accident that I have not the wretched muddler at my elbow and cannot ask him personally? People are always getting things wrong. It is the critic's business to know how and when to believe on insufficient evidence and to know how far to go in the matter of setting people right without going too far; the question of what is too far and what is sufficient evidence can only be settled by the higgling and haggling of the literary market.

So I justify my emendation of the "grotta del toro" at Trapani. [*The Authoress of the Odyssey*, Chap. VIII.] "Il toro macigna un tesoro di oro." [The bull is grinding a treasure of gold] in the grotto in which (for other reasons) I am convinced Ulysses hid the gifts the Phœacians had given him. And so the grotto is called "La grotta del toro" [The grotto of the bull]. I make no doubt it was originally called "La grotta del tesoro" [The grotto of the treasure], but children got it wrong, and corrupted "tesoro" into "toro"; then, it being known that the "tesoro" was in it somehow, the "toro" was made to grind the "tesoro."

XIII
Unprofessional Sermons

Righteousness

According to Mr. Matthew Arnold, as we find the highest traditions of grace, beauty and the heroic virtues among the Greeks and Romans, so we derive our highest ideal of righteousness from Jewish sources. Righteousness was to the Jew what strength and beauty were to the Greek or fortitude to the Roman.

This sounds well, but can we think that the Jews taken as a nation were really more righteous than the Greeks and Romans? Could they indeed be so if they were less strong, graceful and enduring? In some respects they may have been — every nation has its strong points — but surely there has been a nearly unanimous verdict for many generations that the typical Greek or Roman is a higher, nobler person than the typical Jew — and this referring not to the modern Jew, who may perhaps he held to have been injured by centuries of oppression, but to the Hebrew of the time of the old prophets and of the most prosperous eras in the history of the nation. If three men could be set before us as the most perfect Greek, Roman and Jew respectively, and if we could choose which we would have our only son most resemble, is it not likely we should find ourselves preferring the Greek or Roman to the Jew? And does not this involve that we hold the two former to be the more righteous in a broad sense of the word?

I dare not say that we owe no benefits to the Jewish nation, I do not feel sure whether we do or do not, but I can see no good thing that I can point to as a notoriously Hebrew contribution to our moral and intellectual well-being as I can point to our law and say that it is Roman, or to our fine arts and say that they are based on what the Greeks and Italians taught us. On the contrary, if asked what feature of post-Christian life we had derived most distinctly from Hebrew sources I should say at once "intolerance" — the desire to dogmatise about matters whereon the Greek and Roman held certainty to be at once unimportant and unattainable. This, with all its train of bloodshed and family disunion, is chargeable to the Jewish rather than to any other account.

There is yet another vice which occurs readily to any one who reckons up the characteristics which we derive mainly from the Jews; it is one that we call, after a Jewish sect, "Pharisaism." I do not mean to say that no Greek or Roman was ever a sanctimonious hypocrite, still, sanctimoniousness does not readily enter into our notions of Greeks and Romans and it does so enter into our notions of the old Hebrews. Of course, we are all of us sanctimonious sometimes; Horace himself is so when he talks about *aurum irrepertum et sic melius situm*, and as for Virgil he was a prig, pure and simple; still, on the whole, sanctimoniousness was not a Greek and Roman vice and it was a Hebrew one. True, they stoned their prophets freely; but these are not the Hebrews to whom Mr. Arnold is referring, they are the ones whom it is the custom to leave out of sight and out of mind as far as possible, so that they should hardly count as Hebrews at all, and none of our characteristics should be ascribed to them.

Taking their literature I cannot see that it deserves the praises that have been lavished upon it. The Song of Solomon and the book of Esther are the most interesting in the Old Testament, but these are the very ones that make the smallest pretensions to holiness, and even these are neither of them of very transcendent merit. They would stand no chance of being accepted by Messrs. Cassell and Co. or by any biblical publisher of the present day. Chatto and Windus might take the Song of Solomon, but, with this exception, I doubt if there is a publisher in London who would give a guinea for the pair. Ecclesiastes contains some fine things but is strongly tinged with pessimism, cynicism and affectation. Some of the Proverbs are good, but not many of them are in common use. Job contains some fine passages, and so do some of the Psalms; but the Psalms generally are poor and, for the most part, querulous, spiteful and introspective into the bargain. Mudie would not take thirteen copies of the lot if they were to appear now for the first time—unless indeed their royal authorship were to arouse an adventitious interest in them, or unless the author were a rich man who played his cards judiciously with the reviewers. As for the prophets—we know what appears to have been the opinion formed concerning them by those who should have been best acquainted with them; I am no judge as to the merits of the controversy between them and their fellow-countrymen, but I have read their works and am of opinion that they will not hold their own against such masterpieces of modern literature as, we will say, *The Pilgrim's Progress, Robinson Crusoe, Gulliver's Travels* or *Tom Jones.* "Whether there be prophecies," exclaims the Apostle, "they shall fail." On the whole I should say that Isaiah and Jeremiah must be held to have failed.

I would join issue with Mr. Matthew Arnold on yet another point. I understand him to imply that righteousness should be a man's highest aim in life. I do not like setting up righteousness, nor yet anything else, as the highest aim in life; a man should have any number of little aims about which he should be conscious and for which he should have names, but he should have neither name for, nor consciousness concerning the main aim of his life. Whatever we do we must try and do it rightly — this is obvious — but righteousness implies something much more than this: it conveys to our minds not only the desire to get whatever we have taken in hand as nearly right as possible, but also the general reference of our lives to the supposed will of an unseen but supreme power. Granted that there is such a power, and granted that we should obey its will, we are the more likely to do this the less we concern ourselves about the matter and the more we confine our attention to the things immediately round about us which seem, so to speak, entrusted to us as the natural and legitimate sphere of our activity. I believe a man will get the most useful information on these matters from modern European sources; next to these he will get most from Athens and ancient Rome. Mr. Matthew Arnold notwithstanding, I do not think he will get anything from Jerusalem which he will not find better and more easily elsewhere. [1883.]

Wisdom

But where shall wisdom be found? (Job xxviii. 12).

If the writer of these words meant exactly what he said, he had so little wisdom that he might well seek more. He should have known that wisdom spends most of her time crying in the streets and public-houses, and he should have gone thither to look for her. It is written:

"Wisdom crieth without; she uttereth her voice in the streets:

"She crieth in the chief place of concourse, in the openings of the gates: in the city she uttereth her words" (Prov. i. 20, 21.)

If however he meant rather "Where shall wisdom be regarded?" this, again, is not a very sensible question. People have had wisdom before them for some time, and they may be presumed to be the best judges of their own affairs, yet they do not generally show much regard for wisdom. We may conclude, therefore, that they have found her less profitable than by her own estimate she would appear to be. This indeed is what one of the wisest men who ever lived — the author of the Book of Ecclesiastes — definitely concludes to be the case, when he tells his readers that they had better not overdo either their virtue or their wisdom. They must not, on the other hand, overdo their wickedness nor, presumably, their ignorance, still the writer evidently thinks that error is safer on the side of too little than of too much. [203]

Reflection will show that this must always have been true, and must always remain so, for this is the side on which error is both least disastrous and offers most place for repentance. He who finds himself inconvenienced by knowing too little can go to the British Museum, or to the Working Men's College, and learn more; but when a thing is once well learnt it is even harder to unlearn it than it was to learn it. Would it be possible to unlearn the art of speech or the arts of reading and writing even if we wished to do so? Wisdom and knowledge are, like a bad reputation, more easily won than lost; we got on fairly well without knowing that the earth went round the sun; we thought the sun went round the earth until we found it made us uncomfortable to think so any longer, then we altered our opinion; it was not very easy to alter it, but it was easier than it would be to alter it back again. *Vestigia nulla retrorsum*; the earth itself does not pursue its course more steadily than mind does when it has once committed itself, and if we could see the movements of the stars in slow time we should probably find that there was much more throb and tremor in detail than we can take note of.

How, I wonder, will it be if in our pursuit of knowledge we stumble upon some awkward fact as disturbing for the human race as an enquiry into the state of his own finances may sometimes prove to the individual? The pursuit of knowledge can never be anything but a leap in the dark, and a leap in the dark is a very uncomfortable thing. I have sometimes thought that if the human race ever loses its ascendancy it will not be through plague, famine or cataclysm, but by getting to know some little microbe, as it were, of knowledge which shall get into its system and breed there till it makes an end of us. [204] It is well, therefore, that there should be a substratum of mankind who cannot by any inducement be persuaded to know anything whatever at all, and who are resolutely determined to know nothing among us but what the parson tells them, and not to be too sure even about that.

Whence then cometh wisdom and where is the place of understanding? How does Job solve his problem?

"Behold the fear of the Lord, that is wisdom: and to depart from evil is understanding."

The answer is all very well as far as it goes, but it only amounts to saying that wisdom is wisdom. We know no better what the fear of the Lord is than what wisdom is, and we often do not depart from evil simply because we do not know that what we are cleaving to is evil.

Loving and Hating

I have often said that there is no true love short of eating and consequent assimilation; the embryonic processes are but a long course of eating and assimilation — the sperm and germ cells, or the two elements that go to form the new animal, whatever they should be called, eat one another up, and then the mother assimilates them, more or less, through mutual inter-feeding and inter-breeding between her and them. But the curious point is that the more profound our love is the less we are conscious of it as love. True, a nurse tells her child that she would like to eat it, but this is only an expression that shows an instinctive recognition of the fact that eating is a mode of, or rather the acme of, love—no nurse loves her child half well enough to want really to eat it; put to such proof as this the love of which she is so profoundly, as she imagines, sentient proves to be but skin deep. So with our horses and dogs: we think we dote upon them, but we do not really love them.

What, on the other hand, can awaken less consciousness of warm affection than an oyster? Who would press an oyster to his heart, or pat it and want to kiss it? Yet nothing short of its complete absorption into our own being can in the least satisfy us. No merely superficial temporary contact of exterior form to exterior form will serve us. The embrace must be consummate, not achieved by a mocking environment of draped and muffled arms that leaves no lasting trace on organisation or consciousness, but by an enfolding within the bare and warm bosom of an open mouth—a grinding out of all differences of opinion by the sweet persuasion of the jaws, and the eloquence of a tongue that now convinces all the more powerfully because it is inarticulate and deals but with the one universal language of agglutination. Then we become made one with what we love—not heart to heart, but protoplasm to protoplasm, and this is far more to the purpose.

The proof of love, then, like that of any other pleasant pudding, is in the eating, and tested by this proof we see that consciousness of love, like all other consciousness vanishes on becoming intense. While we are yet fully aware of it, we do not love as well as we think we do. When we really mean business and are hungry with affection, we do not know that we are in love, but simply go into the love-shop—for so any eating-house should be more fitly called—ask the price, pay our money down, and love till we can either love or pay no longer.

And so with hate. When we really hate a thing it makes us sick, and we use this expression to symbolise the utmost hatred of which our nature is capable; but when we know we hate, our hatred is in reality mild and inoffensive. I, for example, think I hate all those people whose photographs I see in the shop windows, but I am so conscious of this that I am convinced, in reality, nothing would please me better than to be in the shop windows too. So when I see the universities conferring degrees on any one, or the learned societies moulting the yearly medals as peacocks moult their tails, I am so conscious of disapproval as to feel sure I should like a degree or a medal too if they would only give me one, and hence I conclude that my disapproval is grounded in nothing more serious than a superficial, transient jealousy.

The Roman Empire

Nothing will ever die so long as it knows what to do under the circumstances, in other words so long as it knows its business. The Roman Empire must have died of inexperience of some kind, I should think most likely it was puzzled to death by the Christian religion. But the question is not so much how the Roman Empire or any other great thing came to an end — everything must come to an end some time, it is only scientists who wonder that a state should die — the interesting question is how did the Romans become so great, under what circumstances were they born and bred? We should watch childhood and schooldays rather than old age and death-beds.

As I sit writing on the top of a wild-beast pen of the amphitheatre of Aosta I may note, for one thing, that the Romans were not squeamish, they had no Society for the Prevention of Cruelty to Animals. Again, their ladies did not write in the newspapers. Fancy Miss Cato reviewing Horace! They had no Frances Power Cobbes, no . . . s, no . . . s; yet they seem to have got along quite nicely without these powerful moral engines. The comeliest and most enjoyable races that we know of were the ancient Greeks, the Italians and the South Sea Islanders, and they have none of them been purists.

Italians and Englishmen

Italians, and perhaps Frenchmen, consider first whether they like or want to do a thing and then whether, on the whole, it will do them any harm. Englishmen, and perhaps Germans, consider first whether they ought to like a thing and often never reach the questions whether they do like it and whether it will hurt. There is much to be said for both systems, but I suppose it is best to combine them as far as possible.

On Knowing what Gives us Pleasure

i

One can bring no greater reproach against a man than to say that he does not set sufficient value upon pleasure, and there is no greater sign of a fool than the thinking that he can tell at once and easily what it is that pleases him. To know this is not easy, and how to extend our knowledge of it is the highest and the most neglected of all arts and branches of education. Indeed, if we could solve the difficulty of knowing what gives us pleasure, if we could find its springs, its inception and earliest *modus operandi*, we should have discovered the secret of life and development, for the same difficulty has attended the development of every sense from touch onwards, and no new sense was ever developed without pains. A man had better stick to known and proved pleasures, but, if he will venture in quest of new ones, he should not do so with a light heart.

One reason why we find it so hard to know our own likings is because we are so little accustomed to try; we have our likings found for us in respect of by far the greater number of the matters that concern us; thus we have grown all our limbs on the strength of the likings of our ancestors and adopt these without question.

Another reason is that, except in mere matters of eating and drinking, people do not realise the importance of finding out what it is that gives them pleasure if, that is to say, they would make themselves as comfortable here as they reasonably can. Very few, however, seem to care greatly whether they are comfortable or no. There are some men so ignorant and careless of what gives them pleasure that they cannot be said ever to have been really born as living beings at all. They present some of the phenomena of having been born — they reproduce, in fact, so many of the ideas which we associate with having been born that it is hard not to think of them as living beings — but in spite of all appearances the central idea is wanting. At least one half of the misery which meets us daily might be removed or, at any rate, greatly alleviated, if those who suffer by it would think it worth their while to be at any pains to get rid of it. That they do not so think is proof that they neither know, nor care to know, more than in a very languid way, what it is that will relieve them most effectually or, in other words, that the shoe does not really pinch them so hard as we think it does. For when it really pinches, as when a man is being flogged, he will seek relief by any means in his power. So my great namesake said, "Surely the pleasure is as great Of being cheated as to cheat"; and so, again, I remember to have seen a poem many years ago in *Punch* according to which a certain young lady, being discontented at home, went out into the world in quest to "Some burden make or burden bear, But which she did not greatly care — Oh Miseree!" So long as there was discomfort somewhere it was all right.

To those, however, who are desirous of knowing what gives them pleasure but do not quite know how to set about it I have no better advice to give than that they must take the same pains about acquiring this difficult art as about any other, and must acquire it in the same way — that is by attending to one thing at a time and not being in too great a hurry. Proficiency is not to be attained here, any more than elsewhere, by short cuts or by getting other people to do work that no other than oneself can do. Above all things it is necessary here, as in all other branches of study, not to think we know a thing before we do know it — to make sure of our ground and be quite certain that we really do like a thing before we say we do. When you cannot decide whether you like a thing or not, nothing is easier than to say so and to hang it up among the uncertainties. Or when you know you do not know and are in such doubt as to see no chance of deciding, then you may take one side or the other provisionally and throw yourself into it. This will sometimes make you uncomfortable, and you will feel you have taken the wrong side and thus learn that the other was the right one. Sometimes you will feel you have done right. Any way ere long you will know more about it. But there must have been a secret treaty with yourself to the effect that the decision was provisional only. For, after all, the most important first principle in this matter is the not lightly thinking you know what you like till you have made sure of your ground. I was nearly forty before I felt how stupid it was to pretend to know things that I did not know and I still often catch myself doing so. Not one of my schoolmasters taught me this, but altogether otherwise.

ii

I should like to like Schumann's music better than I do; I dare say I could make myself like it better if I tried; but I do not like having to try to make myself like things; I like things that make me like them at once and no trying at all.

iii

To know whether you are enjoying a piece of music or not you must see whether you find yourself looking at the advertisements of Pear's soap at the end of the programme.

De Minimis non Curat Lex

i

Yes, but what is a minimum? Sometimes a maximum is a minimum, and sometimes the other way about. If you know you know, and if you don't you don't.

ii

Yes, but what is a minimum? So increased material weight involves increased moral weight, but where does there begin to be any weight at all? There is a miracle somewhere. At the point where two very large nothings have united to form a very little something.

iii

There is no such complete assimilation as assimilation of rhythm. In fact it is in assimilation of rhythm that what we see as assimilation consists.

When two liquid bodies come together with nearly the same rhythms, as, say, two tumblers of water, differing but very slightly, the two assimilate rapidly—becoming homogeneous throughout. So with wine and water which assimilate, or at any rate form a new homogeneous substance, very rapidly. Not so with oil and water. Still, I should like to know whether it would not be possible to have so much water and so little oil that the water would in time absorb the oil.

I have not thought about it, but it seems as though the maxim *de minimis non curat lex*—the fact that a wrong, a contradiction in terms, a violation of all our ordinary canons does not matter and should be brushed aside—it seems as though this maxim went very low down in the scale of nature, as though it were the one principle rendering combination (integration) and, I suppose, dissolution (disintegration) also, possible. For combination of any kind involves contradiction in terms; it involves a self-stultification on the part of one or more things, more or less complete in both of them. For one or both cease to be, and to cease to be is to contradict all one's fundamental axioms or terms.

And this is always going on in the mental world as much as in the material; everything is always changing and stultifying itself more or less completely. There is no permanence of identity so absolute, either in the physical world, or in our conception of the word "identity," that it is not crossed with the notion of perpetual change which, *pro tanto*, destroys identity. Perfect, absolute identity is like perfect, absolute anything—as near an approach to nothing, or nonsense, as our minds can grasp. It is, then, in the essence of our conception of identity that nothing should maintain a perfect identity; there is an element of disintegration in the only conception of integration that we can form.

What is it, then, that makes this conflict not only possible and bearable but even pleasant? What is it that so oils the machinery of our thoughts that things which would otherwise cause intolerable friction and heat produce no jar?

Surely it is the principle that a very overwhelming majority rides rough-shod with impunity over a very small minority; that a drop of brandy in a gallon of water is practically no brandy; that a dozen maniacs among a hundred thousand people produce no unsettling effect upon our minds; that a well-written i will go as an i even though the dot be omitted—it seems to me that it is this principle, which is embodied in *de minimis non curat lex*, that makes it possible that there should be *majora* and a *lex* to care about them. This is saying in another form that association does not stick to the letter of its bond.

Saints

Saints are always grumbling because the world will not take them at their own estimate; so they cry out upon this place and upon that, saying it does not know the things belonging to its peace and that it will be too late soon and that people will be very sorry then that they did not make more of the grumbler, whoever he may be, inasmuch as he will make it hot for them and pay them out generally.

All this means: "Put me in a better social and financial position than I now occupy; give me more of the good things of this life, if not actual money yet authority (which is better loved by most men than even money itself), to reward me because I am to have such an extraordinary good fortune and high position in the world which is to come."

When their contemporaries do not see this and tell them that they cannot expect to have it both ways, they lose their tempers, shake the dust from their feet and go sulking off into the wilderness.

This is as regards themselves; to their followers they say: "You must not expect to be able to make the best of both worlds. The thing is absurd; it cannot be done. You must choose which you prefer, go in for it and leave the other, for you cannot have both."

When a saint complains that people do not know the things belonging to their peace, what he really means is that they do not sufficiently care about the things belonging to his own peace.

Prayer

i

Lord, let me know mine end, and the number of my days: that I may be certified how long I have to live (Ps. xxxix. 5).

Of all prayers this is the insanest. That the one who uttered it should have made and retained a reputation is a strong argument in favour of his having been surrounded with courtiers. "Lord, let me not know mine end" would be better, only it would be praying for what God has already granted us. "Lord, let me know A.B.'s end" would be bad enough. Even though A.B. were Mr. Gladstone — we might hear he was not to die yet. "Lord, stop A.B. from knowing my end" would be reasonable, if there were any use in praying that A.B. might not be able to do what he never can do. Or can the prayer refer to the other end of life? "Lord, let me know my beginning." This again would not be always prudent.

The prayer is a silly piece of petulance and it would have served the maker of it right to have had it granted. "A painful and lingering disease followed by death" or "Ninety, a burden to yourself and every one else" — there is not so much to pick and choose between them. Surely, "I thank thee, O Lord, that thou hast hidden mine end from me" would be better. The sting of death is in foreknowledge of the when and the how.

If again he had prayed that he might be able to make his psalms a little more lively, and be saved from becoming the bore which he has been to so many generations of sick persons and young children — or that he might find a publisher for them with greater facility — but there is no end to it. The prayer he did pray was about the worst he could have prayed and the psalmist, being the psalmist, naturally prayed it — unless I have misquoted him.

ii

Prayers are to men as dolls are to children. They are not without use and comfort, but it is not easy to take them very seriously. I dropped saying mine suddenly once for all without malice prepense, on the night of the 29th of September, 1859, when I went on board the *Roman Emperor* to sail for New Zealand. I had said them the night before and doubted not that I was always going to say them as I always had done hitherto. That night, I suppose, the sense of change was so great that it shook them quietly off. I was not then a sceptic; I had got as far as disbelief in infant baptism but no further. I felt no compunction of conscience, however, about leaving off my morning and evening prayers — simply I could no longer say them.

iii

Lead us not into temptation (Matt. vi. 13).

For example; I am crossing from Calais to Dover and there is a well-known popular preacher on board, say Archdeacon Farrar.

I have my camera in my hand and though the sea is rough the sun is brilliant. I see the archdeacon come on board at Calais and seat himself upon the upper deck, looking as though he had just stepped out of a band-box. Can I be expected to resist the temptation of snapping him? Suppose that in the train for an hour before reaching Calais I had said any number of times, "Lead us not into temptation," is it likely that the archdeacon would have been made to take some other boat or to stay in Calais, or that I myself, by being delayed on my homeward journey, should have been led into some other temptation, though perhaps smaller? Had I not better snap him and have done with it? Is there enough chance of good result to make it worth while to try the experiment? The general consensus of opinion is that there is not.

And as for praying for strength to resist temptation — granted that if, when I saw the archdeacon in the band-box stage, I had immediately prayed for strength I might have been enabled to put the evil thing from me for a time, how long would this have been likely to last when I saw his face grow saintlier and saintlier? I am an excellent sailor myself, but he is not, and when I see him there, his eyes closed and his head thrown back, like a sleeping St.

Joseph in a shovel hat, with a basin beside him, can I expect to be saved from snapping him by such a formula as "Deliver us from evil"?

Is it in photographer's nature to do so? When David found himself in the cave with Saul he cut off one of Saul's coattails; if he had had a camera and there had been enough light he would have photographed him; but would it have been in flesh and blood for him neither to cut off his coat-tail nor to snap him?

There is a photographer in every bush, going about like a roaring lion seeking whom he may devour.

iv

Teach me to live that I may dread
The grave as little as my bed.

This is from the evening hymn which all respectable children are taught. It sounds well, but it is immoral.

Our own death is a premium which we must pay for the far greater benefit we have derived from the fact that so many people have not only lived but also died before us. For if the old ones had not in course of time gone there would have been no progress; all our civilisation is due to the arrangement whereby no man shall live for ever, and to this huge mass of advantage we must each contribute our mite; that is to say, when our turn comes we too must die. The hardship is that interested persons should be able to scare us into thinking the change we call death to be the desperate business which they make it out to be. There is no hardship in having to suffer that change.

Bishop Ken, however, goes too far. Undesirable, of course, death must always be to those who are fairly well off, but it is undesirable that any living being should live in habitual indifference to death. The indifference should be kept for worthy occasions, and even then, though death be gladly faced, it is not healthy that it should be faced as though it were a mere undressing and going to bed.

XIV
Higgledy-Piggledy

Preface to Vol. II

On indexing this volume, as with Vols. I and IV which are already indexed and as, no doubt, will be the case with any that I may live to index later, I am alarmed at the triviality of many of these notes, the ineptitude of many and the obvious untenableness of many that I should have done much better to destroy.

Elmsley, in one of his letters to Dr. Butler, says that an author is the worst person to put one of his own works through the press (*Life of Dr. Butler*, I, 88). It seems to me that he is the worst person also to make selections from his own notes or indeed even, in my case, to write them. I cannot help it. They grew as, with little disturbance, they now stand; they are not meant for publication; the bad ones serve as bread for the jam of the good ones; it was less trouble to let them go than to think whether they ought not to be destroyed. The retort, however, is obvious; no thinking should have been required in respect of many—a glance should have consigned them to the waste-paper basket. I know it and I know that many a one of those who look over these books—for that they will be looked over by not a few I doubt not—will think me to have been a greater fool than I probably was. I cannot help it. I have at any rate the consolation of also knowing that, however much I may have irritated, displeased or disappointed them, they will not be able to tell me so; and I think that, to some, such a record of passing moods and thoughts good, bad and indifferent will be more valuable as throwing light upon the period to which it relates than it would have been if it had been edited with greater judgment.

Besides, Vols. I and IV being already bound, I should not have enough to form Vols. II and III if I cut out all those that ought to be cut out. [June, 1898.]

P.S.—If I had re-read my preface to Vol. IV, I need not have written the above.

Waste-Paper Baskets

Every one should keep a mental waste-paper basket and the older he grows the more things he will consign to it—torn up to irrecoverable tatters.

Flies in the Milk-Jug

Saving scraps is like picking flies out of the milk-jug. We do not mind doing this, I suppose, because we feel sure the flies will never want to borrow money off us. We do not feel so sure about anything much bigger than a fly. If it were a mouse that had got into the milk-jug, we should call the cat at once.

My Thoughts

They are like persons met upon a journey; I think them very agreeable at first but soon find, as a rule, that I am tired of them.

Our Ideas

They are for the most part like bad sixpences and we spend our lives in trying to pass them on one another.

Cat-Ideas and Mouse-Ideas

We can never get rid of mouse-ideas completely, they keep turning up again and again, and nibble, nibble — no matter how often we drive them off. The best way to keep them down is to have a few good strong cat-ideas which will embrace them and ensure their not reappearing till they do so in another shape.

Incoherency of New Ideas

An idea must not be condemned for being a little shy and incoherent; all new ideas are shy when introduced first among our old ones. We should have patience and see whether the incoherency is likely to wear off or to wear on, in which latter case the sooner we get rid of them the better.

An Apology for the Devil

It must be remembered that we have only heard one side of the case. God has written all the books.

Hallelujah

When we exclaim so triumphantly "Hallelujah! for the Lord God omnipotent reigneth" we only mean that we think no small beer of ourselves, that our God is a much greater God than any one else's God, that he was our father's God before us, and that it is all right, respectable and as it should be.

Hating

It does not matter much what a man hates provided he hates something.

Hamlet, Don Quixote, Mr. Pickwick and others

The great characters of fiction live as truly as the memories of dead men. For the life after death it is not necessary that a man or woman should have lived.

Reputation

The evil that men do lives after them. Yes, and a good deal of the evil that they never did as well.

Science and Business

The best class of scientific mind is the same as the best class of business mind. The great desideratum in either case is to know how much evidence is enough to warrant action. It is as unbusiness-like to want too much evidence before buying or selling as to be content with too little. The same kind of qualities are wanted in either case. The difference is that if the business man makes a mistake, he commonly has to suffer for it, whereas it is rarely that scientific blundering, so long as it is confined to theory, entails loss on the blunderer. On the contrary it very often brings him fame, money and a pension. Hence the business man, if he is a good one, will take greater care not to overdo or underdo things than the scientific man can reasonably be expected to take.

Scientists

There are two classes, those who want to know and do not care whether others think they know or not, and those who do not much care about knowing but care very greatly about being reputed as knowing.

Scientific Terminology

This is the Scylla's cave which men of science are preparing for themselves to be able to pounce out upon us from it, and into which we cannot penetrate.

Scientists and Drapers

Why should the botanist, geologist or other-ist give himself such airs over the draper's assistant? Is it because he names his plants or specimens with Latin names and divides them into genera and species, whereas the draper does not formulate his classifications, or at any rate only uses his mother tongue when he does? Yet how like the sub-divisions of textile life are to those of the animal and vegetable kingdoms! A few great families—cotton, linen, hempen, woollen, silk, mohair, alpaca—into what an infinite variety of genera and species do not these great families subdivide themselves? And does it take less labour, with less intelligence, to master all these and to acquire familiarity with their various habits, habitats and prices than it does to master the details of any other great branch of science? I do not know. But when I think of Shoolbred's on the one hand and, say, the ornithological collections of the British Museum upon the other, I feel as though it would take me less trouble to master the second than the first.

Men of Science

If they are worthy of the name they are indeed about God's path and about his bed and spying out all his ways.

Sparks

Everything matters more than we think it does, and, at the same time, nothing matters so much as we think it does. The merest spark may set all Europe in a blaze, but though all Europe be set in a blaze twenty times over, the world will wag itself right again.

Dumb-Bells

I regard them with suspicion as academic.

Purgatory

Time is the only true purgatory.

Greatness

He is greatest who is most often in men's good thoughts.

The Vanity of Human Wishes

There is only one thing vainer and that is the having no wishes.

Jones's Conscience

He said he had not much conscience, and what little he had was guilty.

Nihilism

The Nihilists do not believe in nothing; they only believe in nothing that does not commend itself to themselves; that is, they will not allow that anything may be beyond their comprehension. As their comprehension is not great their creed is, after all, very nearly nihil.

On Breaking Habits

To begin knocking off the habit in the evening, then the afternoon as well and, finally, the morning too is better than to begin cutting it off in the morning and then go on to the afternoon and evening. I speak from experience as regards smoking and can say that when one comes to within an hour or two of smoke-time one begins to be impatient for it, whereas there will be no impatience after the time for knocking off has been confirmed as a habit.

Dogs

The great pleasure of a dog is that you may make a fool of yourself with him and not only will he not scold you, but he will make a fool of himself too.

Future and Past

The Will-be and the Has-been touch us more nearly than the Is. So we are more tender towards children and old people than to those who are in the prime of life.

Nature

As the word is now commonly used it excludes nature's most interesting productions—the works of man. Nature is usually taken to mean mountains, rivers, clouds and undomesticated animals and plants. I am not indifferent to this half of nature, but it interests me much less than the other half.

Lucky and Unlucky

People are lucky and unlucky not according to what they get absolutely, but according to the ratio between what they get and what they have been led to expect.

Definitions

i

As, no matter what cunning system of checks we devise, we must in the end trust some one whom we do not check, but to whom we give unreserved confidence, so there is a point at which the understanding and mental processes must be taken as understood without further question or definition in words. And I should say that this point should be fixed pretty early in the discussion.

ii

There is one class of mind that loves to lean on rules and definitions, and another that discards them as far as possible. A faddist will generally ask for a definition of faddism, and one who is not a faddist will be impatient of being asked to give one.

iii

A definition is the enclosing a wilderness of idea within a wall of words.

iv

Definitions are a kind of scratching and generally leave a sore place more sore than it was before.

As Love is too young to know what conscience is, so Truth and Genius are too old to know what definition is.

Money

It has such an inherent power to run itself clear of taint that human ingenuity cannot devise the means of making it work permanent mischief, any more than means can be found of torturing peoplè beyond what they can bear. Even if a man founds a College of Technical Instruction, the chances are ten to one that no one will be taught anything and that it will have been practically left to a number of excellent professors who will know very well what to do with it.

Wit

There is no Professor of Wit at either University. Surely they might as reasonably have a professor of wit as of poetry.

Oxford and Cambridge

The dons are too busy educating the young men to be able to teach them anything.

Cooking

There is a higher average of good cooking at Oxford and Cambridge than elsewhere. The cooking is better than the curriculum. But there is no Chair of Cookery, it is taught by apprenticeship in the kitchens.

Perseus and St. George

These dragon-slayers did not take lessons in dragon-slaying, nor do leaders of forlorn hopes generally rehearse their parts beforehand. Small things may be rehearsed, but the greatest are always do-or-die, neck-or-nothing matters.

Specialism and Generalism

Woe to the specialist who is not a pretty fair generalist, and woe to the generalist who is not also a bit of a specialist.

Silence and Tact

Silence is not always tact and it is tact that is golden, not silence.

Truth-tellers

Professional truth-tellers may be trusted to profess that they are telling the truth.

Street Preachers

These are the costermongers and barrow men of the religious world.

Providence and Othello

Providence, in making the rain fall also upon the sea, was like the man who, when he was to play Othello, must needs black himself all over.

Providence and Improvidence

i

We should no longer say: Put your trust in Providence, but in Improvidence, for this is what we mean.

ii

To put one's trust in God is only a longer way of saying that one will chance it.

iii

There is nothing so imprudent or so improvident as over-prudence or over-providence.

Epiphany

If Providence could be seen at all, he would probably turn out to be a very disappointing person—a little wizened old gentleman with a cold in his head, a red nose and a comforter round his neck, whistling o'er the furrow'd land or crooning to himself as he goes aimlessly along the streets, poking his way about and loitering continually at shop-windows and second-hand book-stalls.

Fortune

Like Wisdom, Fortune crieth in the streets, and no man regardeth. There is not an advertisement supplement to the *Times*—nay, hardly a half sheet of newspaper that comes into a house wrapping up this or that, but it gives information which would make a man's fortune, if he could only spot it and detect the one paragraph that would do this among the 99 which would wreck him if he had anything to do with them.

Gold-Mines

Gold is not found in quartz alone; its richest lodes are in the eyes and ears of the public, but these are harder to work and to prospect than any quartz vein.

Things and Purses

Everything is like a purse — there may be money in it, and we can generally say by the feel of it whether there is or is not. Sometimes, however, we must turn it inside out before we can be quite sure whether there is anything in it or no. When I have turned a proposition inside out, put it to stand on its head, and shaken it, I have often been surprised to find how much came out of it.

Solomon in all his Glory

But, in the first place, the lilies do toil and spin after their own fashion, and, in the next, it was not desirable that Solomon should be dressed like a lily of the valley.

David's Teachers

David said he had more understanding than his teachers. If his teachers were anything like mine this need not imply much understanding on David's part. And if his teachers did not know more than the Psalms — it is absurd. It is merely swagger, like the German Emperor. [1897.]

S. Michael

He contended with the devil about the body of Moses. Now, I do not believe that any reasonable person would contend about the body of Moses with the devil or with any one else.

One Form of Failure

From a worldly point of view there is no mistake so great as that of being always right.

Andromeda

The dragon was never in better health and spirits than on the morning when Perseus came down upon him. It is said that Andromeda told Perseus she had been thinking how remarkably well he was looking. He had got up quite in his usual health — and so on.

When I said this to Ballard [a fellow art-student at Heatherley's] and that other thing which I said about Andromeda in *Life and Habit*, [225] he remarked that he wished it had been so in the poets.

I looked at him. "Ballard," I said, "I also am 'the poets.'"

Self-Confidence

Nothing is ever any good unless it is thwarted with self-distrust though in the main self-confident.

Wandering

When the inclination is not obvious, the mind meanders, or maunders, as a stream in a flat meadow.

Poverty

I shun it because I have found it so apt to become contagious; but I fancy my constitution is more seasoned against it now than formerly. I hope that what I have gone through may have made me immune.

Pedals or Drones

The discords of every age are rendered possible by being taken on a drone or pedal of cant, common form and conventionality. This drone is, as it were, the flour and suet of a plum pudding.

Evasive Nature

She is one long This-way-and-it-isness and, at the same time, That-way-and-it-isn'tness. She flies so like a snipe that she is hard to hit.

Fashion

Fashion is like God, man cannot see it in its holy of holies and live. And it is, like God, increate, springing out of nothing, yet the maker of all things — ever changing yet the same yesterday, to-day and for ever.

Doctors and Clergymen

A physician's physiology has much the same relation to his power of healing as a cleric's divinity has to his power of influencing conduct.

God is Love

I dare say. But what a mischievous devil Love is!

Common Chords

If Man is the tonic and God the dominant, the Devil is certainly the sub-dominant and Woman is the relative minor.

God and the Devil

God and the Devil are an effort after specialisation and division of labour.

Sex

The sexes are the first — or are among the first great experiments in the social subdivision of labour.

Women

If you choose to insist on the analogies and points of resemblance between men and women, they are so great that the differences seem indeed small. If, on the other hand, you are in a mood for emphasising the points of difference, you can show that men and women have hardly anything in common. And so with anything: if a man wants to make a case he can generally find a way of doing so.

Offers of Marriage

Women sometimes say that they have had no offers, and only wish that some one had ever proposed to them. This is not the right way to put it. What they should say is that though, like all women, they have been proposing to men all their lives, yet they grieve to remember that they have been invariably refused.

Marriage

i

The question of marriage or non-marriage is only the question of whether it is better to be spoiled one way or another.

ii

In matrimony, to hesitate is sometimes to be saved.

iii

Inoculation, or a hair of the dog that is going to bite you—this principle should be introduced in respect of marriage and speculation.

Life and Love

To live is like to love—all reason is against it, and all healthy instinct for it.

The Basis of Life

We may say what we will, but Life is, *au fond*, sensual.

Woman Suffrage

I will vote for it when women have left off making a noise in the reading-room of the British Museum, when they leave off wearing high head-dresses in the pit of a theatre and when I have seen as many as twelve women in all catch hold of the strap or bar on getting into an omnibus.

Manners Makyth Man

Yes, but they make woman still more.

Women and Religion

It has been said that all sensible men are of the same religion and that no sensible man ever says what that religion is. So all sensible men are of the same opinion about women and no sensible man ever says what that opinion is.

Happiness

Behold and see if there be any happiness like unto the happiness of the devils when they found themselves cast out of Mary Magdalene.

Sorrow within Sorrow

He was in reality damned glad; he told people he was sorry he was not more sorry, and here began the first genuine sorrow, for he was really sorry that people would not believe he was sorry that he was not more sorry.

Going Away

I can generally bear the separation, but I don't like the leave-taking.

XV
Titles and Subjects

Titles

A good title should aim at making what follows as far as possible superfluous to those who know anything of the subject.

"The Ancient Mariner"

This poem would not have taken so well if it had been called "The Old Sailor," so that Wardour Street has its uses.

For Unwritten Articles, Essays, Stories

The Art of Quarrelling.

Christian Death-beds.

The Book of Babes and Sucklings.

Literary Struldbrugs.

The Life of the World to Come.

The Limits of Good Faith.

Art, Money and Religion.

The Third Class Excursion Train, or Steam-boat, as the Church of the Future.

The Utter Speculation involved in much of the good advice that is commonly given—as never to sell a reversion, etc.

Tracts for Children, warning them against the virtues of their elders.

Making Ready for Death as a Means of Prolonging Life. An Essay concerning Human Misunderstanding. So McCulloch [a fellow art-student at Heatherley's, a very fine draughtsman] used to say that he drew a great many lines and saved the best of them. Illusion, mistake, action taken in the dark—these are among the main sources of our progress.

The Elements of Immorality for the Use of Earnest Schoolmasters.

Family Prayers: A series of perfectly plain and sensible ones asking for what people really do want without any kind of humbug.

A Penitential Psalm as David would have written it if he had been reading Herbert Spencer.

A Few Little Crows which I have to pick with various people.

The Scylla of Atheism and the Charybdis of Christianity.

The Battle of the Prigs and Blackguards.

That Good may Come.

The Marriage of Inconvenience.

The Judicious Separation.

Fooling Around.

Higgledy-Piggledy.

The Diseases and Ordinary Causes of Mortality among Friendships.

The finding a lot of old photographs at Herculaneum or Thebes; and they should turn out to be of no interest.

On the points of resemblance and difference between the dropping off of leaves from a tree and the dropping off of guests from a dinner or a concert.

The Sense of Touch: An essay showing that all the senses resolve themselves ultimately into a sense of touch, and that eating is touch carried to the bitter end. So there is but one sense—touch—and the amœba has it. When I look upon the foraminifera I look upon myself.

The China Shepherdess with Lamb on public-house chimney-pieces in England as against the Virgin with Child in Italy.

For a Medical pamphlet: Cant as a means of Prolonging Life.

For an Art book: The Complete Pot-boiler; or what to paint and how to paint it, with illustrations reproduced from contemporary exhibitions and explanatory notes.

For a Picture: St. Francis preaching to Silenus. Fra Angelico and Rubens might collaborate to produce this picture.

The Happy Mistress. Fifteen mistresses apply for three cooks and the mistress who thought herself nobody is chosen by the beautiful and accomplished cook.

The Complete Drunkard. He would not give money to sober people, he said they would only eat it and send their children to school with it.

The Contented Porpoise. It knew it was to be stuffed and set up in a glass case after death, and looked forward to this as to a life of endless happiness.

The Flying Balance. The ghost of an old cashier haunts a ledger, so that the books always refuse to balance by the sum of, say, £1.15.11. No matter how many accountants are called in, year after year the same error always turns up; sometimes they think they have it right and it turns out there was a mistake, so the old error reappears. At last a son and heir is born, and at some festivities the old cashier's name is mentioned with honour. This lays his ghost. Next morning the books are found correct and remain so.

A Dialogue between Isaac and Ishmael on the night that Isaac came down from the mountain with his father. The rebellious Ishmael tries to stir up Isaac, and that good young man explains the righteousness of the transaction — without much effect.

Bad Habits: on the dropping them gradually, as one leaves off requiring them, on the evolution principle.

A Story about a Freethinking Father who has an illegitimate son which he considers the proper thing; he finds this son taking to immoral ways, e.g. he turns Christian, becomes a clergyman and insists on marrying.

For a Ballad: Two sets of rooms in some alms-houses at Cobham near Gravesend have an inscription stating that they belong to "the Hundred of Hoo in the Isle of Grain." These words would make a lovely refrain for a ballad.

A story about a man who suffered from atrophy of the purse, or atrophy of the opinions; but whatever the disease some plausible Latin, or imitation-Latin name must be found for it and also some cure.

A Fairy Story modelled on the Ugly Duckling of Hans Andersen about a bumptious boy whom all the nice boys hated. He finds out that he was really at last caressed by the Huxleys and Tyndalls as one of themselves.

A Collection of the letters of people who have committed suicide; and also of people who only threaten to do so. The first may be got abundantly from reports of coroners' inquests, the second would be harder to come by.

The Structure and Comparative Anatomy of Fads, Fancies and Theories; showing, moreover, that men and women exist only as the organs and tools of the ideas that dominate them; it is the fad that is alone living.

An Astronomical Speculation: Each fixed star has a separate god whose body is his own particular solar system, and these gods know each other, move about among each other as we do, laugh at each other and criticise one another's work. Write some of their discourses with and about one another.

Imaginary Worlds

A world exactly, to the minutest detail, a duplicate of our own, but as we shall be five hundred, or from that to twenty thousand, years hence. Let there be also another world, a duplicate of what we were five hundred to twenty thousand years ago. There should be many worlds of each kind at different dates behind us and ahead of us.

I send a visitor from a world ahead of us to a world behind us, after which he comes to us, and so we learn what happened in the Homeric age. My visitor will not tell me what has happened in his own world since the time corresponding to the present moment in our world, because the knowledge of the future would be not only fatal to ourselves but would upset the similarity between the two worlds, so they would be no longer able to refer to us for information on any point of history from the moment of the introduction of the disturbing element.

When they are in doubt about a point in their past history that we have not yet reached they make preparation and forecast its occurrence in our world as we foretell eclipses and transits of Venus, and all their most accomplished historians investigate it; but if the conditions for observation have been unfavourable, or if they postpone consideration of the point till the time of its happening here has gone by, then they must wait for many years till the same combination occurs in some other world. Thus they say, "The next beheading of King Charles I will be in Ald. b. x. 231c/d" — or whatever the name of the star may be — "on such and such a day of such and such a year, and there will not be another in the lifetime of any man now living," or there will, in such and such a star, as the case may be.

Communication with a world twenty thousand years ahead of us might ruin the human race as effectually as if we had fallen into the sun. It would be too wide a cross. The people in my supposed world know this and if, for any reason, they want to kill a civilisation, stuff it and put it into a museum, they tell it something that is too much ahead of its other ideas, something that travels faster than thought, thus setting an avalanche of new ideas tumbling in upon it and utterly destroying everything. Sometimes they merely introduce a little poisonous microbe of thought which the cells in the world where it is introduced do not know how to deal with — some such trifle as that two and two make seven, or that you can weigh time in scales by the pound; a single such microbe of knowledge placed in the brain of a fitting subject would breed like wild fire and kill all that came in contact with it.

And so on.

An Idyll

I knew a South Italian of the old Greek blood whose sister told him when he was a boy that he had eyes like a cow.

Raging with despair and grief he haunted the fountains and looked into the mirror of their waters. "Are my eyes," he asked himself with horror, "are they really like the eyes of a cow?" "Alas!" he was compelled to answer, "they are only too sadly, sadly like them."

And he asked those of his playmates whom he best knew and trusted whether it was indeed true that his eyes were like the eyes of a cow, but he got no comfort from any of them, for they one and all laughed at him and said that they were not only like, but very like. Then grief consumed his soul, and he could eat no food, till one day the loveliest girl in the place said to him:

"Gaetano, my grandmother is ill and cannot get her firewood; come with me to the bosco this evening and help me to bring her a load or two, will you?"

And he said he would go.

So when the sun was well down and the cool night air was sauntering under the chestnuts, the pair sat together cheek to cheek and with their arms round each other's waists.

"O Gaetano," she exclaimed, "I do love you so very dearly. When you look at me your eyes are like—they are like the eyes"—here she faltered a little—"the eyes of a cow."

Thenceforward he cared not . . .

And so on.

A Divorce Novelette

The hero and heroine are engaged against their wishes. They like one another very well but each is in love with some one else; nevertheless, under an uncle's will, they forfeit large property unless they marry one another, so they get married, making no secret to one another that they dislike it very much.

On the evening of their wedding day they broach the subject that has long been nearest to their hearts—the possibility of being divorced. They discuss it tearfully, but the obstacles seem insuperable. Nevertheless they agree that faint heart never yet got rid of fair lady, "None but the brave," exclaims the husband, "deserve to lose the fair," and they plight their most solemn vows that they will henceforth live but for the object of getting divorced from one another.

But the course of true divorce never did run smooth, and the plot turns upon the difficulties that meet them and how they try to overcome them. At one time they seem almost certain of success, but the cup is dashed from their lips and is farther off than ever.

At last an opportunity occurs in an unlooked-for manner. They are divorced and live happily apart ever afterwards.

The Moral Painter—A Tale of Double Personality

Once upon a time there was a painter who divided his life into two halves; in the one half he painted pot-boilers for the market, setting every consideration aside except that of doing for his master, the public, something for which he could get paid the money on which he lived. He was great at floods and never looked at nature except in order to see what would make most show with least expense. On the whole he found nothing so cheap to make and easy to sell as veiled heads.

The other half of his time he studied and painted with the sincerity of Giovanni Bellini, Rembrandt, Holbein or De Hooghe. He was then his own master and thought only of doing his work as well as he could, regardless of whether it would bring him anything but debt and abuse or not. He gave his best without receiving so much as thanks.

He avoided the temptation of telling either half about the other.

Two Writers

One left little or nothing about himself and the world complained that it was puzzled. Another, mindful of this, left copious details about himself, whereon the world said that it was even more puzzled about him than about the man who had left nothing, till presently it found out that it was also bored, and troubled itself no more about either.

The Archbishop of Heligoland

The Archbishop of Heligoland believes his faith, and it makes him so unhappy that he finds it impossible to advise any one to accept it. He summons the Devil, makes a compact with him and is relieved by being made to see that there was nothing in it—whereon he is very good and happy and leads a most beneficent life, but is haunted by the thought that on his death the Devil will claim his bond. This terror grows greater and greater, and he determines to see the Devil again.

The upshot of it all is that the Devil turns out to have been Christ who has a dual life and appears sometimes as Christ and sometimes as the Devil. [235]

XVI
Written Sketches

Literary Sketch-Books

The true writer will stop everywhere and anywhere to put down his notes, as the true painter will stop everywhere and anywhere to sketch.

I do not see why an author should not have a sale of literary sketches, each one short, slight and capable of being framed and glazed in small compass. They would make excellent library decorations and ought to fetch as much as an artist's sketches. They might be cut up in suitable lots, if the fashion were once set, and many a man might be making provision for his family at odd times with his notes as an artist does with his sketches.

London

If I were asked what part of London I was most identified with after Clifford's Inn itself, I should say Fetter Lane—every part of it. Just by the Record Office is one of the places where I am especially prone to get ideas; so also is the other end, about the butcher's shop near Holborn. The reason in both cases is the same, namely, that I have about had time to settle down to reflection after leaving, on the one hand, my rooms in Clifford's Inn and, on the other, Jones's rooms in Barnard's Inn where I usually spend the evening. The subject which has occupied my mind during the day being approached anew after an interval and a shake, some fresh idea in connection with it often strikes me. But long before I knew Jones, Fetter Lane was always a street which I was more in than perhaps any other in London. Leather Lane, the road through Lincoln's Inn Fields to the Museum, the Embankment, Fleet Street, the Strand and Charing Cross come next.

A Clifford's Inn Euphemism

People when they want to get rid of their cats, and do not like killing them, bring them to the garden of Clifford's Inn, drop them there and go away. In spite of all that is said about cats being able to find their way so wonderfully, they seldom do find it, and once in Clifford's Inn the cat generally remains there. The technical word among the laundresses in the inn for this is, "losing" a cat:

"Poor thing, poor thing," said one old woman to me a few days ago, "it's got no fur on its head at all, and no doubt that's why the people she lived with lost her."

London Trees

They are making a great outcry about the ventilators on the Thames Embankment, just as they made a great outcry about the Griffin in Fleet Street. [See *Alps and Sanctuaries*. Introduction.] They say the ventilators have spoiled the Thames Embankment. They do not spoil it half so much as the statues do—indeed, I do not see that they spoil it at all. The trees that are planted everywhere are, or will be, a more serious nuisance. Trees are all very well where there is plenty of room, otherwise they are a mistake; they keep in the moisture, exclude light and air, and their roots disturb foundations; most of our London Squares would look much better if the trees were thinned. I should like to cut down all the plane trees in the garden of Clifford's Inn and leave only the others.

What I Said to the Milkman

One afternoon I heard a knock at the door and found it was the milkman. Mrs. Doncaster [his laundress] was not there, so I took in the milk myself. The milkman is a very nice man, and, by way of making himself pleasant, said, rather complainingly, that the weather kept very dry.

I looked at him significantly and said: "Ah, yes, of course for your business you must find it very inconvenient," and laughed.

He saw he had been caught and laughed too. It was a very old joke, but he had not expected it at that particular moment, and on the top of such an innocent remark.

The Return of the Jews to Palestine

A man called on me last week and proposed gravely that I should write a book upon an idea which had occurred to a friend of his, a Jew living in New Bond Street. It was a plan requiring the co-operation of a brilliant writer and that was why he had come to me. If only I would help, the return of the Jews to Palestine would be rendered certain and easy. There was no trouble about the poor Jews, he knew how he could get them back at any time; the difficulty lay with the Rothschilds, the Oppenheims and such; with my assistance, however, the thing could be done.

I am afraid I was rude enough to decline to go into the scheme on the ground that I did not care twopence whether the Rothschilds and Oppenheims went back to Palestine or not. This was felt to be an obstacle; but then he began to try and make me care, whereupon, of course, I had to get rid of him. [1883.]

The Great Bear's Barley-Water

Last night Jones was walking down with me from Staple Inn to Clifford's Inn, about 10 o'clock, and we saw the Great Bear standing upright on the tip of his tail which was coming out of a chimney pot. Jones said it wanted attending to. I said:

"Yes, but to attend to it properly we ought to sit up with it all night, and if the Great Bear thinks that I am going to sit by his bed-side and give him a spoonful of barley-water every ten minutes, he will find himself much mistaken." [1892.]

The Cock Tavern

I went into Fleet Street one Sunday morning last November [1882] with my camera lucida to see whether I should like to make a sketch of the gap made by the demolition of the Cock Tavern. It was rather pretty, with an old roof or two behind and scaffolding about and torn paper hanging to an exposed party-wall and old fireplaces and so on, but it was not very much out of the way. Still I would have taken it if it had not been the Cock. I thought of all the trash that has been written about it and of Tennyson's plump head waiter (who by the way used to swear that he did not know Tennyson and that Tennyson never did resort to the Cock) and I said to myself:

"No—you may go. I will put out no hand to save you."

Myself in Dowie's Shop

I always buy ready-made boots and insist on taking those which the shopman says are much too large for me. By this means I keep free from corns, but I have a great deal of trouble generally with the shopman. I had got on a pair once which I thought would do, and the shopman said for the third or fourth time:

"But really, sir, these boots are much too large for you." I turned to him and said rather sternly, "Now, you made that remark before."

There was nothing in it, but all at once I became aware that I was being watched, and, looking up, saw a middle-aged gentleman eyeing the whole proceedings with much amusement. He was quite polite but he was obviously exceedingly amused. I can hardly tell why, nor why I should put such a trifle down, somehow or other an impression was made upon me by the affair quite out of proportion to that usually produced by so small a matter.

My Dentist

Mr. Forsyth had been stopping a tooth for me and then talked a little, as he generally does, and asked me if I knew a certain distinguished literary man, or rather journalist. I said No, and that I did not want to know him. The paper edited by the gentleman in question was not to my taste. I was a literary Ishmael, and preferred to remain so. It was my rôle.

"It seems to me," I continued, "that if a man will only be careful not to write about things that he does not understand, if he will use the tooth-pick freely and the spirit twice a day, and come to you again in October, he will get on very well without knowing any of the big-wigs."

"The tooth-pick freely" and "the spirit twice a day" being tags of Mr. Forsyth's, he laughed.

Furber the Violin-Maker

From what my cousin [Reginald E. Worsley] and Gogin both tell me I am sure that Furber is one of the best men we have. My cousin did not like to send Hyam to him for a violin: he did not think him worthy to have one. Furber does not want you to buy a violin unless you can appreciate it when you have it. My cousin says of him:

"He is generally a little tight on a Saturday afternoon. He always speaks the truth, but on Saturday afternoons it comes pouring out more."

"His joints [i.e. the joints of the violins he makes] are the closest and neatest that were ever made."

"He always speaks of the corners of a fiddle; Haweis would call them the points. Haweis calls it the neck of a fiddle. Furber always the handle."

My cousin says he would like to take his violins to bed with him.

Speaking of Strad violins Furber said: "Rough, rough linings, but they look as if they grew together."

One day my cousin called and Furber, on opening the door, before saying "How do you do?" or any word of greeting, said very quietly:

"The dog is dead."

My cousin, having said what he thought sufficient, took up a violin and played a few notes. Furber evidently did not like it. Rose, the dog, was still unburied; she was laid out in that very room. My cousin stopped. Then Mrs. Furber came in.

R. E. W. "I am very sorry, Mrs. Furber, to hear about Rose."

Mrs. F. "Well, yes sir. But I suppose it is all for the best."

R. E. W. "I am afraid you will miss her a great deal."

Mrs. F. "No doubt we shall, sir; but you see she is only gone a little while before us."

R. E. W. "Oh, Mrs. Furber, I hope a good long while."

Mrs. F. (brightening). "Well, yes sir, I don't want to go just yet, though Mr. Furber does say it is a happy thing to die."

My cousin says that Furber hardly knows any one by their real name. He identifies them by some nickname in connection with the fiddles they buy from him or get him to repair, or by some personal peculiarity.

"There is one man," said my cousin, "whom he calls 'diaphragm' because he wanted a fiddle made with what he called a diaphragm in it. He knows Dando and Carrodus and Jenny Lind, but hardly any one else."

"Who is Dando?" said I.

"Why, Dando? Not know Dando? He was George the Fourth's music master, and is now one of the oldest members of the profession."

Window Cleaning in the British Museum Reading-Room

Once a year or so the figures on the Assyrian bas-reliefs break adrift and may be seen, with their scaling ladders and all, cleaning the outside of the windows in the dome of the reading-room. It is very pretty to watch them and they would photograph beautifully. If I live to see them do it again I must certainly snapshot them. You can see them smoking and sparring, and this year they have left a little hole in the window above the clock.

The Electric Light in its Infancy

I heard a woman in a 'bus boring her lover about the electric light. She wanted to know this and that, and the poor lover was helpless. Then she said she wanted to know how it was regulated. At last she settled down by saying that she knew it was in its infancy. The word "infancy" seemed to have a soothing effect upon her, for she said no more but, leaning her head against her lover's shoulder, composed herself to slumber.

Fire

I was at one the other night and heard a man say: "That corner stack is alight now quite nicely." People's sympathies seem generally to be with the fire so long as no one is in danger of being burned.

Adam and Eve

A little boy and a little girl were looking at a picture of Adam and Eve.

"Which is Adam and which is Eve?" said one.

"I do not know," said the other, "but I could tell if they had their clothes on."

Does Mamma Know?

A father was telling his eldest daughter, aged about six, that she had a little sister, and was explaining to her how nice it all was. The child said it was delightful and added:

"Does Mamma know? Let's go and tell her."

Mr. Darwin in the Zoological Gardens

Frank Darwin told me his father was once standing near the hippopotamus cage when a little boy and girl, aged four and five, came up. The hippopotamus shut his eyes for a minute.

"That bird's dead," said the little girl; "come along."

Terbourg

Gogin told me that Berg, an impulsive Swede whom he had known in Laurens's studio in Paris and who painted very well, came to London and was taken by an artist friend [Henry Scott Tuke, A.R.A.] to the National Gallery where he became very enthusiastic about the Terbourgs. They then went for a walk and, in Kensington Gore, near one of the entrances to Hyde Park or Kensington Gardens, there was an old Irish apple-woman sitting with her feet in a basket, smoking a pipe and selling oranges.

"Arranges two a penny, sorr," said the old woman in a general way.

And Berg, turning to her and throwing out his hands appealingly, said:

"O, madame, avez-vous vu les Terbourgs? Allez voir les Terbourgs."

He felt that such a big note had been left out of the life of any one who had not seen them.

At Doctors' Commons

A woman once stopped me at the entrance to Doctors' Commons and said:

"If you please, sir, can you tell me — is this the place that I came to before?"

Not knowing where she had been before I could not tell her.

The Sack of Khartoum

As I was getting out of a 'bus the conductor said to me in a confidential tone:

"I say, what does that mean? 'Sack of Khartoum'? What does 'Sack of Khartoum' mean?"

"It means," said I, "that they've taken Khartoum and played hell with it all round."

He understood that and thanked me, whereon we parted.

Missolonghi

Ballard [a fellow art-student with Butler at Heatherley's] told me that an old governess, some twenty years since, was teaching some girls modern geography. One of them did not know the name Missolonghi. The old lady wrung her hands:

"Why, me dear," she exclaimed, "when I was your age I could never hear the name mentioned without bursting into tears."

I should perhaps add that Byron died there.

Memnon

I saw the driver of the Hampstead 'bus once, near St. Giles's Church — an old, fat, red-faced man sitting bolt upright on the top of his 'bus in a driving storm of snow, fast asleep with a huge waterproof over his great-coat which descended with sweeping lines on to a tarpaulin. All this rose out of a cloud of steam from the horses. He had a short clay pipe in his mouth but, for the moment, he looked just like Memnon.

Manzi the Model

They had promised him sittings at the Royal Academy and then refused him on the ground that his legs were too hairy. He complained to Gogin:

"Why," said he, "I sat at the Slade School for the figure only last week, and there were five ladies, but not one of them told me my legs were too hairy."

A Sailor Boy and Some Chickens

A pretty girl in the train had some chirping chickens about ten days' old in a box labelled "German egg powders. One packet equal to six eggs." A sailor boy got in at Basingstoke, a quiet, reserved youth, well behaved and unusually good-looking. By and by the chickens were taken out of the box and fed with biscuit on the carriage seat. This thawed the boy who, though he fought against it for some lime, yielded to irresistible fascination and said:

"What are they?"

"Chickens," said the girl.

"Will they grow bigger?"

"Yes."

Then the boy said with an expression of infinite wonder: "And did you hatch them from they powders?"

We all laughed till the boy blushed and I was very sorry for him. If we had said they had been hatched from the powders he would have certainly believed us.

Gogin, the Japanese Gentleman and the Dead Dog

Gogin was one day going down Cleveland Street and saw an old, lean, careworn man crying over the body of his dog which had been just run over and killed by the old man's own cart. I have no doubt it was the dog's fault, for the man was in great distress; as for the dog there it lay all swelled and livid where the wheel had gone over it, its eyes protruded from their sockets and its tongue lolled out, but it was dead. The old man gazed on it, helplessly weeping, for some time and then got a large piece of brown paper in which he wrapped up the body of his favourite; he tied it neatly with a piece of string and, placing it in his cart, went homeward with a heavy heart. The day was dull, the gutters were full of cabbage stalks and the air resounded with the cry of costermongers.

On this a Japanese gentleman, who had watched the scene, lifted up his voice and made the bystanders a set oration. He was very yellow, had long black hair, gold spectacles and a top hat; he was a typical Japanese, but he spoke English perfectly. He said the scene they had all just witnessed was a very sad one and that it ought not to be passed over entirely without comment. He explained that it was very nice of the good old man to be so sorry about his dog and to be so careful of its remains and that he and all the bystanders must sympathise with him in his grief, and as the expression of their sympathy, both with the man and with the poor dog, he had thought fit, with all respect, to make them his present speech.

I have not the man's words but Gogin said they were like a Japanese drawing, that is to say, wonderfully charming, and showing great knowledge but not done in the least after the manner in which a European would do them. The bystanders stood open-mouthed and could make nothing of it, but they liked it, and the Japanese gentleman liked addressing them. When he left off and went away they followed him with their eyes, speechless.

St. Pancras' Bells

Gogin lives at 164 Euston Road, just opposite St. Pancras Church, and the bells play doleful hymn tunes opposite his window which worries him. My

St. Dunstan's bells near Clifford's Inn play doleful hymn tunes which enter in at my window; I not only do not dislike them, but rather like them; they are so silly and the bells are out of tune. I never yet was annoyed by either bells or street music except when a loud piano organ strikes up outside the public-house opposite my bedroom window after I am in bed and when I am just going to sleep. However, Jones was at Gogin's one summer evening and the bells struck up their dingy old burden as usual. The tonic bell on which the tune concluded was the most stuffy and out of tune. Gogin said it was like the smell of a bug.

At Eynsford

I saw a man painting there the other day but passed his work without looking at it and sat down to sketch some hundred of yards off. In course of time he came strolling round to see what I was doing and I, not knowing but what he might paint much better than I, was apologetic and said I was not a painter by profession.

"What are you?" said he.

I said I was a writer.

"Dear me," said he. "Why that's my line—I'm a writer."

I laughed and said I hoped he made it pay better than I did. He said it paid very well and asked me where I lived and in what neighbourhood my connection lay. I said I had no connection but only wrote books.

"Oh! I see. You mean you are an author. I'm not an author; I didn't mean that. I paint people's names up over their shops, and that's what we call being a writer. There isn't a touch on my work as good as any touch on yours."

I was gratified by so much modesty and, on my way back to dinner, called to see his work. I am afraid that he was not far wrong—it was awful.

Omne ignotum pro magnifico holds with painters perhaps more than elsewhere; we never see a man sketching, or even carrying a paint-box, without rushing to the conclusion that he can paint very well. There is no cheaper way of getting a reputation than that of going about with easel, paint-box, etc., provided one can ensure one's work not being seen. And the more traps one carries the cleverer people think one.

Mrs. Hicks

She and her husband, an old army sergeant who was all through the Indian Mutiny, are two very remarkable people; they keep a public-house where we often get our beer when out for our Sunday walk. She owns to sixty-seven, I should think she was a full seventy-five, and her husband, say, sixty-five. She is a tall, raw-boned Gothic woman with a strong family likeness to the crooked old crusader who lies in the church transept, and one would expect to find her body scrawled over with dates ranging from 400 years ago to the present time, just as the marble figure itself is. She has a great beard and moustaches and three projecting teeth in her lower jaw but no more in any part of her mouth. She moves slowly and is always a little in liquor besides being singularly dirty in her person. Her husband is like unto her.

For all this they are hard-working industrious people, keep no servant, pay cash for everything, are clearly going up rather than down in the world and live well. She always shows us what she is going to have for dinner and it is excellent—"And I made the stuffing over night and the gravy first thing this morning." Each time we go we find the house a little more done up. She dotes on Mr. Hicks—we never go there without her wedding day being referred to. She has earned her own living ever since she was ten years old, and lived twenty-nine and a half years in the house from which Mr. Hicks married her. "I am as happy," she said, "as the day is long." She dearly loves a joke and a little flirtation. I always say something perhaps a little impudently broad to her and she likes it extremely. Last time she sailed smilingly out of the room, doubtless to tell Mr. Hicks, and came back still smiling.

When we come we find her as though she had lien among the pots, but as soon as she has given us our beer, she goes upstairs and puts on a cap and a clean apron and washes her face—that is to say, she washes a round piece in the middle of her face, leaving a great glory of dirt showing all round it. It is plain the pair are respected by the manner in which all who come in treat them.

Last time we were there she said she hoped she should not die yet.

"You see," she said, "I am beginning now to know how to live."

These were her own words and, considering the circumstances under which they were spoken, they are enough to stamp the speaker as a remarkable woman. She has got as much from age and lost as little from youth as woman can well do. Nevertheless, to look at, she is like one of the witches in *Macbeth*.

New-Laid Eggs

When I take my Sunday walks in the country, I try to buy a few really new-laid eggs warm from the nest. At this time of the year (January) they are very hard to come by, and I have long since invented a sick wife who has implored me to get her a few eggs laid not earlier than the self-same morning. Of late, as I am getting older, it has become my daughter who has just had a little baby. This will generally draw a new-laid egg, if there is one about the place at all.

At Harrow Weald it has always been my wife who for years has been a great sufferer and finds a really new-laid egg the one thing she can digest in the way of solid food. So I turned her on as movingly as I could not long since, and was at last sold some eggs that were no better than common shop eggs, if so good. Next time I went I said my poor wife had been made seriously ill by them; it was no good trying to deceive her; she could tell a new-laid egg from a bad one as well as any woman in London, and she had such a high temper that it was very unpleasant for me when she found herself disappointed.

"Ah! sir," said the landlady, "but you would not like to lose her."

"Ma'am," I replied, "I must not allow my thoughts to wander in that direction. But it's no use bringing her stale eggs, anyhow."

"The Egg that Hen Belonged to"

I got some new-laid eggs a few Sundays ago. The landlady said they were her own, and talked about them a good deal.

She pointed to one of them and said:

"Now, would you believe it? The egg that hen belonged to laid 53 hens running and never stopped."

She called the egg a hen and the hen an egg. One would have thought she had been reading *Life and Habit* [and passim].

At Englefield Green

As an example of how anything can be made out of anything or done with anything by those who want to do it (as I said in *Life and Habit* that a bullock can take an eyelash out of its eye with its hind-foot—which I saw one of my bullocks in New Zealand do), at the Barley Mow, Englefield Green, they have a picture of a horse and dog talking to one another, made entirely of butterflies' wings, and very well and spiritedly done too.

They have another picture, done in the same way, of a greyhound running after a hare, also good but not so good.

At Abbey Wood

I heard a man say to another: "I went to live there just about the time that beer came down from 5d. to 4d. a pot. That will give you an idea when it was."

At Ightham Mote

We took Ightham on one of our Sunday walks about a fortnight ago, and Jones and I wanted to go inside over the house.

My cousin said, "You'd much better not, it will only unsettle your history."

We felt, however, that we had so little history to unsettle that we left him outside and went in.

Dr. Mandell Creighton and Mr. W. S. Rockstro

"The Bishop had been reading Mr. Samuel Butler's enchanting book Alps and Sanctuaries *and determined to visit some of the places there described. We divided our time between the Italian lakes and the lower slopes of the Alps and explored many mountain sanctuaries . . . As a result of this journey the Bishop got to know Mr. S. Butler. He wrote to tell him the pleasure his books had given us and asked him to visit us. After this he came frequently and the Bishop was much attracted by his original mind and stores of out-of-the-way knowledge."* (The Life and Letters of Dr. Mandell Creighton *by his Wife, Vol. II, p. 83.*)

The first time that Dr. Creighton asked me to come down to Peterborough in 1894 before he became Bishop of London, I was a little doubtful whether to go or not. As usual, I consulted my good clerk, Alfred, who said:

"Let me have a look at his letter, sir." I gave him the letter, and he said:

"I see, sir, there is a crumb of tobacco in it; I think you may go."

I went and enjoyed myself very much. I should like to add that there are very few men who have ever impressed me so profoundly and so favourably as Dr. Creighton. I have often seen him since, both at Peterborough and at Fulham, and like and admire him most cordially. [251]

I paid my first visit to Peterborough at a time when that learned musician and incomparable teacher, Mr. W. S. Rockstro, was giving me lessons in medieval counterpoint; so I particularly noticed the music at divine service. The hymns were very silly, and of the usual Gounod-Barnby character. Their numbers were posted up in a frame and I saw there were to be five, so I called the first Farringdon Street, the second King's Cross, the third Gower Street, the fourth Portland Road, and the fifth Baker Street, those being stations on my way to Rickmansworth, where I frequently go for a walk in the country.

In his private chapel at night the bishop began his verse of the psalms always well before we had done the response to the preceding verse. It reminded me of what Rockstro had said a few weeks earlier to the effect that a point of imitation was always more effective if introduced before the other voices had finished. I told Rockstro about it and said that the bishop's instinct had guided him correctly — certainly I found his method more satisfactory than if he had waited till we had finished. Rockstro smiled, and knowing that I was at the time forbidden to work, said:

"Satan finds some mischief still for idle brains to do."

Talking of Rockstro, he scolded me once and said he wondered how I could have done such a thing as to call Handel "one of the greatest of all musicians," referring to the great chords in *Erewhon*. I said that if he would look again at the passage he would find I had said not that Handel was "one of the greatest" but that he was "the greatest of all musicians," on which he apologised.

Pigs

We often walk from Rickmansworth across Moor Park to Pinner. On getting out of Moor Park there is a public-house just to the left where we generally have some shandy-gaff and buy some eggs. The landlord had a noble sow which I photographed for him; some months afterwards I asked how the sow was. She had been sold. The landlord knew she ought to be killed and made into bacon, but he had been intimate with her for three years and some one else must eat her, not he.

"And what," said I, "became of her daughter?"

"Oh, we killed her and ate her. You see we had only known her eighteen months."

I wonder how he settled the exact line beyond which intimacy with a pig must not go if the pig is to be eaten.

Mozart

An old Scotchman at Boulogne was holding forth on the beauties of Mozart, which he exemplified by singing thus:

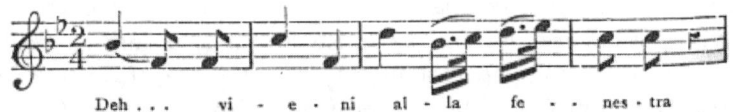

Deh . . . vi - e - ni al - la fe . . . nes - tra

I maliciously assented, but said it was strange how strongly that air always reminded me of "Voi che sapete."

Divorce

There was a man in the hotel at Harwich with an ugly disagreeable woman who I supposed was his wife. I did not care about him, but he began to make up to me in the smoking-room.

"This divorce case," said he, referring to one that was being reported in the papers, "doesn't seem to move very fast."

I put on my sweetest smile and said: "I have not observed it. I am not married myself, and naturally take less interest in divorce."

He dropped me.

Ravens

Mr. Latham, the Master of Jones's College, Trinity Hall, Cambridge, has two ravens named Agrippa and Agrippina. Mr. Latham throws Agrippa a piece of cheese; Agrippa takes it, hides it carefully and then goes away contented; but Agrippina has had her eye upon him and immediately goes and steals it, hiding it somewhere else; Agrippa, however, has always one eye upon Agrippina and no sooner is her back turned than he steals it and buries it anew; then it becomes Agrippina's turn, and thus they pass the time, making believe that they want the cheese though neither of them really wants it. One day Agrippa had a small fight with a spaniel and got rather the worst of it. He immediately flew at Agrippina and gave her a beating. Jones said he could almost hear him say, "It's all your fault."

Calais to Dover

When I got on board the steamer at Calais I saw Lewis Day, who writes books about decoration, and began to talk with him. Also I saw A. B., Editor of the *X.Y.Z. Review.* I met him some years ago at Phipson Beale's, but we do not speak. Recently I wanted him to let me write an article in his review and he would not, so I was spiteful and, when I saw him come on board, said to Day:

"I see we are to have the Editor of the *X.Y.Z.* on board."

"Yes," said Day.

"He's an owl," said I sententiously.

"I wonder," said Day, "how he got the editorship of his review?"

"Oh," said I, "I suppose he married some one."

On this the conversation dropped, and we parted. Later on we met again and Day said:

"Do you know who that lady was — the one standing at your elbow when we were talking just now?"

"No," said I.

"That," he replied, "was Mrs. A. B."

And it was so.

Snapshotting a Bishop

I must some day write about how I hunted the late Bishop of Carlisle with my camera, hoping to shoot him when he was sea-sick crossing from Calais to Dover, and how St. Somebody protected him and said I might shoot him when he was well, but not when he was sea-sick. I should like to do it in the manner of the *Odyssey*:

. . . And the steward went round and laid them all on the sofas and benches and he set a beautiful basin by each, variegated and adorned with flowers, but it contained no water for washing the hands, and Neptune sent great waves that washed over the eyelet-holes of the cabin. But when it was now the middle of the passage and a great roaring arose as of beasts in the Zoological Gardens, and they promised hecatombs to Neptune if he would still the raging of the waves . . .

At any rate I shot him and have him in my snap-shot book, but he was not sea-sick. [1892.]

Homer and the Basins

When I returned from Calais last December, after spending Christmas at Boulogne according to my custom, the sea was rough as I crossed to Dover and, having a cold upon me, I went down into the second-class cabin, cleared the railway books off one of the tables, spread out my papers and continued my translation, or rather analysis, of the *Iliad*. Several people of all ages and sexes were on the sofas and they soon began to be sea-sick. There was no steward, so I got them each a basin and placed it for them as well as I could; then I sat down again at my table in the middle and went on with my translation while they were sick all round me. I had to get the *Iliad* well into my head before I began my lecture on *The Humour of Homer* and I could not afford to throw away a couple of hours, but I doubt whether Homer was ever before translated under such circumstances. [1892.]

The Channel Passage

How holy people look when they are sea-sick! There was a patient Parsee near me who seemed purified once and for ever from all taint of the flesh. Buddha was a low, worldly minded, music-hall comic singer in comparison. He sat like this for a long time until . . . and he made a noise like cows coming home to be milked on an April evening.

The Two Barristers at Ypres

When Gogin and I were taking our Easter holiday this year we went, among other places, to Ypres. We put up at the Hôtel Tête d'Or and found it exquisitely clean, comfortable and cheap, with a charming old-world, last-century feeling. It was Good Friday, and we were to dine *maigre*; this was so clearly *de rigueur* that we did not venture even the feeblest protest.

When we came down to dinner we were told that there were two other gentlemen, also English, who were to dine with us, and in due course they appeared — the one a man verging towards fifty-eight, a kind of cross between Cardinal Manning and the late Mr. John Parry, the other some ten years younger, amiable-looking and, I should say, not so shining a light in his own sphere as his companion. These two sat on one side of the table and we opposite them. There was an air about them both which said: "You are not to try to get into conversation with us; we shall not let you if you do; we dare say you are very good sort of people, but we have nothing in common; so long as you keep quiet we will not hurt you; but if you so much as ask us to pass the melted butter we will shoot you." We saw this and so, during the first two courses, talked *sotto voce* to one another, and made no attempt to open up communications.

With the third course, however, there was a new arrival in the person of a portly gentleman of about fifty-five, or from that to sixty, who was told to sit at the head of the table, and accordingly did so. This gentleman had a decided manner and carried quite as many guns as the two barristers (for barristers they were) who sat opposite to us. He had rather a red nose, he dined *maigre* because he had to, but he did not like it. I do not think he dined *maigre* often. He had something of the air of a half, if not wholly, broken-down blackguard of a gambler who had seen much but had moved in good society and been accustomed to have things more or less his own way.

This gentleman, who before he went gave us his card, immediately opened up conversation both with us and with our neighbours, addressing his remarks alternately and impartially to each. He said he was an Italian who had the profoundest admiration for England. I said at once—

"Lei non può amare l'Inghilterra più che io amo ed ammiro l'Italia."

The Manning-Parry barrister looked up with an air of slightly offended surprise. Conversation was from this point carried on between both parties through the Italian who acted, as Gogin said afterwards, like one of those stones in times of plague on which people from the country put their butter and eggs and people from the town their money.

By and by dealings became more direct between us and at last, I know not how, I found myself in full discussion with the elder barrister as to whether Jean Van Eyck's picture in the National Gallery commonly called "Portrait of John Arnolfini and his Wife" should not properly be held to be a portrait of Van Eyck himself (which, by the way, I suppose there is no doubt that it should not, though I have never gone into the evidence for the present inscription). Then they spoke of the tricks of light practised by De Hooghe; so we rebelled, and said De Hooghe had no tricks — no one less — and that what they called trick was only observation and direct rendering of nature. Then they applauded Tintoretto, and so did we, but still as men who were bowing the knee to Baal. We put in a word for Gaudenzio Ferrari, but they had never heard of him. Then they played Raffaelle as a safe card and we said he was a master of line and a facile decorator, but nothing more.

On this all the fat was in the fire, for they had invested in Raffaelle as believing him to be the Three per Cents of artistic securities. Did I not like the "Madonna di S. Sisto"? I said, "No." I said the large photo looked well at a distance because the work was so concealed under a dark and sloppy glaze that any one might see into it pretty much what one chose to bring, while the small photo looked well because it had gained so greatly by reduction. I said the Child was all very well as a child but a failure as a Christ, as all infant Christs must be to the end of time. I said the Pope and female saint, whoever she was, were commonplace, as also the angels at the bottom. I admitted the beauty of line in the Virgin's drapery and also that the work was an effective piece of decoration, but I said it was not inspired by devotional or serious feeling of any kind and for impressiveness could not hold its own with even a very average Madonna by Giovanni Bellini. They appealed to the Italian, but he said there was a great reaction against Raffaelle in Italy now and that few of the younger men thought of him as their fathers had done. Gogin, of course, backed me up, so they were in a minority. It was not at all what they expected or were accustomed to. I yielded wherever I could and never differed without giving a reason which they could understand. They must have seen that there was no malice prepense, but it always came round to this in the end that we did not agree with them.

Then they played Leonardo Da Vinci. I had not intended saying how cordially I dislike him, but presently they became enthusiastic about the head of the Virgin in the "Vierge aux Rochers" in our Gallery. I said Leonardo had not succeeded with this head; he had succeeded with the angel's head lower down to the right (I think) of the picture, but had failed with the Madonna. They did not like my talking about Leonardo Da Vinci as now succeeding and now failing, just like other people. I said it was perhaps fortunate that we knew the "Last Supper" only by engravings and might fancy the original to have been more full of individuality than the engravings are, and I greatly questioned whether I should have liked the work if I had seen it as it was when Leonardo left it. As for his caricatures he should not have done them, much less preserved them; the fact of his having set store by them was enough to show that there was a screw loose about him somewhere and that he had no sense of humour. Still, I admitted that I liked him better than I did Michael Angelo.

Whatever we touched upon the same fatality attended us. Fortunately neither evolution nor politics came under discussion, nor yet, happily, music, or they would have praised Beethoven and very likely Mendelssohn too. They did begin to run Nuremberg and it was on the tip of my tongue to say, "Yes, but there's the flavour of *Faust* and Goethe"; however, I did not. In course of time the séance ended, though not till nearly ten o'clock, and we all went to bed.

Next morning we saw them at breakfast and they were quite tame. As Gogin said afterwards:

"They came and sat on our fingers and ate crumbs out of our hands." [1887.]

At Montreuil-sur-Mer

Jones and I lunched at the Hôtel de France where we found everything very good. As we were going out, the landlady, getting on towards eighty, with a bookish nose, pale blue eyes and a Giovanni Bellini's Loredano Loredani kind of expression, came up to us and said, in sweetly apologetic accents: —

"Avez-vous donc déjeuné à peu près selon vos idées, Messieurs?"

It would have been too much for her to suppose that she had been able to give us a repast that had fully realised our ideals, still she hoped that these had been, at any rate, adumbrated in the luncheon she had provided. Dear old thing: of course they had and a great deal more than adumbrated. [26 December, 1901.]

XVII
Material for a Projected Sequel
to Alps and Sanctuaries

Mrs. Dowe on Alps and Sanctuaries

After reading *Alps and Sanctuaries* Mrs. Dowe said to Ballard: "You seem to hear him talking to you all the time you are reading."

I don't think I ever heard a criticism of my books which pleased me better, especially as Mrs. Dowe is one of the women I have always liked.

Not to be Omitted

I must get in about the people one meets. The man who did not like parrots because they were too intelligent. And the man who told me that Handel's *Messiah* was "très chic," and the smell of the cyclamens "stupendous." And the man who said it was hard to think the world was not more than 6000 years old, and we encouraged him by telling him we thought it must be even more than 7000. And the English lady who said of some one that "being an artist, you know, of course he had a great deal of poetical feeling." And the man who was sketching and said he had a very good eye for colour in the light, but would I be good enough to tell him what colour was best for the shadows.

"An amateur," he said, "might do very decent things in water-colour, but oils require genius."

So I said: "What is genius?"

"Millet's picture of the *Angelus* sold for 700,000 francs. Now that," he said, "is genius."

After which I was very civil to him.

At Bellinzona a man told me that one of the two towers was built by the Visconti and the other by Julius Cæsar, a hundred years earlier. So, poor old Mrs. Barratt at Langar could conceive no longer time than a hundred years. The Trojan war did not last ten years, but ten years was as big a lie as Homer knew.

We went over the Albula Pass to St. Moritz in two diligences and could not settle which was tonic and which was dominant; but the carriage behind us was the relative minor.

There was a picture in the dining-room but we could not get near enough to see it; we thought it must be either Christ disputing with the Doctors or Louis XVI saying farewell to his family — or something of that sort.

The Sacro Monte at Varese

The Sacro Monte is a kind of ecclesiastical Rosherville Gardens, eminently the place to spend a happy day.

The processions were best at the last part of the ascent; there were pilgrims, all decked out with coloured feathers, and priests and banners and music and crimson and gold and white and glittering brass against the cloudless blue sky. The old priest sat at his open window to receive the offerings of the devout as they passed, but he did not seem to get more than a few bambini modelled in wax. Perhaps he was used to it. And the band played the barocco music on the barocco little piazza and we were all barocco together. It was as though the clergymen at Ladywell had given out that, instead of having service as usual, the congregation would go in procession to the Crystal Palace with all their traps, and that the band had been practising "Wait till the clouds roll by" for some time, and on Sunday, as a great treat, they should have it.

The Pope has issued an order saying he will not have masses written like operas. It is no use. The Pope can do much, but he will not be able to get contrapuntal music into Varese. He will not be able to get anything more solemn than *La Fille de Madame Angot* into Varese. As for fugues —! I would as soon take an English bishop to the Surrey pantomime as to the Sacro Monte on a festa.

Then the pilgrims went into the shadow of a great rock behind the sanctuary, spread themselves out over the grass and dined.

The Albergo Grotta Crimea

The entrance to this hotel at Chiavenna is through a covered court-yard; steps lead up to the roof of the court-yard, which is a terrace where one dines in fine weather. A great tree grows in the court-yard below, its trunk pierces the floor of the terrace, and its branches shade the open-air dining-room. The walls of the house are painted in fresco, with a check pattern like the late Lord Brougham's trousers, and there are also pictures. One represents Mendelssohn. He is not called Mendelssohn, but I knew him by his legs. He is in the costume of a dandy of some five-and-forty years ago, is smoking a cigar and appears to be making an offer of marriage to his cook. [261] Down below is a fresco of a man sitting on a barrel with a glass in his hand. A more absolutely worldly minded, uncultured individual it would be impossible to conceive. When I saw these frescoes I knew I should get along all right and not be over-charged.

Public Opinion

The public buys its opinions as it buys its meat, or takes in its milk, on the principle that it is cheaper to do this than to keep a cow. So it is, but the milk is more likely to be watered.

These Notes

I make them under the impression that I may use them in my books, but I never do unless I happen to remember them at the right time. When I wrote "Ramblings in Cheapside" [in the *Universal Review*, reprinted in *Essays on Life, Art and Science*] the preceding note about Public Opinion would have come in admirably; it was in my pocket, in my little black note-book, but I forgot all about it till I came to post my pocket-book into my note-book.

The Wife of Bath

There are Canterbury Pilgrims every Sunday in summer who start from close to the old Tabard, only they go by the South-Eastern Railway and come back the same day for five shillings. And, what is more, they are just the same sort of people. If they do not go to Canterbury they go by the *Clacton Belle* to Clacton-on-Sea. There is not a Sunday the whole summer through but you may find all Chaucer's pilgrims, man and woman for man and woman, on board the *Lord of the Isles* or the *Clacton Belle*. Why, I have seen the Wife of Bath on the *Lord of the Isles* myself. She was eating her luncheon off an *Ally Sloper's Half-Holiday*, which was spread out upon her knees. Whether it was I who had had too much beer or she I cannot tell, God knoweth; and whether or no I was caught up into Paradise, again I cannot tell; but I certainly did hear unspeakable words which it is not lawful for a man to utter, and that not above fourteen years ago but the very last Sunday that ever was. The Wife of Bath heard them too, but she never turned a hair. Luckily I had my detective camera with me, so I snapped her there and then. She put her hand up to her mouth at that very moment and rather spoiled herself, but not much. [1891.]

Horace at the Post-Office in Rome

When I was in Rome last summer whom should I meet but Horace.

I did not know him at first, and told him enquiringly that the post-office was in the Piazza Venezia?

He smiled benignly, shrugged his shoulders, said "Prego" and pointed to the post-office itself, which was over the way and, of course, in the Piazza S. Silvestro.

Then I knew him. I believe he went straight home and wrote an epistle to Mecænas, or whatever the man's name was, asking how it comes about that people who travel hundreds of miles to see things can never see what is all the time under their noses. In fact, I saw him take out his note-book and begin making notes at once. He need not talk. He was not a good man of business and I do not believe his books sold much better than my own. But this does not matter to him now, for he has not the faintest idea that he ever wrote any of them and, more likely than not, has never even refreshed his memory by reading them.

Beethoven at Faido and at Boulogne

I have twice seen people so unmistakably like Beethoven (just as Madame Patey is unmistakably like Handel and only wants dressing in costume to be the image of him not in features only but in figure and air and manner) that I always think of them as Beethoven.

Once, at Faido in the Val Leventina, in 1876 or 1877, when the engineers were there surveying for the tunnel, there was among them a rather fine-looking young German with wild, ginger hair that rang out to the wild sky like the bells in *In Memoriam*, and a strong Edmund Gurney cut, [263] who played Wagner and was great upon the overture to *Lohengrin*; as for Handel — he was not worth consideration, etc. Well, this young man rather took a fancy to me and I did not dislike him, but one day, to tease him, I told him that a little insignificant-looking engineer, the most commonplace mortal imaginable, who was sitting at the head of the table, was like Beethoven. He was very like him indeed, and Müller saw it, smiled and flushed at the same time. He was short, getting on in years and was a little thick, though not fat. A few days afterwards he went away and Müller and I happened to meet his box — an enormous cube of a trunk — coming down the stairs.

"That's Beethoven's box," said Müller to me.

"Oh," I said, and, looking at it curiously for a moment, asked gravely, "And is he inside it?" It seemed to fit him and to correspond so perfectly with him in every way that one felt as though if he were not inside it he ought to be.

The second time was at Boulogne this spring. There were three Germans at the Hôtel de Paris who sat together, went in and out together, smoked together and did everything as though they were a unity in trinity and a trinity in unity. We settled that they must be the Heckmann Quartet, minus

Heckmann: we had not the smallest reason for thinking this but we settled it at once. The middle one of these was like Beethoven also. On Easter Sunday, after dinner, when he was a little—well, it was after dinner and his hair went rather mad—Jones said to me:

"Do you see that Beethoven has got into the posthumous quartet stage?" [1885.]

Silvio

In the autumn of 1884, Butler spent some time at Promontogno and Soglio in the Val Bregaglia, sketching and making notes. Among the children of the Italian families in the albergo was Silvio, a boy of ten or twelve. He knew a little English and was very fond of poetry. He could repeat, "How doth the little buzzy bee." The poem which pleased him best, however, was:

> *Hey diddle diddle,*
> *The Cat and the Fiddle,*
> *The Cow jumped over the Moon.*

They had nothing, he said, in Italian literature so good as this. Silvio used to talk to Butler while he was sketching.

"And you shall read Longfellow much in England?"

"No," I replied, "I don't think we read him very much."

"But how is that? He is a very pretty poet."

"Oh yes, but I don't greatly like poetry myself."

"Why don't you like poetry?"

"You see, poetry resembles metaphysics, one does not mind one's own, but one does not like any one else's."

"Oh! And what you call metaphysic?"

This was too much. It was like the lady who attributed the decline of the Italian opera to the fact that singers would no longer "podge" their voices.

"And what, pray, is 'podging'?" enquired my informant of the lady.

"Why, don't you understand what 'podging' is? Well, I don't know that I can exactly tell you, but I am sure Edith and Blanche podge beautifully."

However, I said that metaphysics were *la filosofia* and this quieted him. He left poetry and turned to prose.

"Then you shall like much the works of Washington Irving?"

I was grieved to say that I did not; but I dislike Washington Irving so cordially that I determined to chance another "No."

"Then you shall like better Fenimore Cooper?"

I was becoming reckless. I could not go on saying "No" after "No," and yet to ask me to be ever so little enthusiastic about Fenimore Cooper was laying a burden upon me heavier than I could bear, so I said I did not like him.

"Oh, I see," said the boy; "then it is *Uncle Tom's Cabin* that you shall like?"

Here I gave in. More "Noes" I could not say, so, thinking I might as well be hung for a sheep as for a mutton chop, I said that I thought *Uncle Tom's Cabin* one of the most wonderful and beautiful books that ever were written.

Having got at a writer whom I admired, he was satisfied, but not for long.

"And you think very much of the theories of Darwin in England, do you not?"

I groaned inwardly and said we did.

"And what are the theories of Darwin?"

Imagine what followed!

After which:

"Why do you not like poetry? — You shall have a very good university in London?" and so on.

Sunday Morning at Soglio

The quarantine men sat on the wall, dangling their legs over the parapet and singing the same old tune over and over again and the same old words over and over again. "Fu tradito, fu tradito da una donna." To them it was a holiday.

Two gnomes came along and looked at me. I asked the first how old it was; it said fourteen. They both looked about eight. I said that the flies and the fowls ought to be put into quarantine, and the gnomes grinned and showed their teeth till the corners of their mouths met at the backs of their heads.

The skeleton of a bird was nailed up against a barn, and I said to a man: "Aquila?"

He replied: "Aquila," and I passed on.

The village boys came round me and sighed while they watched me sketching. And the women came and exclaimed: "Oh! che testa, che testa!"

And the bells in the windows of the campanile began, and I turned and looked up at their beautiful lolling and watched their fitful tumble-aboutiness. They swung open-mouthed like elephants with uplifted trunks, and I wished I could have fed them with buns. They were not like English bells, and yet they rang more all 'Inglese than bells mostly do in Italy—they had got it, but they had not got it right.

There used to be two crows, and when one disappeared the other came to the house where it had not been for a month. While I was sketching it played with a woman who was weeding; it got on her back and tried to bite her hat; then it got down and pecked at the nails in her boots and tried to steal them. It let her catch it, and then made a little fuss, but it did not fly away when she let it go, it continued playing with her. Then it came to exploit me but would not come close up. Signor Scartazzini says it will play with all the women of the place but not with men or boys, except with him.

Then there came a monk and passed by me, and I knew I had seen him before but could not think where till, of a sudden, it flashed across me that he was Valoroso XXIV, King of Paphlagonia, no doubt expiating his offences.

And I watched the ants that were busy near my feet, and listened to them as they talked about me and discussed whether man has instinct.

"What is he doing here?" they said; "he wasn't here yesterday. Certainly they have no instinct. They may have a low kind of reason, but nothing approaching to instinct. Some of the London houses show signs of instinct—Gower Street, for example, does really seem to suggest instinct; but it is all delusive. It is curious that these cities of theirs should always exist in places where there are no ants. They certainly anthropomorphise too freely. Or is it perhaps that we formicomorphise more than we should?"

And Silvio came by on his way to church. It was he who taught all the boys in Soglio to make a noise. Before he came up there was no sound to be heard in the streets, except the fountains and the bells. I asked him whether the curate was good to him.

"Si," he replied, "è abbastanza buono."

I should think Auld Robin Gray was "abbastanza buono" to Mrs. Gray.

One of the little girls told me that Silvio had so many centesimi and she had none. I said at once:

"You don't want any centesimi."

As soon as these words fell from my lips, I knew I must be getting old.

And presently the Devil came up to me. He was a nice, clean old man, but he dropped his h's, and that was where he spoiled himself—or perhaps it was just this that threw me off my guard, for I had always heard that the Prince of Darkness was a perfect gentleman. He whispered to me that in the winter the monks of St. Bernard sometimes say matins overnight.

The blue of the mountains looks bluer through the chestnuts than through the pines. The river is snowy against the "Verdi prati e selve amene." The great fat tobacco plant agrees with itself if not with us; I never saw any plant look in better health. The briar knows perfectly well what it wants to do and that it does not want to be disturbed; it knows, in fact, all that it cares to know. The question is how and why it got to care to know just these things and no others. Two cheeky goats came tumbling down upon me and demanded salt, and the man came from the saw-mill and, with his great brown hands, scooped the mud from the dams of the rills that watered his meadow, for the hour had come when it was his turn to use the stream.

There were cow-bells, mountain elder-berries and lots of flowers in the grass. There was the glacier, the roar of the river and a plaintive little chapel on a green knoll under the great cliff of ice which cut the sky. There was a fat, crumby woman making hay. She said:

"Buon giorno."

And the "i o r" of the "giorno" came out like oil and honey. I saw she wanted a gossip. She and her husband tuned their scythes in two-part, note-against-note counterpoint; but I could hear that it was she who was the canto fermo and he who was the counterpoint. I peered down over the edge of the steep slippery slope which all had to be mown from top to bottom; if hay grew on the dome of St. Paul's these dreadful traders would gather it in, and presently the autumn crocuses would begin to push up their delicate, naked snouts through the closely shaven surface. I expressed my wonder.

"Siamo esatti," said the fat, crumby woman.

For what little things will not people risk their lives? So Smith and I crossed the Rangitata. So Esau sold his birthright.

It was noon, and I was so sheer above the floor of the valley and the sun was so sheer above me that the chestnuts in the meadow of Bondo squatted upon their own shadows and the gardens were as though the valley had been paved with bricks of various colours. The old grass-grown road ran below, nearer the river, where many a good man had gone up and down on his journey to that larger road where the reader and the writer shall alike join him.

Fascination

I know a man, and one whom people generally call a very clever one, who, when his eye catches mine, if I meet him at an at home or an evening party, beams upon me from afar with the expression of an intellectual rattlesnake on having espied an intellectual rabbit. Through any crowd that man will come sidling towards me, ruthless and irresistible as fate; while I, foreknowing my doom, sidle also him-wards, and flatter myself that no sign of my inward apprehension has escaped me.

Supreme Occasions

Men are seldom more commonplace than on supreme occasions. I knew of an old gentleman who insisted on having the original polka played to him as he lay upon his death-bed. In the only well-authenticated words I have ever met with as spoken by a man who knew he was going to be murdered, there is a commonness which may almost be called Shakespearean. There had been many murders on or near some gold-fields in New Zealand about the years 1863 or 1864, I forget where but I think near the Nelson gold-fields, and at last the murderers were taken. One was allowed to turn Queen's evidence and gave an account of the circumstances of each murder. One of the victims, it appeared, on being told they were about to kill him, said:

"If you murder me, I shall be foully murdered."

Whereupon they murdered him and he was foully murdered. It is a mistake to expect people to rise to the occasion unless the occasion is only a little above their ordinary limit. People seldom rise to their greater occasions, they almost always fall to them. It is only supreme men who are supreme at supreme moments. They differ from the rest of us in this that, when the moment for rising comes, they rise at once and instinctively.

The Aurora Borealis

I saw one once in the Gulf of the St. Lawrence off the island of Anticosti. We were in the middle of it, and seemed to be looking up through a great cone of light millions and millions of miles into the sky. Then we saw it farther off and the pillars of fire stalked up and down the face of heaven like one of Handel's great basses.

In front of my room at Montreal there was a verandah from which a rope was stretched across a small yard to a chimney on a stable roof over the way. Clothes were hung to dry on this rope. As I lay in bed of a morning I could see the shadows and reflected lights from these clothes moving on the ceiling as the clothes were blown about by the wind. The movement of these shadows and reflected lights was exactly that of the rays of an Aurora Borealis, minus colour. I can conceive no resemblance more perfect. They stalked across the ceiling with the same kind of movement absolutely.

A Tragic Expression

The three occasions when I have seen a really tragic expression upon a face were as follows: —

(1) When Mrs. Inglis in my room at Montreal heard my sausages frying, as she thought, too furiously in the kitchen, she left me hurriedly with a glance, and the folds of her dress as she swept out of the room were Niobean.

(2) Once at dinner I sat opposite a certain lady who had a tureen of soup before her and also a plate of the same to which she had just helped herself. There was meat in the soup and I suppose she got a bit she did not like; instead of leaving it, she swiftly, stealthily, picked it up from her plate when she thought no one was looking and, with an expression which Mrs. Siddons might have studied for a performance of Clytemnestra, popped it back into the tureen.

(3) There was an alarm of fire on an emigrant ship in mid-ocean when I was going to New Zealand and the women rushed aft with faces as in a Massacre of the Innocents.

The Wrath to Come

On the Monte Generoso a lady who sat next me at the table-d'hôte was complaining of a man in the hotel. She said he was a nuisance because he practised on the violin. I excused him by saying that I supposed some one had warned him to fly from the wrath to come, meaning that he had conceptions of an ideal world and was trying to get into it. (I heard a man say something like this many years ago and it stuck by me.)

The Beauties of Nature

A man told me that at some Swiss hotel he had been speaking enthusiastically about the beauty of the scenery to a Frenchman who said to him:

"Aimez-vous donc les beautés de la nature? Pour moi je les abborre."

The Late King Vittorio Emanuele

Cavaliere Negri, at Casale-Monferrato, told me not long since that when he was a child, during the troubles of 1848 and 1849, the King was lunching with his (Cav. Negri's) father who had provided the best possible luncheon in honour of his guest. The King said:

"I can eat no such luncheon in times like these — give me some garlic."

The garlic being brought, he ate it along with a great hunch of bread, but would touch nothing else.

The Bishop of Chichester at Faido

When I was at Faido in the Val Leventina last summer there was a lady there who remembered me in New Zealand; she had brought her children to Switzerland for their holiday; good people, all of them. They had friends coming to them, a certain canon and his sister, and there was a talk that the Bishop of Chichester might possibly come too. In course of time the canon and his sister came. At first the sister, who was put to sit next me at dinner, was below zero and her brother opposite was hardly less freezing; but as dinner wore on they thawed and, from regarding me as the monster which in the first instance they clearly did, began to see that I agreed with them in much more than they had thought possible. By and by they were reassured, became cordial and proved on acquaintance to be most kind and good. They soon saw that I liked them, and the canon let me take him where I chose. I took him to the place where the Woodsias grow and we found some splendid specimens. I took him to Mairengo and showed him the double chancel. Coming back he said I had promised to show him some Alternifolium. I stopped him and said:

"Here is some," for there happened to be a bit in the wall by the side of the path.

This quite finished the conquest, and before long I was given to understand that the bishop really would come and we were to take him pretty near the Woodsias and not tell him, and he was to find them out for himself. I have no doubt that the bishop had meant coming with the canon, but then the canon had heard from the New Zealand lady that I was there, and this would not do at all for the bishop. Anyhow the canon had better exploit me by going first and seeing how bad I was. So the canon came, said I was all right and in a couple of days or so the bishop and his daughters arrived.

The bishop did not speak to me at dinner, but after dinner, in the salon, he made an advance in the matter of the newspaper and, I replying, he began a conversation which lasted the best part of an hour, and during which I trust I behaved discreetly. Then I bade him "Good-night" and left the room.

Next morning I saw him eating his breakfast and said "Good-morning" to him. He was quite ready to talk. We discussed the Woodsia Ilvensis and agreed that it was a mythical species. It was said in botany books to grow near Guildford. We dismissed this assertion. But he remarked that it was extraordinary in what odd places we sometimes do find plants; he knew a single plant of Asplenium Trichomanes which had no other within thirty miles of it; it was growing on a tombstone which had come from a long distance and from a Trichomanes country. It almost seemed as if the seeds and germs were always going about in the air and grew wherever they found a suitable environment. I said it was the same with our thoughts; the germs of all manner of thoughts and ideas are always floating about unperceived in our minds and it was astonishing sometimes in what strange places they found the soil which enabled them to take root and grow into perceived thought and action. The bishop looked up from his egg and said:

"That is a very striking remark," and then he went on with his egg as though if I were going to talk like that he should not play any more.

Thinking I was not likely to do better than this, I retreated immediately and went away down to Claro where there was a confirmation and so on to Bellinzona.

In the morning I had asked the waitress how she liked the bishop.

"Oh! beaucoup, beaucoup," she exclaimed, "et je trouve son nez vraiment noble." [1886.]

At Piora

I am confident that I have written the following note in one or other of the earlier of these volumes, but I have searched my precious indexes in vain to find it. No doubt as soon as I have retold the story I shall stumble upon it.

One day in the autumn of 1886 I walked up to Piora from Airolo, returning the same day. At Piora I met a very nice quiet man whose name I presently discovered, and who, I have since learned, is a well-known and most liberal employer of labour somewhere in the north of England. He told me that he had been induced to visit Piora by a book which had made a great impression upon him. He could not recollect its title, but it had made a great impression upon him; nor yet could he recollect the author's name, but the book had made a great impression upon him; he could not remember even what else there was in the book; the only thing he knew was that it had made a great impression upon him.

This is a good example of what is called a residuary impression. Whether or no I told him that the book which had made such a great impression upon him was called *Alps and Sanctuaries* (see Chap. VI), and that it had been written by the person he was addressing, I cannot tell. It would be very like me to have blurted it all out and given him to understand how fortunate he had been in meeting me; this would be so fatally like me that the chances are ten to one that I did it; but I have, thank Heaven, no recollection of sin in this respect, and have rather a strong impression that, for once in my life, I smiled to myself and said nothing.

At Ferentino

After dinner I ordered a coffee; the landlord, who also had had his dinner, asked me to be good enough to defer it for another year and I assented. I then asked him which was the best inn at Segni. He replied that it did not matter, that when a man had quattrini one albergo was as good as another. I said, No; that more depended on what kind of blood was running about inside the albergatore than on how many quattrini the guest had in his pocket. He smiled and offered me a pinch of the most delicious snuff. His wife came and cleared the table, having done which she shed the water bottle over the floor to keep the dust down. I am sure she did it all to all the blessed gods that live in heaven, though she did not say so.

The Imperfect Lady

There was one at a country house in Sicily where I was staying. She had been lent to my host for change of air by his friend the marchese. She dined at table with us and we all liked her very much. She was extremely pretty and not less amiable than pretty. In order to reach the dining-room we had to go through her bedroom as also through my host's. When the monsignore came, she dined with us just the same, and the old priest evidently did not mind at all. In Sicily they do not bring the scent of the incense across the dining-room table. And one would hardly expect the attempt to be made by people who use the oath "Santo Diavolo."

Siena and S. Gimignano

At Siena last spring, prowling round outside the cathedral, we saw an English ecclesiastic in a stringed, sub-shovel hat. He had a young lady with him, presumably a daughter or niece. He eyed us with much the same incurious curiosity as that with which we eyed him. We passed them and went inside the duomo. How far less impressive is the interior (indeed I had almost said also the exterior) than that of San Domenico! Nothing palls so soon as over-ornamentation.

A few minutes afterwards my Lord and the young lady came in too. It was Sunday and mass was being celebrated. The pair passed us and, when they reached the fringe of the kneeling folk, the bishop knelt down too on the bare floor, kneeling bolt upright from the knees, a few feet in front of where we stood. We saw him and I am sure he knew we were looking at him. The lady seemed to hesitate but, after a minute or so, she knuckled down by his side and we left them kneeling bolt upright from the knees on the hard floor.

I always cross myself and genuflect when I go into a Roman Catholic church, as a mark of respect, but Jones and Gogin say that any one can see I am not an old hand at it. How rudimentary is the action of an old priest! I saw one once at Venice in the dining-room of the Hotel la Luna who crossed himself by a rapid motion of his fork just before he began to eat, and Miss Bertha Thomas told me she saw an Italian lady at Varallo at the table-d'hôte cross herself with her fan. I do not cross myself before eating nor do I think it incumbent upon me to kneel down on the hard floor in church—perhaps because I am not an English bishop. We were sorry for this one and for his young lady, but it was their own doing.

We then went into the Libreria to see the frescoes by Pinturicchio — which we did not like — and spent some little time in attending to them. On leaving we were told to sign our names in a book and did so. As we were going out we met the bishop and his lady coming in; whether they had been kneeling all the time, or whether they had got up as soon we were gone and had spent the time in looking round I cannot say, but, when they had seen the frescoes, they would be told to sign their names and, when they signed, they would see ours and, I flatter myself, know who we were.

On returning to our hotel we were able to collect enough information to settle in our own minds which particular bishop he was.

A day or two later we went to Poggibonsi, which must have been an important place once; nothing but the walls remain now, the city within them having been razed by Charles V. At the station we took a carriage, and our driver, Ulisse Pogni, was a delightful person, second baritone at the Poggibonsi Opera and principal fly-owner of the town. He drove us up to S. Gimignano and told us that the people still hold the figures in Benozzo Gozzoli's frescoes to be portraits of themselves and say: "That's me," and "That's so and so."

Of course we went to see the frescoes, and as we were coming down the main street, from the Piazza on which the Municipio stands, who should be mounting the incline but our bishop and his lady. The moment he saw us, he looked cross, stood still and began inspecting the tops of the houses on the other side of the street; so also did the lady. There was nothing of the smallest interest in these and we neither of us had the smallest doubt that he was embarrassed at meeting us and was pretending not to notice us. I have seldom seen any like attempt more clumsily and fatuously done. Whether he was saying to himself, "Good Lord! that wretch will be putting my kneeling down into another *Alps and Sanctuaries* or *Ex Voto*"; or whether it was only that we were a couple of blackguard atheists who contaminated the air all round us, I cannot tell; but on venturing to look back a second or two after we had passed them, the bishop and the lady had got a considerable distance away.

As we returned our driver took us about 4 kilometres outside Poggibonsi to San Lucchese, a church of the 12th or 13th century, greatly decayed, but still very beautiful and containing a few naïf frescoes. He told us he had sung the Sanctus here at the festa on the preceding Sunday. In a room adjoining the church, formerly, we were told, a refectory, there is a very good fresco representing the "Miraculous Draught of Fishes" by Gerino da Pistoja (I think, but one forgets these names at once unless one writes them down then and there). It is dated — I think (again!) — about 1509, betrays the influence of Perugino but is more lively and interesting than anything I know by that painter, for I cannot call him master. It is in good preservation and deserves to be better, though perhaps not very much better, known than it is. Our driver pointed out that the baskets in which the fishes are being collected are portraits of the baskets still in use in the neighbourhood.

After we had returned to London we found, in the Royal Academy Exhibition, a portrait of our bishop which, though not good, was quite good enough to assure us that we had not been mistaken as to his diocese.

The Etruscan Urns at Volterra

As regards the way in which the Etruscan artists kept to a few stock subjects, this has been so in all times and countries.

When Christianity convulsed the world and displaced the older mythology, she did but introduce new subjects of her own, to which her artists kept as closely as their pagan ancestors had kept to their heathen gods and goddesses. We now make believe to have freed ourselves from these trammels, but the departure is more apparent than real. Our works of art fall into a few well-marked groups and the pictures of each group, though differing in detail, present the same general characters. We have, however, broken much new ground, whereas until the last three or four hundred years it almost seems either as if artists had thought subject a detail beneath their notice, or publics had insisted on being told only what they knew already.

The principle of living only to see and to hear some new thing, and the other principle of avoiding everything with which we are not perfectly familiar are equally old, equally universal, equally useful. They are the principles of conservation and accumulation on the one hand, and of adventure, speculation and progress on the other, each equally indispensable. The money has been, and will probably always be more persistently in the hands of the first of these two groups. But, after all, is not money an art? Nay, is it not the most difficult on earth and the parent of all? And if life is short and art long, is not money still longer? And are not works of art, for the most part, more or less works of money also? In so far as a work of art is a work of money, it must not complain of being bound by the laws of money; in so far as it is a work of art, it has nothing to do with money and, again, cannot complain.

It is a great help to the spectator to know the subject of a picture and not to be bothered with having to find out all about the story. Subjects should be such as either tell their own story instantly on the face of them, or things with which all spectators may be supposed familiar. It must not be forgotten that a work exposed to public view is addressed to a great many people and should accordingly consider many people rather than one. I saw an English family not long since looking at a fine collection of the coins of all nations. They hardly pretended even to take a languid interest in the French, German, Dutch and Italian coins, but brightened up at once on being shown a shilling, a florin and a half-crown. So children do not want new stories; they look for old ones.

"Mamma dear, will you please tell us the story of 'The Three Bears'?"

"No, my love, not to-day, I have told it you very often lately and I am busy."

"Very well, Mamma dear, then we will tell you the story of 'The Three Bears.'"

The *Iliad* and the *Odyssey* are only "The Three Bears" upon a larger scale. Just as the life of a man is only the fission of two amœbas on a larger scale. *Cui non dictus Hylas puer et Latonia Delos?* That was no argument against telling it again, but rather for repeating it. So people look out in the newspapers for what they know rather than for what they do not know, and the better they know it the more interested they are to see it in print and, as a general rule, unless they get what they expect — or think they know already — they are angry. This tendency of our nature culminates in the well-known lines repeated for ever and ever:

> The battle of the Nile
> I was there all the while;
> I was there all the while
> At the battle of the Nile.
> The battle of . . .

And so on ad lib. Even this will please very young children. As they grow older they want to hear about nothing but "The Three Bears." As they mature still further they want the greater invention and freer play of fancy manifested by such people as Homer and our west-end upholsterers, beyond which there is no liberty, but only eccentricity and extravagance.

So it is with all fashion. Fashions change, but not radically except after convulsion and, even then, the change is more apparent than real, the older fashions continually coming back as new ones.

So it is not only as regards choice of subject but also as regards treatment of subject within the limits of the work itself, after the subject is chosen. No matter whether the utterance of a man's inner mind is attempted by way of words, painting, or music, the same principle underlies all these three arts and, of course, also those arts that are akin to them. In each case a man should have but one subject easily recognisable as the main motive, and in each case he must develop, treat and illustrate this by means of episodes and details that are neither so alien to the subject as to appear lugged in by the heels, nor yet so germane to it as to be identical. The treatment grows out of the subject as the family from the parents and the race from the family—each new-born member being the same and yet not the same with those that have preceded him. So it is with all the arts and all the sciences—they flourish best by the addition of but little new at a time in comparison with the old.

And so, lastly, it is with the *ars artium* itself, that art of arts and science of sciences, that guild of arts and crafts which is comprised within each one of us, I mean our bodies. In the detail they are nourished from day to day by food which must not be too alien from past food or from the body itself, nor yet too germane to either; and in the gross, that is to say, in the history of the development of a race or species, the evolution is admittedly for the most part exceedingly gradual, by means of many generations, as it were, of episodes that are kindred to and yet not identical with the subject.

And when we come to think of it, we find in the evolution of bodily form (which along with modification involves persistence of type) the explanation why persistence of type in subjects chosen for treatment in works of art should be so universal. It is because we are so averse to great changes and at the same time so averse to no change at all, that we have a bodily form, in the main, persistent and yet, at the same time, capable of modifications. Without a strong aversion to change its habits and, with its habits, the pabulum of its mind, there would be no fixity of type in any species and, indeed, there would be no life at all, as we are accustomed to think of life, for organs would disappear before they could be developed, and to try to build life on such a shifting foundation would be as hopeless as it would be to try and build a material building on an actual quicksand. Hence the habits, cries, abodes, food, hopes and fears of each species (and what are these but the realities of which human arts are as the shadow?) tell the same old tales in the same old ways from generation to generation, and it is only because they do so that they appear to us as species at all.

Returning now to the Etruscan cinerary urns—I have no doubt that, perhaps three or four thousand years hence, a collection of the tombstones from some of our suburban cemeteries will be thought exceedingly interesting, but I confess to having found the urns in the Museum at Volterra a little monotonous and, after looking at about three urns, I hurried over the remaining 397 as fast as I could. [1889.]

The Quick and the Dead

The walls of the houses [in an Italian village] are built of brick and the roofs are covered with stone. They call the stone "vivo." It is as though they thought bricks were like veal or mutton and stones like bits out of the living calf or sheep. [279]

The Grape-Filter

When the water of a place is bad, it is safest to drink none that has not been filtered through either the berry of a grape, or else a tub of malt. These are the most reliable filters yet invented.

Bertoli and his Bees

Giacomo Bertoli of Varallo-Sesia keeps a watch and clock shop in the street. He is a cheery little old gentleman, though I do not see why I should call him old for I doubt his being so old as I am. He and I have been very good friends for years and he is always among the first to welcome me when I go to Varallo.

He is one of the most famous bee-masters in Europe. He keeps some of his bees during the winter at Camasco not very far from Varallo, others in other places near and moves them up to Alagna, at the head of the Val Sesia, towards the end of May that they may make their honey from the spring flowers—and excellent honey they make.

About a fortnight ago I happened to meet him bringing down ten of his hives. He was walking in front and was immediately followed by two women each with crates on their backs, and each carrying five hives. They seemed to me to be ordinary deal boxes, open at the top, but covered over with gauze which would keep the bees in but not exclude air. I asked him if the bees minded the journey, and he replied that they were very angry and had a great deal to say about it; he was sure to be stung when he let them out. He said it was "un lavoro improbo," and cost him a great deal of anxiety.

"The Lost Chord"

It should be "The Lost Progression," for the young lady was mistaken in supposing she had ever heard any single chord "like the sound of a great Amen." Unless we are to suppose that she had already found the chord of C Major for the final syllable of the word and was seeking the chord for the first syllable; and there she is on the walls of a Milanese restaurant arpeggioing experimental harmonies in a transport of delight to advertise Somebody and Someone's pianos and holding the loud pedal solidly down all the time. Her family had always been unsympathetic about her music. They said it was like a loose bundle of fire-wood which you never can get across the room without dropping sticks; they said she would have been so much better employed doing anything else.

Fancy being in the room with her while she was strumming about and hunting after her chord! Fancy being in heaven with her when she had found it!

Introduction of Foreign Plants

I have brought back this year some mountain auriculas and the seed of some salvia and Fusio tiger-lily, and mean to plant the auriculas and to sow the seeds in Epping Forest and elsewhere round about London. I wish people would more generally bring back the seeds of pleasing foreign plants and introduce them broadcast, sowing them by our waysides and in our fields, or in whatever situation is most likely to suit them. It is true, this would puzzle botanists, but there is no reason why botanists should not be puzzled. A botanist is a person whose aim is to uproot, kill and exterminate every plant that is at all remarkable for rarity or any special virtue, and the rarer it is the more bitterly he will hunt it down.

Saint Cosimo and Saint Damiano at Siena

Sano di Pietro shows us a heartless practical joke played by these two very naughty saints, both medical men, who should be uncanonised immediately. It seems they laid their heads together and for some reason, best known to themselves, resolved to cut a leg off a dead negro and put it on to a white man. In the one compartment they are seen in high glee cutting the negro's leg off. In the next they have gone to the white man who is in bed, obviously asleep, and are substituting the black leg for his own. Then, no doubt, they will stand behind the door and see what he does when he wakes. They must be saints because they have glories on, but it looks as though a glory is not much more to be relied on than a gig as a test of respectability. [1889.]

At Pienza

At Pienza, after having seen the Museum with a custode whom I photoed as being more like death, though in excellent health and spirits, than any one I ever saw, I was taken to the leading college for young ladies, the Conservatorio di S. Carlo, under the direction of Signora (or Signorina, I do not know which) Cesira Carletti, to see the wonderful Viale of the twelfth or thirteenth century given to Pienza by Pope Æneas Sylvius Piccolomini (Pius II) and stolen a few years since, but recovered. Signora Carletti was copying parts of it in needlework, nor can I think that the original was ever better than the parts which she had already done. The work would take weeks or even months to examine with any fullness, and volumes to describe. It is as prodigal of labour, design and colour as nature herself is. In fact it is one of those things that nature has a right to do but not art. It fatigues one to look at it or think upon it and, bathos though it be to say so, it won the first prize at the Exhibitions of Ecclesiastical Art Work held a few years ago at Rome and at Siena. It has taken Signora Carletti months to do even the little she has done, but that little must be seen to be believed, for no words can do justice to it.

Having seen the Viale, I was shown round the whole establishment, and can imagine nothing better ordered. I was taken over the dormitories — very nice and comfortable — and, finally, not without being much abashed, into the room where the young ladies were engaged upon needlework. It reminded me of nothing so much as of the Education of the Virgin Chapel at Oropa. [282] I was taken to each young lady and did my best to acquit myself properly in praising her beautiful work but, beautiful as the work of one and all was, it could not compare with that of Signora Carletti. I asked her if she could not get some of the young ladies to help her in the less important parts of her work, but she said she preferred doing it all herself. They all looked well and happy and as though they were well cared for, as I am sure they are.

Then Signora Carletti took me to the top of the house to show me the meteorological room of which she is superintendent, and which is in connection with the main meteorological observatory at Rome. Again I found everything in admirable order, and left the house not a little pleased and impressed with everything I had seen. [1889.]

Homer's Hot and Cold Springs

The following extract is taken from a memorandum Butler made of a visit he paid to Greece and the Troad in the spring of 1895. In the Iliad (xxii. 145) Homer mentions hot and cold springs where the Trojan women used to wash their clothes. There are no such springs near Hissarlik, where they ought to be, but the American Consul at the Dardanelles told Butler there was something of the kind on Mount Ida, at the sources of the Scamander, and he determined to see them after visiting Hissarlik. He was provided with an interpreter, Yakoub, an attendant, Ahmed, an escort of one soldier and a horse. He went first to the Consul's farm at Thymbra, about five miles from Hissarlik, where he spent the night and found it "all very like a first-class New Zealand sheep-station." The next day he went to Hissarlik and saw no reason for disagreeing with the received opinion that it is the site of Troy. He then proceeded to Bunarbashi and so to Bairemitch, passing on the way a saw-mill where there was a Government official with twenty soldiers under him. This official was much interested in the traveller and directed his men to take carpets and a dish of trout, caught that morning in the Scamander, and carry them up to the hot and cold springs while he himself accompanied Butler. So they set off and the official, Ismail, showed him the way and pointed out the springs, and there is a long note about the hot and cold water.

And now let me return to Ismail Gusbashi, the excellent Turkish official who, by the way, was with me during all my examination of the springs, and whose assurances of their twofold temperature I should have found it impossible to doubt, even though I had not caught one warmer cupful myself. His men, while we were at the springs, had spread a large Turkey carpet on the flower-bespangled grass under the trees, and there were three smaller rugs at three of the corners. On these Ismail and Yakoub and I took our places. The other two were cross-legged, but I reclining anyhow. The sun shimmered through the spring foliage. I saw two hoopoes and many beautiful birds whose names I knew not. Through the trees I could see the snow-fields of Ida far above me, but it was hopeless to think of reaching them. The soldiers and Ahmed cooked the trout and the eggs all together; then we had boiled eggs, bread and cheese and, of course, more lamb's liver done on skewers like cats' meat. I ate with my pocket-knife, the others using their fingers in true Homeric fashion.

When we had put from us "the desire of meat and drink," Ismail began to talk to me. He said he had now for the first time in his life found himself in familiar conversation with Wisdom from the West (that was me), and that, as he greatly doubted whether such another opportunity would be ever vouchsafed to him, he should wish to consult me upon a matter which had greatly exercised him. He was now fifty years old and had never married. Sometimes he thought he had done a wise thing, and sometimes it seemed to him that he had been very foolish. Would I kindly tell him which it was and advise him as to the future? I said he was addressing one who was in much the same condition as himself, only that I was some ten years older. We had a saying in England that if a man marries he will regret it, and that if he does not marry he will regret it.

"Ah!" said Ismail, who was leaning towards me and trying to catch every word I spoke, though he could not understand a syllable till Yakoub interpreted my Italian into Turkish. "Ah!" he said, "that is a true word."

In my younger days, I said (may Heaven forgive me!), I had been passionately in love with a most beautiful young lady, but—and here my voice faltered, and I looked very sad, waiting for Yakoub to interpret what I had said—but it had been the will of Allah that she should marry another gentleman, and this had broken my heart for many years. After a time, however, I concluded that these things were all settled for us by a higher Power.

"Ah! that is a true word."

"And so, my dear sir, in your case I should reflect that if Allah" (and I raised my hand to Heaven) "had desired your being married, he would have signified his will to you in some way that you could hardly mistake. As he does not appear to have done so, I should recommend you to remain single until you receive some distinct intimation that you are to marry."

"Ah! that is a true word."

"Besides," I continued, "suppose you marry a woman with whom you think you are in love and then find out, after you have been married to her for three months, that you do not like her. This would be a very painful situation."

"Ah, yes, indeed! that is a true word."

"And if you had children who were good and dutiful, it would be delightful; but suppose they turned out disobedient and ungrateful — and I have known many such cases — could anything be more distressing to a parent in his declining years?"

"Ah! that is a true word that you have spoken."

"We have a great Imaum," I continued, "in England; he is called the Archbishop of Canterbury and gives answers to people who are in any kind of doubt or difficulty. I knew one gentleman who asked his advice upon the very question that you have done me the honour of propounding to myself."

"Ah! and what was his answer?"

"He told him," said I, "that it was cheaper to buy the milk than to keep a cow."

"Ah! ah! that is a most true word."

Here I closed the conversation, and we began packing up to make a start. When we were about to mount, I said to him, hat in hand:

"Sir, it occurs to me with great sadness that, though you will, no doubt, often revisit this lovely spot, yet it is most certain that I shall never do so. Promise me that when you come here you will sometimes think of the stupid old Englishman who has had the pleasure of lunching with you to-day, and I promise that I will often think of you when I am at home again in London."

He was much touched, and we started. After we had gone about a mile, I suddenly missed my knife. I knew I should want it badly many a time before we got to the Dardanelles, and I knew perfectly well where I should find it: so I stopped the cavalcade and said I must ride back for it. I did so, found it immediately and returned. Then I said to Ismail:

"Sir, I understand now why I was led to leave my knife behind me. I had said it was certain I should never see that enchanting spot again, but I spoke presumptuously, forgetting that if Allah" (and I raised my hand to Heaven) "willed it I should assuredly do so. I am corrected, and with great leniency."

Ismail was much affected. The good fellow immediately took off his watch-chain (happily of brass and of no intrinsic value) and gave it me, assuring me that it was given him by a very dear friend, that he had worn it for many years, and valued it greatly — would I keep it as a memorial of himself? Fortunately I had with me a little silver match-box which Alfred had given me and which had my name engraved on it. I gave it to him, but had some difficulty in making him accept it. Then we rode on till we came to the saw-mills. I ordered two lambs for the ten soldiers who had accompanied us, having understood from Yakoub that this would be an acceptable present. And so I parted from this most kind and friendly gentleman with every warm expression of cordiality on both sides.

I sent him his photograph which I had taken, and I sent his soldiers their groups also — one for each man — and in due course I received the following letter of thanks. Alas! I have never written in answer. I knew not how to do it. I knew, however, that I could not keep up a correspondence, even though I wrote once. But few unanswered letters more often rise up and smite me. How the Post Office people ever read "Bueter, Ciforzin St." into "Butler, Clifford's Inn" I cannot tell. What splendid emendators of a corrupt text they ought to make! But I could almost wish that they had failed, for it has pained me not a little that I have not replied.

Mr. Samuel Bueter,
    No. 15 Ciforzin St. London, England.

Dardanelles,
August 4/95.

Mr. Samuel. England.

My dear Friend,

Many thanks for the phothograph you have send me. It was very kind of you to think of me to send me this token of your remembrance. I certainly, appreciate it, and shall think of you whenever I look at it. Ah My Dear Brother, it is impossible for me to forget you. under favorable circumstance I confess I must prefer you. I have a grate desire to have the beautifull chance to meet you. Ah then with the tears of gladness to be the result of the great love of our friendness A my Sir what pen can describe the meeting that shall be come with your second visit if it please God.

It is my pray to Our Lord God to protect you and to keep you glad and happy for ever.

Though we are far from each other yet we can speak with letters.

Thank God to have your love of friendness with me and mine with your noble person.

Hopeing to hear from you,

Yours truly,

Ismayel, from
Byramich hizar memuerue iuse bashi.

XVIII
Material for Erewhon Revisited

Apologise for the names in *Erewhon*. I was an unpractised writer and had no idea the names could matter so much.

Give a map showing the geography of Erewhon in so far as the entrance into the country goes, and explain somewhere, if possible, about Butler's stones.

Up as far as the top of the pass, where the statues are, keeps to the actual geography of the upper Rangitata district except that I have doubled the gorge. There was no gorge up above my place [Mesopotamia] and I wanted one, so I took the gorge some 10 or a dozen miles lower down and repeated it and then came upon my own country again, but made it bare of grass and useless instead of (as it actually was) excellent country. Baker and I went up the last saddle we tried and thought it was a pass to the West Coast, but found it looked down on to the headwaters of the Rakaia: however we saw a true pass opposite, just as I have described in *Erewhon*, only that there were no clouds and we never went straight down as I said I did, but took two days going round by Lake Heron. And there is no lake at the top of the true pass. This is the pass over which, in consequence of our report, Whitcombe was sent and got drowned on the other side. We went up to the top of the pass but found it too rough to go down without more help than we had. I rather think I have told this in *A First Year in Canterbury Settlement*, but am so much ashamed of that book that I dare not look to see. I don't mean to say that the later books are much better; still they are better.

They show a lot of stones on the Hokitika pass, so Mr. Slade told me, which they call mine and say I intended them in *Erewhon* [for the statues]. I never saw them and knew nothing about them.

Refer to the agony and settled melancholy with which unborn children in the womb regard birth as the extinction of their being, and how some declare that there is a world beyond the womb and others deny this. "We must all one day be born," "Birth is certain" and so on, just as we say of death. Birth involves with it an original sin. It must be sin, for the wages of sin is death (what else, I should like to know, is the wages of virtue?) and assuredly the wages of birth is death.

They consider "wilful procreation," as they call it, much as we do murder and will not allow it to be a moral ailment at all. Sometimes a jury will recommend to mercy and sometimes they bring in a verdict of "justifiable baby-getting," but they treat these cases as a rule with great severity.

Every baby has a month of heaven and a month of hell before birth, so that it may make its choice with its eyes open.

The hour of birth should be prayed for in the litany as well as that of death, and so it would be if we could remember the agony of horror which, no doubt, we felt at birth—surpassing, no doubt, the utmost agony of apprehension that can be felt on death.

Let automata increase in variety and ingenuity till at last they present so many of the phenomena of life that the religious world declares they were designed and created by God as an independent species. The scientific world, on the other hand, denies that there is any design in connection with them, and holds that if any slight variation happened to arise by which a fortuitous combination of atoms occurred which was more suitable for advertising purposes (the automata were chiefly used for advertising) it was seized upon and preserved by natural selection.

They have schools where they teach the arts of forgetting and of not seeing. Young ladies are taught the art of proposing. Lists of successful matches are advertised with the prospectuses of all the girls' schools.

They have professors of all the languages of the principal beasts and birds. I stayed with the Professor of Feline Languages who had invented a kind of Ollendorffian system for teaching the Art of Polite Conversation among cats.

They have an art-class in which the first thing insisted on is that the pupils should know the price of all the leading modern pictures that have been sold during the last twenty years at Christie's, and the fluctuations in their values. Give an examination paper on this subject. The artist being a picture-dealer, the first thing he must do is to know how to sell his pictures, and therefore how to adapt them to the market. What is the use of being able to paint a picture unless one can sell it when one has painted it?

Add that the secret of the success of modern French art lies in its recognition of values.

Let there be monks who have taken vows of modest competency (about £1000 a year, derived from consols), who spurn popularity as medieval monks spurned money—and with about as much sincerity. Their great object is to try and find out what they like and then get it. They do not live in one building, and there are no vows of celibacy, but, in practice, when any member marries he drifts away from the society. They have no profession of faith or articles of association, but, as they who hunted for the Holy Grail, so do these hunt in all things, whether of art or science, for that which commends itself to them as comfortable and worthy to be accepted. Their liberty of thought and speech and their reasonable enjoyment of the good things of this life are what they alone live for.

Let the Erewhonians have Westminster Abbeys of the first, second and third class, and in one of these let them raise monuments to dead theories which were once celebrated.

Let them study those arts whereby the opinions of a minority may be made to seem those of a majority.

Introduce an Erewhonian sermon to the effect that if people are wicked they may perhaps have to go to heaven when they die.

Let them have a Regius Professor of Studied Ambiguity.

Let the Professor of Worldly Wisdom pluck a man for want of sufficient vagueness in his saving-clauses paper.

Another poor fellow may be floored for having written an article on a scientific subject without having made free enough use of the words "patiently" and "carefully," and for having shown too obvious signs of thinking for himself.

Let them attach disgrace to any who do not rapidly become obscure after death.

Let them have a Professor of Mischief. They found that people always did harm when they meant well and that all the professorships founded with an avowedly laudable object failed, so they aim at mischief in the hope that they may miss the mark here as when they aimed at what they thought advantageous.

The Professor of Worldly Wisdom plucked a man for buying an egg that had a date stamped upon it. And another for being too often and too seriously in the right. And another for telling people what they did not want to know. He plucked several for insufficient mistrust in printed matter. It appeared that the Professor had written an article teeming with plausible blunders, and had had it inserted in a leading weekly. He then set his paper so that the men were sure to tumble into these blunders themselves; then he plucked them. This occasioned a good deal of comment at the time.

One man who entered for the Chancellor's medal declined to answer any of the questions set. He said he saw they were intended more to show off the ingenuity of the examiner than either to assist or test the judgment of the examined. He observed, moreover, that the view taken of his answers would in great measure depend upon what the examiner had had for dinner and, since it was not in his power to control this, he was not going to waste time where the result was, at best, so much a matter of chance. Briefly, his view of life was that the longer you lived and the less you thought or talked about it the better. He should go pretty straight in the main himself because it saved trouble on the whole, and he should be guided mainly by a sense of humour in deciding when to deviate from the path of technical honesty, and he would take care that his errors, if any, should be rather on the side of excess than of asceticism

This man won the Chancellor's medal.

They have a review class in which the pupils are taught not to mind what is written in newspapers. As a natural result they grow up more keenly sensitive than ever.

Round the margin of the newspapers sentences are printed cautioning the readers against believing the criticisms they see, inasmuch as personal motives will underlie the greater number.

They defend the universities and academic bodies on the ground that, but for them, good work would be so universal that the world would become clogged with masterpieces to an extent that would reduce it to an absurdity. Good sense would rule over all, and merely smart or clever people would be unable to earn a living.

They assume that truth is best got at by the falling out of thieves. "Well then, there must be thieves, or how can they fall out? Our business is to produce the raw material from which truth may be elicited."

"And you succeed, sir," I replied, "in a way that is beyond all praise, and it seems as though there would be no limit to the supply of truth that ought to be available. But, considering the number of your thieves, they show less alacrity in flying at each other's throats than might have been expected."

They live their lives backwards, beginning, as old men and women, with little more knowledge of the past than we have of the future, and foreseeing the future about as clearly as we see the past, winding up by entering into the womb as though being buried. But delicacy forbids me to pursue this subject further: the upshot is that it comes to much the same thing, provided one is used to it.

Paying debts is a luxury which we cannot all of us afford.

"It is not every one, my dear, who can reach such a counsel of perfection as murder."

There was no more space for the chronicles and, what was worse, there was no more space in which anything could happen at all, the whole land had become one vast cancerous growth of chronicles, chronicles, chronicles, nothing but chronicles.

The catalogue of the Browne medals alone will in time come to occupy several hundreds of pages in the *University Calendar*.

There was a professor who was looked upon as such a valuable man because he had done more than any other living person to suppress any kind of originality.

"It is not our business," he used to say, "to help students to think for themselves — surely this is the very last thing that one who wishes them well would do by them. Our business to make them think as we do, or at any rate as we consider expedient to say we do."

He was President of the Society for the Suppression of Useless Knowledge and for the Complete Obliteration of the Past.

They have professional mind-dressers, as we have hair-dressers, and before going out to dinner or fashionable At-homes, people go and get themselves primed with smart sayings or moral reflections according to the style which they think will be most becoming to them in the kind of company they expect.

They deify as God something which I can only translate by a word as underivable as God — I mean Gumption. But it is part of their religion that there should be no temple to Gumption, nor are there priests or professors of Gumption — Gumption being too ineffable to hit the sense of human definition and analysis.

They hold that the function of universities is to make learning repellent and thus to prevent its becoming dangerously common. And they discharge this beneficent function all the more efficiently because they do it unconsciously and automatically. The professors think they are advancing healthy intellectual assimilation and digestion when they are in reality little better than cancer on the stomach.

Let them be afflicted by an epidemic of the fear-of-giving-themselves-away disease. Enumerate its symptoms. There is a new discovery whereby the invisible rays that emanate from the soul can be caught and all the details of a man's spiritual nature, his character, disposition, principles, &c. be photographed on a plate as easily as his face or the bones of his hands, but no cure for the f. o. g. th. a. disease has yet been discovered.

They have a company for ameliorating the condition of those who are in a future state, and for improving the future state itself.

People are buried alive for a week before they are married so that their offspring may know something about the grave, of which, otherwise, heredity could teach it nothing.

It has long been held that those constitutions are best which promote most effectually the greatest happiness of the greatest number. Now the greatest number are none too wise and none too honest, and to arrange our systems with a view to the greater happiness of sensible straightforward people—indeed to give these people a chance at all if it can be avoided—is to interfere with the greatest happiness of the greatest number. Dull, slovenly and arrogant people do not like those who are quick, painstaking and unassuming; how can we then consistently with the first principles of either morality or political economy encourage such people when we can bring sincerity and modesty fairly home to them?

Much we have to tolerate, partly because we cannot always discover in time who are really insincere and who are only masking sincerity under a garb of flippancy, and partly also because we wish to err on the side of letting the guilty escape rather than of punishing the innocent. Thus many people who are perfectly well known to belong to the straightforward class are allowed to remain at large and may even be seen hobnobbing and on the best of possible terms with the guardians of public immorality. We all feel, as indeed has been said in other nations, that the poor abuses of the time want countenance, and this moreover in the interests of the uses themselves, for the presence of a small modicum of sincerity acts as a wholesome stimulant and irritant to the prevailing spirit of academicism; moreover, we hold it useful to have a certain number of melancholy examples whose notorious failure shall serve as a warning to those who do not cultivate a power of immoral self-control which shall prevent them from saying, or indeed even thinking, anything that shall not be to their immediate and palpable advantage with the greatest number.

It is a point of good breeding with the Erewhonians to keep their opinions as far as possible in the background in all cases where controversy is even remotely possible, that is to say whenever conversation gets beyond the discussion of the weather. It is found necessary, however, to recognise some means of ventilating points on which differences of opinion may exist, and the convention adopted is that whenever a man finds occasion to speak strongly he should express himself by dwelling as forcibly as he can on the views most opposed to his own; even this, however, is tolerated rather than approved, for it is counted the perfection of scholarship and good breeding not to express, and much more not even to have a definite opinion upon any subject whatsoever.

Thus their "yea" is "nay" and their "nay," "yea," but it comes to the same thing in the end, for it does not matter whether "yea" is called "yea" or "nay" so long as it is understood as "yea." They go a long way round only to find themselves at the point from which they started, but there is no accounting for tastes. With us such tactics are inconceivable, but so far do the Erewhonians carry them that it is common for them to write whole reviews and articles between the lines of which a practised reader will detect a sense exactly contrary to that ostensibly put forward; nor is a man held to be more than a tyro in the arts of polite society unless he instinctively suspects a hidden sense in every proposition that meets him. I was more than once misled by these plover-like tactics, and on one occasion was near getting into a serious scrape. It happened thus: —

A man of venerable aspect was maintaining that pain was a sad thing and should not be permitted under any circumstances. People ought not even to be allowed to suffer for the consequences of their own folly, and should be punished for it severely if they did. If they could only be kept from making fools of themselves by the loss of freedom or, if necessary, by some polite and painless method of extinction—which meant hanging—then they ought to be extinguished. If permanent improvement can only be won through ages of mistake and suffering, which must be all begun *de novo* for every fresh improvement, let us be content to forego improvement, and let those who suffer their lawless thoughts to stray in this direction be improved from off the face of the earth as fast as possible. No remedy can be too drastic for such a disease as the pain felt by another person. We find we can generally bear the pain ourselves when we have to do so, but it is intolerable that we should know it is being borne by any one else. The mere sight of pain unfits people for ordinary life, the wear and tear of which would be very much reduced if we would be at any trouble to restrain the present almost unbounded licence in the matter of suffering—a licence that people take advantage of to make themselves as miserable as they please, without so much as a thought for the feelings of others. Hence, he maintained, the practice of putting dupes in the same category as the physically diseased or the unlucky was founded on the eternal and inherent nature of things, and could no more be interfered with than the revolution of the earth on its axis.

He said a good deal more to the same effect, and I was beginning to wonder how much longer he would think it necessary to insist on what was so obvious, when his hearers began to differ from him. One dilated on the correlation between pain and pleasure which ensured that neither could be extinguished without the extinguishing along with it of the other. Another said that throughout the animal and vegetable worlds there was found what might be counted as a system of rewards and punishments; this, he contended, must cease to exist (and hence virtue must cease) if the pain attaching to misconduct were less notoriously advertised. Another maintained that the horror so freely expressed by many at the sight of pain was as much selfish as not—and so on.

Let Erewhon be revisited by the son of the original writer—let him hint that his father used to write the advertisements for Mother Seigel's Syrup. He gradually worked his way up to this from being a mere writer of penny tracts. [Dec. 1896.]

On reaching the country he finds that divine honours are being paid him, churches erected to him, and a copious mythology daily swelling, with accounts of the miracles he had worked and all his sayings and doings. If any child got hurt he used to kiss the place and it would get well at once.

Everything has been turned topsy-turvy in consequence of his flight in the balloon being ascribed to miraculous agency.

Among other things, he had maintained that sermons should be always preached by two people, one taking one side and another the opposite, while a third summed up and the congregation decided by a show of hands.

This system had been adopted and he goes to hear a sermon On the Growing Habit of Careful Patient Investigation as Encouraging Casuistry. [October 1897.]

XIX
Truth and Convenience

Opposites

You may have all growth or nothing growth, just as you may have all mechanism or nothing mechanism, all chance or nothing chance, but you must not mix them. Having settled this, you must proceed at once to mix them.

Two Points of View

Everything must be studied from the point of view of itself, as near as we can get to this, and from the point of view of its relations, as near as we can get to them. If we try to see it absolutely in itself, unalloyed with relations, we shall find, by and by, that we have, as it were, whittled it away. If we try to see it in its relations to the bitter end, we shall find that there is no corner of the universe into which it does not enter. Either way the thing eludes us if we try to grasp it with the horny hands of language and conscious thought. Either way we can think it perfectly well—so long as we don't think about thinking about it. The pale cast of thought sicklies over everything.

Practically everything should be seen as itself pure and simple, so far as we can comfortably see it, and at the same time as not itself, so far as we can comfortably see it, and then the two views should be combined, so far as we can comfortably combine them. If we cannot comfortably combine them, we should think of something else.

Truth

i

We can neither define what we mean by truth nor be in doubt as to our meaning. And this I suppose must be due to the antiquity of the instinct that, on the whole, directs us towards truth. We cannot self-vivisect ourselves in respect of such a vital function, though we can discharge it normally and easily enough so long as we do not think about it.

ii

The pursuit of truth is chimerical. That is why it is so hard to say what truth is. There is no permanent absolute unchangeable truth; what we should pursue is the most convenient arrangement of our ideas.

iii

There is no such source of error as the pursuit of absolute truth.

iv

A. B. was so impressed with the greatness and certain ultimate victory of truth that he considered it unnecessary to encourage her or do anything to defend her.

v

He who can best read men best knows all truth that need concern him; for it is not what the thing is, apart from man's thoughts in respect of it, but how to reach the fairest compromise between men's past and future opinions that is the fittest object of consideration; and this we get by reading men and women.

vi

Truth should not be absolutely lost sight of, but it should not be talked about.

vii

Some men love truth so much that they seem to be in continual fear lest she should catch cold on over-exposure.

viii

The firmest line that can be drawn upon the smoothest paper has still jagged edges if seen through a microscope. This does not matter until important deductions are made on the supposition that there are no jagged edges.

ix

Truth should never be allowed to become extreme; otherwise it will be apt to meet and to run into the extreme of falsehood. It should be played pretty low down—to the pit and gallery rather than the stalls. Pit-truth is more true to the stalls than stall-truth to the pit.

x

An absolute lie may live—for it is a true lie, and is saved by being flecked with a grain of its opposite. Not so absolute truth.

xi

Whenever we push truth hard she runs to earth in contradiction in terms, that is to say, in falsehood. An essential contradiction in terms meets us at the end of every enquiry.

xii

In *Alps and Sanctuaries* (Chapter V) I implied that I was lying when I told the novice that Handel was a Catholic. But I was not lying; Handel was a Catholic, and so am I, and so is every well-disposed person. It shows how careful we ought to be when we lie—we can never be sure but what we may be speaking the truth.

xiii

Perhaps a little bit of absolute truth on any one question might prove a general solvent, and dissipate the universe.

xiv

Truth generally is kindness, but where the two diverge or collide, kindness should override truth.

Falsehood

i

Truth consists not in never lying but in knowing when to lie and when not to do so. *De minimis non curat veritas.*

Yes, but what is a minimum? Sometimes a maximum is a minimum and sometimes it is the other way.

ii

Lying is like borrowing or appropriating in music. It is only a good, sound, truthful person who can lie to any good purpose; if a man is not habitually truthful his very lies will be false to him and betray him. The converse also is true; if a man is not a good, sound, honest, capable liar there is no truth in him.

iii

Any fool can tell the truth, but it requires a man of some sense to know how to lie well.

iv

I do not mind lying, but I hate inaccuracy.

v

A friend who cannot at a pinch remember a thing or two that never happened is as bad as one who does not know how to forget.

vi

Cursed is he that does not know when to shut his mind. An open mind is all very well in its way, but it ought not to be so open that there is no keeping anything in or out of it. It should be capable of shutting its doors sometimes, or it may be found a little draughty.

vii

He who knows not how to wink knows not how to see; and he who knows not how to lie knows not how to speak the truth. So he who cannot suppress his opinions cannot express them.

viii

There can no more be a true statement without falsehood distributed through it, than a note on a well-tuned piano that is not intentionally and deliberately put out of tune to some extent in order to have the piano in the most perfect possible tune. Any perfection of tune as regards one key can only be got at the expense of all the rest.

ix

Lying has a kind of respect and reverence with it. We pay a person the compliment of acknowledging his superiority whenever we lie to him.

x

I seem to see lies crowding and crushing at a narrow gate and working their way in along with truths into the domain of history.

Nature's Double Falsehood

That one great lie she told about the earth being flat when she knew it was round all the time! And again how she stuck to it that the sun went round us when it was we who were going round the sun! This double falsehood has irretrievably ruined my confidence in her. There is no lie which she will not tell and stick to like a Gladstonian. How plausibly she told her tale, and how many ages was it before she was so much as suspected! And then when things did begin to look bad for her, how she brazened it out, and what a desperate business it was to bring her shifts and prevarications to book!

Convenience

i

We wonder at its being as hard often to discover convenience as it is to discover truth. But surely convenience is truth.

ii

The use of truth is like the use of words; both truth and words depend greatly upon custom.

iii

We do with truth much as we do with God. We create it according to our own requirements and then say that it has created us, or requires that we shall do or think so and so—whatever we find convenient.

"What is Truth?" is often asked, as though it were harder to say what truth is than what anything else is. But what is Justice? What is anything? An eternal contradiction in terms meets us at the end of every enquiry. We are not required to know what truth is, but to speak the truth, and so with justice.

The search after truth is like the search after perpetual motion or the attempt to square the circle. All we should aim at is the most convenient way of looking at a thing — the way that most sensible people are likely to find give them least trouble for some time to come. It is not true that the sun used to go round the earth until Copernicus's time, but it is true that until Copernicus's time it was most convenient to us to hold this. Still, we had certain ideas which could only fit in comfortably with our other ideas when we came to consider the sun as the centre of the planetary system.

Obvious convenience often takes a long time before it is fully recognised and acted upon, but there will be a *nisus* towards it as long and as widely spread as the desire of men to be saved trouble. If truth is not trouble-saving in the long run it is not truth: truth is only that which is most largely and permanently trouble-saving. The ultimate triumph, therefore, of truth rests on a very tangible basis — much more so than when it is made to depend upon the will of an unseen and unknowable agency. If my views about the *Odyssey*, for example, will, in the long run, save students from perplexity, the students will be sure to adopt them, and I have no wish that they should adopt them otherwise.

It does not matter much what the truth is, but our knowing the truth — that is to say our hitting on the most permanently convenient arrangement of our ideas upon a subject whatever it may be — matters very much; at least it matters, or may matter, very much in some relations. And however little it matters, yet it matters, and however much it matters yet it does not matter. In the utmost importance there is unimportance, and in the utmost unimportance there is importance. So also it is with certainty, life, matter, necessity, consciousness and, indeed, with everything which can form an object of human sensation at all, or of those after-reasonings which spring ultimately from sensations. This is a round-about way of saying that every question has two sides.

Our concern is with the views we shall choose to take and to let other people take concerning things, and as to the way of expressing those views which shall give least trouble. If we express ourselves in one way we f nd our ideas in confusion and our action impotent: if in another our ideas cohere harmoniously, and our action is edifying. The convenience of least disturbing vested ideas, and at the same time rearranging our views in accordance with new facts that come to our knowledge, this is our proper care. But it is idle to say we do not know anything about things—perhaps we do, perhaps we don't—but we at any rate know what sane people think and are likely to think about things, and this to all intents and purposes is knowing the things themselves. For the things only are what sensible people agree to say and think they are.

vii

The arrangement of our ideas is as much a matter of convenience as the packing of goods in a druggist's or draper's store and leads to exactly the same kind of difficulties in the matter of classifying them. We all admit the arbitrariness of classifications in a languid way, but we do not think of it more than we can help—I suppose because it is so inconvenient to do so. The great advantage of classification is to conceal the fact that subdivisions are as arbitrary as they are.

Classification

There can be no perfect way, for classification presupposes that a thing has absolute limits whereas there is nothing that does not partake of the universal infinity—nothing whose boundaries do not vary. Everything is one thing at one time and in some respects, and another at other times and in other respects. We want a new mode of measurement altogether; at present we take what gaps we can find, set up milestones, and declare them irremovable. We want a measure which shall express, or at any rate recognise, the harmonics of resemblance that lurk even in the most absolute differences and vice versa.

Attempts at Classification

are like nailing battens of our own flesh and blood upon ourselves as an inclined plane that we may walk up ourselves more easily; and yet it answers very sufficiently.

A Clergyman's Doubts

Under this heading a correspondence appeared in the Examiner, *15th February to 14th June, 1879. Butler wrote all the letters under various signatures except one or perhaps two. His first letter purported to come from "An Earnest Clergyman" aged forty-five, with a wife, five children, a country living worth £400 a year, and a house, but no private means. He had ceased to believe in the doctrines he was called upon to teach. Ought he to continue to lead a life that was a lie or ought he to throw up his orders and plunge himself, his wife and children into poverty? The dilemma interested Butler deeply: he might so easily have found himself in it if he had not begun to doubt the efficacy of infant baptism when he did. Fifteen letters followed, signed "Cantab," "Oxoniensis," and so forth, some recommending one course, some another. One, signed "X.Y.Z.," included "The Righteous Man" which will be found in the last group of this volume, headed "Poems." From the following letter signed "Ethics" Butler afterwards took two passages (which I have enclosed, one between single asterisks the other between double asterisks), and used them for the "Dissertation on Lying" which is in Chapter V of* Alps and Sanctuaries.

To the Editor of the *Examiner.*

Sir: I am sorry for your correspondent "An Earnest Clergyman" for, though he may say he has "come to smile at his troubles," his smile seems to be a grim one. We must all of us eat a peck of moral dirt before we die, but some must know more precisely than others when they are eating it; some, again, can bolt it without wry faces in one shape, while they cannot endure even the smell of it in another. "An Earnest Clergyman" admits that he is in the habit of telling people certain things which he does not believe, but says he has no great fancy for deceiving himself. "Cantab" must, I fear, deceive himself before he can tolerate the notion of deceiving other people. For my own part I prefer to be deceived by one who does not deceive himself rather than by one who does, for the first will know better when to stop, and will not commonly deceive me more than he can help. As for the other — if he does not know how to invest his own thoughts safely he will invest mine still worse; he will hold God's most precious gift of falsehood too cheap; he has come by it too easily; cheaply come, cheaply go will be his maxim. The good liar should be the converse of the poet; he should be made, not born.

It is not loss of confidence in a man's strict adherence to the letter of truth that shakes my confidence in him. I know what I do myself and what I must lose all social elasticity if I were not to do. * Turning for moral guidance to my cousins the lower animals — whose unsophisticated instinct proclaims what God has taught them with a directness we may sometimes study — I find the plover lying when she reads us truly and, knowing that we shall hit her if we think her to be down, lures us from her young ones under the fiction of a broken wing. Is God angry, think you, with this pretty deviation from the letter of strict accuracy? or was it not He who whispered to her to tell the falsehood, to tell it with a circumstance, without conscientious scruples, and not once only but to make a practice of it, so as to be an habitual liar for at least six weeks in the year? I imagine so. When I was young I used to read in good books that it was God who taught the bird to make her nest, and, if so, He probably taught each species the other domestic arrangements which should be best suited to it. Or did the nest-building information come from God and was there an Evil One among the birds also who taught them to steer clear of pedantry? Then there is the spider—an ugly creature, but I suppose God likes it—can anything be meaner than that web which naturalists extol as such a marvel of Providential ingenuity?

Ingenuity! The word reeks with lying. Once, on a summer afternoon, in a distant country I met one of those orchids whose main idea consists in the imitation of a fly; this lie they dispose so plausibly upon their petals that other flies who would steal their honey leave them unmolested. Watching intently and keeping very still, methought I heard this person speaking to the offspring which she felt within her though I saw them not.

"My children," she exclaimed, "I must soon leave you; think upon the fly, my loved ones; make it look as terrible as possible; cling to this thought in your passage through life, for it is the one thing needful; once lose sight of it and you are lost."

Over and over again she sang this burden in a small, still voice, and so I left her. Then straightway I came upon some butterflies whose profession it was to pretend to believe in all manner of vital truths which in their inner practice they rejected; thus, pretending to be certain other and hateful butterflies which no bird will eat by reason of their abominable smell, these cunning ones conceal their own sweetness, live long in the land and see good days. Think of that, O Earnest Clergyman, my friend! No. Lying is like Nature, you may expel her with a fork, but she will always come back again. Lying is like the poor, we must have it always with us. The question is, How much, when, where, to whom and under what circumstances is lying right? For, once admit that a plover may pretend to have a broken wing and yet be without sin if she have pretended well enough, and the thin edge of the wedge has been introduced so that there is no more saying that we must never lie. *

It is not, then, the discovery that a man has the power to lie that shakes my confidence in him; it is loss of confidence in his mendacity that I find it impossible to get over. I forgive him for telling me lies, but I cannot forgive him for not telling me the same lies, or nearly so, about the same things. This shows he has a slipshod memory, which is unpardonable, or else that he tells so many lies that he finds it impossible to remember all of them, and this is like having too many of the poor always with us. The plover and the spider have each of them their stock of half a dozen lies or so which we may expect them to tell when occasion arises; they are plausible and consistent, but we know where to have them; otherwise, if they were liable, like self-deceivers, to spring mines upon us in unexpected places, man would soon make it his business to reform them—not from within, but from without.

And now it is time I came to the drift of my letter, which is that if "An Earnest Clergyman" has not cheated himself into thinking he is telling the truth, he will do no great harm by stopping where he is. Do not let him make too much fuss about trifles. The solemnity of the truths which he professes to uphold is very doubtful; there is a tacit consent that it exists more on paper than in reality. If he is a man of any tact, he can say all he is compelled to say and do all the Church requires of him—like a gentleman, with neither undue slovenliness nor undue unction—yet it shall be perfectly plain to all his parishioners who are worth considering that he is acting as a mouthpiece and that his words are spoken dramatically. As for the unimaginative, they are as children; they cannot and should not be taken into account. Men must live as they must write or act—for a certain average standard which each must guess at for himself as best he can; those who are above this standard he cannot reach; those, again, who are below it must be so at their own risk.

Pilate did well when he would not stay for an answer to his question, What is truth? for there is no such thing apart from the sayer and the sayee. ** There is that irony in nature which brings it to pass that if the sayer be a man with any stuff in him, provided he tells no lies wittingly to himself and is never unkindly, he may lie and lie and lie all the day long, and he will no more be false to any man than the sun will shine by night; his lies will become truths as they pass into the hearer's soul. But if a man deceives himself and is unkind, the truth is not in him, it turns to falsehood while yet in his mouth, like the quails in the wilderness of Sinai. How this is so or why, I know not, but that the Lord hath mercy on whom He will have mercy and whom He willeth He hardeneth, and that the bad man can do no right and the good no wrong. **

A great French writer has said that the mainspring of our existence does not lie in those veins and nerves and arteries which have been described with so much care—these are but its masks and mouthpieces through which it acts but behind which it is for ever hidden; so in like manner the faiths and formulæ of a Church may be as its bones and animal mechanism, but they are not the life of the Church, which is something rather that cannot be holden in words, and one should know how to put them off, yet put them off gracefully, if they wish to come too prominently forward. Do not let "An Earnest Clergyman" take things too much *au sérieux*. He seems to be contented where he is; let him take the word of one who is old enough to be his father, that if he has a talent for conscientious scruples he will find plenty of scope for them in other professions as well as in the Church. I, for aught he knows, may be a doctor and I might tell my own story; or I may be a barrister and have found it my duty to win a case which I thought a very poor one, whereby others, whose circumstances were sufficiently pitiable, lost their all; yet doctors and barristers do not write to the newspapers to air their poor consciences in broad daylight. Why should An Earnest (I hate the word) Clergyman do so? Let me give him a last word or two of fatherly advice.

Men may settle small things for themselves—as what they will have for dinner or where they will spend the vacation—but the great ones—such as the choice of a profession, of the part of England they will live in, whether they will marry or no—they had better leave the force of circumstances to settle for them; if they prefer the phraseology, as I do myself, let them leave these matters to God. When He has arranged things for them, do not let them be in too great a hurry to upset His arrangement in a tiff. If they do not like their present and another opening suggests itself easily and naturally, let them take that as a sign that they make a change; otherwise, let them see to it that they do not leave the frying-pan for the fire. A man, finding himself in the field of a profession, should do as cows do when they are put into a field of grass. They do not like any field; they like the open prairie of their ancestors. They walk, however, all round their new abode, surveying the hedges and gates with much interest. If there is a gap in any hedge they will commonly go through it at once, otherwise they will resign themselves contentedly enough to the task of feeding.

I am, Sir,

One who thinks he knows a thing or two about
Ethics.

XX
First Principles

The Baselessness of Our Ideas

That our ideas are baseless, or rotten at the roots, is what few who study them will deny; but they are rotten in the same way as property is robbery, and property is robbery in the same way as our ideas are rotten at the roots, that is to say it is a robbery and it is not. No title to property, no idea and no living form (which is the embodiment of idea) is indefeasible if search be made far enough. Granted that our thoughts are baseless, yet they are so in the same way as the earth itself is both baseless and most firmly based, or again most stable and yet most in motion.

Our ideas, or rather, I should say, our realities, are all of them like our Gods, based on superstitious foundations. If man is a microcosm then kosmos is a megalanthrope and that is how we come to anthropomorphise the deity. In the eternal pendulum swing of thought we make God in our own image, and then make him make us, and then find it out and cry because we have no God and so on, over and over again as a child has new toys given to it, tires of them, breaks them and is disconsolate till it gets new ones which it will again tire of and break. If the man who first made God in his own image had been a good model, all might have been well; but he was impressed with an undue sense of his own importance and, as a natural consequence, he had no sense of humour. Both these imperfections he has fully and faithfully reproduced in his work and with the result we are familiar. All our most solid and tangible realities are but as lies that we have told too often henceforth to question them. But we have to question them sometimes. It is not the sun that goes round the world but we who go round the sun.

If any one is for examining and making requisitions on title we can search too, and can require the title of the state as against any other state, or against the world at large. But suppose we succeed in this, we must search further still and show by what title mankind has ousted the lower animals, and by what title we eat them, or they themselves eat grass or one another.

See what quicksands we fall into if we wade out too far from the *terra firma* of common consent! The error springs from supposing that there is any absolute right or absolute truth, and also from supposing that truth and right are any the less real for being not absolute but relative. In the complex of human affairs we should aim not at a supposed absolute standard but at the greatest coming-together-ness or convenience of all our ideas and practices; that is to say, at their most harmonious working with one another. Hit ourselves somewhere we are bound to do: no idea will travel far without colliding with some other idea. Thus, if we pursue one line of probable convenience, we find it convenient to see all things as ultimately one: that is, if we insist rather on the points of agreement between things than on those of disagreement. If we insist on the opposite view, namely, on the points of disagreement, we find ourselves driven to the conclusion that each atom is an individual entity, and that the unity between even the most united things is apparent only. If we did not unduly insist upon—that is to say, emphasise and exaggerate—the part which concerns us for the time, we should never get to understand anything; the proper way is to exaggerate first one view and then the other, and then let the two exaggerations collide, but good-temperedly and according to the laws of civilised mental warfare. So we see first all things as one, then all things as many and, in the end, a multitude in unity and a unity in multitude. Care must be taken not to accept ideas which though very agreeable at first disagree with us afterwards, and keep rising on our mental stomachs, as garlic does upon our bodily.

Imagination

i

Imagination depends mainly upon memory, but there is a small percentage of creation of something out of nothing with it. We can invent a trifle more than can be got at by mere combination of remembered things.

ii

When we are impressed by a few only, or perhaps only one of a number of ideas which are bonded pleasantly together, there is hope; when we see a good many there is expectation; when we have had so many presented to us that we have expected confidently and the remaining ideas have not turned up, there is disappointment. So the sailor says in the play:

"Here are my arms, here is my manly bosom, but where's my Mary?"

iii

What tricks imagination plays! Thus, if we expect a person in the street we transform a dozen impossible people into him while they are still too far off to be seen distinctly; and when we expect to hear a footstep on the stairs — as, we will say, the postman's — we hear footsteps in every sound. Imagination will make us see a billiard hall as likely to travel farther than it will travel, if we hope that it will do so. It will make us think we feel a train begin to move as soon as the guard has said "All right," though the train has not yet begun to move if another train alongside begins to move exactly at this juncture, there is no man who will not be deceived. And we omit as much as we insert. We often do not notice that a man has grown a beard.

iv

I read once of a man who was cured of a dangerous illness by eating his doctor's prescription which he understood was the medicine itself. So William Sefton Moorhouse [in New Zealand] imagined he was being converted to Christianity by reading Burton's *Anatomy of Melancholy*, which he had got by mistake for Butler's *Analogy*, on the recommendation of a friend. But it puzzled him a good deal.

v

At Ivy Hatch, while we were getting our beer in the inner parlour, there was a confused mêlée of voices in the bar, amid which I distinguished a voice saying:

"Imagination will do any bloody thing almost."

I was writing *Life and Habit* at the time and was much tempted to put this passage in. Nothing truer has ever been said about imagination. Then the voice was heard addressing the barman and saying:

"I suppose you wouldn't trust me with a quart of beer, would you?"

Inexperience

Kant says that all our knowledge is founded on experience. But each new small increment of knowledge is not so founded, and our whole knowledge is made up of the accumulation of these small new increments not one of which is founded upon experience. Our knowledge, then, is founded not on experience but on inexperience; for where there is no novelty, that is to say no inexperience, there is no increment in experience. Our knowledge is really founded upon something which we do not know, but it is converted into experience by memory.

It is like species — we do not know the cause of the variations whose accumulation results in species and any explanation which leaves this out of sight ignores the whole difficulty. We want to know the cause of the effect that inexperience produces on us.

Ex Nihilo Nihil Fit

We say that everything has a beginning. This is one side of the matter. There is another according to which everything is without a beginning—beginnings, and endings also, being, but as it were, steps cut in a slope of ice without which we could not climb it. They are for convenience and the hardness of the hearts of men who make an idol of classification, but they do not exist apart from our sense of our own convenience.

It was a favourite saying with William Sefton Moorhouse [in New Zealand] that men cannot get rich by swopping knives. Nevertheless nature does seem to go upon this principle. Everybody does eat everybody up. Man eats birds, birds eat worms and worms eat man again. It is a vicious circle, yet, somehow or other, there is an increment. I begin to doubt the principle *ex nihilo nihil fit*.

We very much want a way of getting something out of nothing and back into it again. Whether or no we ever shall get such a way, we see the clearly perceptible arising out of and returning into the absolutely imperceptible and, so far as we are concerned, this is much the same thing. To assume an unknowable substratum as the source from which all things proceed or are evolved is equivalent to assuming that they come up out of nothing; for that which does not exist for us is for us nothing; that which we do not know does not exist *qua* us, and therefore it does not exist. When I say "we," I mean mankind generally, for things may exist *qua* one man and not *qua* another. And when I say "nothing" I postulate something of which we have no experience.

And yet we cannot say that a thing does not exist till it is known to exist. The planet Neptune existed though, *qua* us, it did not exist before Adams and Leverrier discovered it, and we cannot hold that its continued non-existence to my laundress and her husband makes it any the less an entity. We cannot say that it did not exist at all till it was discovered, that it exists only partially and vaguely to most of us, that to many it still does not exist at all, that there are few to whom it even exists in any force or fullness and none who can realise more than the broad facts of its existence. Neptune has been disturbing the orbits of the planets nearest to him for more centuries than we can reckon, and whether or not he is known to have been doing so has nothing to do with the matter. If A is robbed, he is robbed, whether he knows it or not.

In one sense, then, we cannot say that the planet Neptune did not exist till he was discovered, but in another we can and ought to do so. *De non apparentibus et non existentibus eadem est ratio*; as long, therefore, as Neptune did not appear he did not exist *qua* us. The only way out of it is through the contradiction in terms of maintaining that a thing exists and does not exist at one and the same time. So A may be both robbed, and not robbed.

We consider, therefore, that things have assumed their present shape by course of evolution from a something which, *qua* us, is a nothing, from a potential something but not an actual, from an actual nothing but a potential not-nothing, from a nothing which might become a something to us with any modification on our parts but which, till such modification has arisen, does not exist in relation to us, though very conceivably doing so in relation to other entities. But this Protean nothing, capable of appearing as something, is not the absolute, eternal, unchangeable nothing that we mean when we say *ex nihilo nihil fit.*

The alternative is that something should not have come out of nothing, and this is saying that something has always existed. But the eternal increateness of matter seems as troublesome to conceive as its having been created out of nothing. I say "seems," for I am not sure how far it really is so. We never saw something come out of nothing, that is to say, we never saw a beginning of anything except as the beginning of a new phase of something pre-existent. We ought therefore to find the notion of eternal being familiar, it ought to be the only conception of matter which we are able to form: nevertheless, we are so carried away by being accustomed to see phases have their beginnings and endings that we forget that the matter, of which we see the phase begin and end, did not begin or end with the phase.

Eternal matter permeated by eternal mind, matter and mind being functions of one another, is the least uncomfortable way of looking at the universe; but as it is beyond our comprehension, and cannot therefore be comfortable, sensible persons will not look at the universe at all except in such details as may concern them.

Contradiction in Terms

We pay higher and higher in proportion to the service rendered till we get to the highest services, such as becoming a Member of Parliament, and this must not be paid at all. If a man would go yet higher and found a new and permanent system, or create some new idea or work of art which remains to give delight to ages—he must not only not be paid, but he will have to pay very heavily out of his own pocket into the bargain.

Again, we are to get all men to speak well of us if we can; yet we are to be cursed if all men speak well of us.

So when the universe has gathered itself into a single ball (which I don't for a moment believe it ever will, but I don't care) it will no sooner have done so, than the bubble will burst and it will go back to its gases again.

Contradiction in terms is so omnipresent that we treat it as we treat death, or free-will, or fate, or air, or God, or the Devil—taking these things so much as matters of course that, though they are visible enough if we choose to see them, we neglect them normally altogether, without for a moment intending to deny their existence. This neglect is convenient as preventing repetitions the monotony of which would defeat their own purpose, but people are tempted nevertheless to forget the underlying omnipresence in the superficial omniabsence. They forget that its opposite lurks in everything—that there are harmonics of God in the Devil and harmonics of the Devil in God.

Contradiction in terms is not only to be excused but there can be no proposition which does not more or less involve one.

It is the fact of there being contradictions in terms, which have to be smoothed away and fused into harmonious acquiescence with their surroundings, that makes life and consciousness possible at all. Unless the unexpected were sprung upon us continually to enliven us we should pass life, as it were, in sleep. To a living being no "It is" can be absolute; wherever there is an "Is," there, among its harmonics, lurks an "Is not." When there is absolute absence of "Is not" the "Is" goes too. And the "Is not" does not go completely till the "Is" is gone along with it. Every proposition has got a skeleton in its cupboard.

Extremes

i

Intuition and evidence seem to have something of the same relation that faith and reason, luck and cunning, freewill and necessity and demand and supply have. They grow up hand in hand and no man can say which comes first. It is the same with life and death, which lurk one within the other as do rest and unrest, change and persistence, heat and cold, poverty and riches, harmony and counterpoint, night and day, summer and winter.

And so with pantheism and atheism; loving everybody is loving nobody, and God everywhere is, practically, God nowhere. I once asked a man if he was a free-thinker; he replied that he did not think he was. And so, I have heard of a man exclaiming "I am an atheist, thank God!" Those who say there is a God are wrong unless they mean at the same time that there is no God, and vice versa. The difference is the same as that between plus nothing and minus nothing, and it is hard to say which we ought to admire and thank most—the first theist or the first atheist. Nevertheless, for many reasons, the plus nothing is to be preferred.

ii

To be poor is to be contemptible, to be very poor is worse still, and so on; but to be actually at the point of death through poverty is to be sublime. So "when weakness is utter, honour ceaseth." [*The Righteous Man, post.*]

iii

The meeting of extremes is never clearer than in the case of moral and intellectual strength and weakness. We may say with Hesiod "How much the half is greater than the whole!" or with S. Paul "My strength is made perfect in weakness"; they come to much the same thing. We all know strength so strong as to be weaker than weakness and weakness so great as to be stronger than strength.

iv

The Queen travels as the Countess of Balmoral and would probably be very glad, if she could, to travel as plain Mrs. Smith. There is a good deal of the Queen lurking in every Mrs. Smith and, conversely, a good deal of Mrs. Smith lurking in every queen.

Free-Will and Necessity

As I am tidying up, and the following beginning of a paper on the above subject has been littering about my table since December 1889, which is the date on the top of page i, I will shoot it on to this dust-heap and bury it out of my sight. It runs:

The difficulty has arisen from our forgetting that contradiction in terms lies at the foundation of all our thoughts as a condition and *sine qua non* of our being able to think at all. We imagine that we must either have all free-will and no necessity, or all necessity and no free-will, and, it being obvious that our free-will is often overridden by force of circumstances while the evidence that necessity is overridden by free-will is harder to find (if indeed it can be found, for I have not fully considered the matter), most people who theorise upon this question will deny in theory that there is any free-will at all, though in practice they take care to act as if there was. For if we admit that like causes are followed by like effects (and everything that we do is based upon this hypothesis), it follows that every combination of causes must have some one consequent which can alone follow it and which free-will cannot touch.

(Yes, but it will generally be found that free-will entered into the original combination and the repetition of the combination will not be exact unless a like free-will is repeated along with all the other factors.)

From which it follows that free-will is apparent only, and that, as I said years ago in *Erewhon*, we are not free to choose what seems best on each occasion but bound to do so, being fettered to the freedom of our wills throughout our lives.

But to deny free-will is to deny moral responsibility, and we are landed in absurdity at once—for there is nothing more patent than that moral responsibility exists. Nevertheless, at first sight, it would seem as though we ought not to hang a man for murder if there was no escape for him but that he must commit one. Of course the answer to one who makes this objection is that our hanging him is as much a matter of necessity as his committing the murder.

If, again, necessity, as involved in the certainty that like combinations will be followed by like consequence, is a basis on which all our actions are founded, so also is freewill. This is quite as much a *sine qua non* for action as necessity is; for who would try to act if he did not think that his trying would influence the result?

We have therefore two apparently incompatible and mutually destructive faiths, each equally and self-evidently demonstrable, each equally necessary for salvation of any kind, and each equally entering into every thought and action of our whole lives, yet utterly contradictory and irreconcilable.

Can any dilemma seem more hopeless? It is not a case of being able to live happily with either were t'other dear charmer away; it is indispensable that we should embrace both, and embrace them with equal cordiality at the same time, though each annihilates the other. It is as though it were indispensable to our existence to be equally dead and equally alive at one and the same moment.

Here we have an illustration which may help us. For, after all, we are both dead and alive at one and the same moment. There is no life without a taint of death and no death that is not instinct with a residuum of past life and with germs of the new that is to succeed it. Let those who deny this show us an example of pure life and pure death. Any one who has considered these matters will know this to be impossible. And yet in spite of this, the cases where we are in doubt whether a thing is to be more fitly called dead or alive are so few that they may be disregarded.

I take it, then, that as, though alive, we are in part dead and, though dead, in part alive, so, though bound by necessity, we are in part free, and, though free, yet in part bound by necessity. At least I can think of no case of such absolute necessity in human affairs as that free-will should have no part in it, nor of such absolute free-will that no part of the action should be limited and controlled by necessity.

Thus, when a man walks to the gallows, he is under large necessity, yet he retains much small freedom; when pinioned, he is less free, but he can open his eyes and mouth and pray aloud or no as he pleases; even when the drop has fallen, so long as he is "he" at all, he can exercise some, though infinitely small, choice.

It may be answered that throughout the foregoing chain of actions, the freedom, what little there is of it, is apparent only, and that even in the small freedoms, which are not so obviously controlled by necessity, the necessity is still present as effectually as when the man, though apparently free to walk to the gallows, is in reality bound to do so. For in respect of the small details of his manner of walking to the gallows, which compulsion does not so glaringly reach, what is it that the man is free to do? He is free to do as he likes, but he is not free to do as he does not like; and a man's likings are determined by outside things and by antecedents, pre-natal and post-natal, whose effect is so powerful that the individual who makes the choice proves to be only the resultant of certain forces which have been brought to bear upon him but which are not the man. So that it seems there is no detail, no nook or corner of action, into which necessity does not penetrate.

This seems logical, but it is as logical to follow instinct and common sense as to follow logic, and both instinct and common sense assure us that there is no nook or corner of action into which free-will does not penetrate, unless it be those into which mind does not enter at all, as when a man is struck by lightning or is overwhelmed suddenly by an avalanche.

Besides, those who maintain that action is bound to follow choice, while choice can only follow opinion as to advantage, neglect the very considerable number of cases in which opinion as to advantage does not exist—when, for instance, a man feels, as we all of us sometimes do, that he is utterly incapable of forming any opinion whatever as to his most advantageous course.

But this again is fallacious. For suppose he decides to toss up and be guided by the result, this is still what he has chosen to do, and his action, therefore, is following his choice. Or suppose, again, that he remains passive and does nothing—his passivity is his choice.

I can see no way out of it unless either frankly to admit that contradiction in terms is the bedrock on which all our thoughts and deeds are founded, and to acquiesce cheerfully in the fact that whenever we try to go below the surface of any enquiry we find ourselves utterly baffled—or to redefine freedom and necessity, admitting each as a potent factor of the other. And this I do not see my way to doing. I am therefore necessitated to choose freely the admission that our understanding can burrow but a very small way into the foundations of our beliefs, and can only weaken rather than strengthen them by burrowing at all.

Free-Will otherwise Cunning

The element of free-will, cunning, spontaneity, individuality—so omnipresent, so essential, yet so unreasonable, and so inconsistent with the other element not less omnipresent and not less essential, I mean necessity, luck, fate—this element of free-will, which comes from the unseen kingdom within which the writs of our thoughts run not, must be carried down to the most tenuous atoms whose action is supposed most purely chemical and mechanical; it can never be held as absolutely eliminated, for if it be so held, there is no getting it back again, and that it exists, even in the lowest forms of life, cannot be disputed. Its existence is one of the proofs of the existence of an unseen world, and a means whereby we know the little that we do know of that world.

Necessity otherwise Luck

It is all very well to insist upon the free-will or cunning side of living action, more especially now when it has been so persistently ignored, but though the fortunes of birth and surroundings have all been built up by cunning, yet it is by ancestral, vicarious cunning, and this, to each individual, comes to much the same as luck pure and simple; in fact, luck is seldom seriously intended to mean a total denial of cunning, but is for the most part only an expression whereby we summarise and express our sense of a cunning too complex and impalpable for conscious following and apprehension.

When we consider how little we have to do with our parentage, country and education, or even with our genus and species, how vitally these things affect us both in life and death, and how, practically, the cunning in connection with them is so spent as to be no cunning at all, it is plain that the drifts, currents, and storms of what is virtually luck will be often more than the little helm of cunning can control. And so with death. Nothing can affect us less, but at the same time nothing can affect us more; and how little can cunning do against it? At the best it can only defer it. Cunning is nine-tenths luck, and luck is nine-tenths cunning; but the fact that nine-tenths of cunning is luck leaves still a tenth part unaccounted for.

Choice

Our choice is apparently most free, and we are least obviously driven to determine our course, in those cases where the future is most obscure, that is, when the balance of advantage appears most doubtful.

Where we have an opinion that assures us promptly which way the balance of advantage will incline—whether it be an instinctive, hereditarily acquired opinion or one rapidly and decisively formed as the result of post-natal experience—then our action is determined at once by that opinion, and freedom of choice practically vanishes.

Ego and Non-Ego

You can have all ego, or all non-ego, but in theory you cannot have half one and half the other—yet in practice this is exactly what you must have, for everything is both itself and not itself at one and the same time.

A living thing is itself in so far as it has wants and gratifies them. It is not itself in so far as it uses itself as a tool for the gratifying of its wants. Thus an amœba is aware of a piece of meat which it wants to eat. It has nothing except its own body to fling at the meat and catch it with. If it had a little hand-net, or even such an organ as our own hand, it would use it, but it has only got itself; so it takes itself by the scruff of its own neck, as it were, and flings itself at the piece of meat, as though it were not itself but something which it is using in order to gratify itself. So we make our own bodies into carriages every time we walk. Our body is our tool-box — and our bodily organs are the simplest tools we can catch hold of.

When the amœba has got the piece of meat and has done digesting it, it leaves off being not itself and becomes itself again. A thing is only itself when it is doing nothing; as long as it is doing something it is its own tool and not itself.

Or you may have it that everything is itself in respect of the pleasure or pain it is feeling, but not itself in respect of the using of itself by itself as a tool with which to work its will. Or perhaps we should say that the ego remains always ego in part; it does not become all non-ego at one and the same time. We throw our fist into a man's face as though it were a stick we had picked up to beat him with. For the moment, our fist is hardly "us," but it becomes "us" again as we feel the resistance it encounters from the man's eye. Anyway, we can only chuck about a part of ourselves at a time, we cannot chuck the lot — and yet I do not know this, for we may jump off the ground and fling ourselves on to a man.

The fact that both elements are present and are of such nearly equal value explains the obstinacy of the conflict between the upholders of Necessity and Free-Will which, indeed, are only luck and cunning under other names.

For, on the one hand, the surroundings so obviously and powerfully mould us, body and soul, and even the little modifying power which at first we seem to have is found, on examination, to spring so completely from surroundings formerly beyond the control of our ancestors, that a logical thinker, who starts with these premises, is soon driven to the total denial of free-will, except, of course, as an illusion; in other words, he perceives the connection between ego and non-ego, tries to disunite them so as to know when he is talking about what, and finds to his surprise that he cannot do so without violence to one or both. Being, above all things, a logical thinker, and abhorring the contradiction in terms involved in admitting anything to be both itself and something other than itself at one and the same time, he makes the manner in which the one is rooted into the other a pretext for merging the ego, as the less bulky of the two, in the non-ego; hence practically he declares the ego to have no further existence, except as a mere appendage and adjunct of the non-ego the existence of which he alone recognises (though how he can recognise it without recognising also that he is recognising it as something foreign to himself it is not easy to see). As for the action and interaction that goes on in the non-ego, he refers it to fate, fortune, chance, luck, necessity, immutable law, providence (meaning generally improvidence) or to whatever kindred term he has most fancy for. In other words, he is so much impressed with the connection between luck and cunning, and so anxious to avoid contradiction in terms, that he tries to abolish cunning, and dwells, as Mr. Darwin did, almost exclusively upon the luck side of the matter.

Others, on the other hand, find the ego no less striking than their opponents find the non-ego. Every hour they mould things so considerably to their pleasure that, even though they may for argument's sake admit free-will to be an illusion, they say with reason that no reality can be more real than an illusion which is so strong, so persistent and so universal; this contention, indeed, cannot be disputed except at the cost of invalidating the reality of all even our most assured convictions. They admit that there is an apparent connection between their ego and non-ego, their necessity and free-will, their luck and cunning; they grant that the difference is resolvable into a difference of degree and not of kind; but, on the other hand, they say that in each degree there still lurks a little kind, and that a difference of many degrees makes a difference of kind — there being, in fact, no difference between differences of degree and those of kind, except that the second are an accumulation of the first. The all-powerfulness of the surroundings is declared by them to be as completely an illusion, if examined closely, as the power of the individual was declared to be by their opponents, inasmuch as the antecedents of the non-ego, when examined by them, prove to be not less due to the personal individual element everywhere recognisable, than the ego, when examined by their opponents, proved to be mergeable in the universal. They claim, therefore, to be able to resolve everything into spontaneity and free-will with no less logical consistency than that with which freewill can be resolved into an outcome of necessity.

Two Incomprehensibles

You may assume life of some kind omnipresent for ever throughout matter. This is one way. Another way is to assume an act of spontaneous generation, i.e. a transition somewhere and somewhen from absolutely non-living to absolutely living. You cannot have it both ways. But it seems to me that you must have it both ways. You must not begin with life (or potential life) everywhere alone, nor must you begin with a single spontaneous generation alone, but you must carry your spontaneous generation (or denial of the continuity of life) down, *ad infinitum*, just as you must carry your continuity of life (or denial of spontaneous generation) down *ad infinitum* and, compatible or incompatible, you must write a scientific Athanasian Creed to comprehend these two incomprehensibles.

If, then, it is only an escape from one incomprehensible position to another, *cui bono* to make a change? Why not stay quietly in the Athanasian Creed as we are? And, after all, the Athanasian Creed is light and comprehensible reading in comparison with much that now passes for science.

I can give no answer to this as regards the unintelligible clauses, for what we come to in the end is just as abhorrent to and inconceivable by reason as what they offer us; but as regards what may be called the intelligible parts — that Christ was born of a Virgin, died, rose from the dead — we say that, if it were not for the prestige that belief in these alleged facts has obtained, we should refuse attention to them. Out of respect, however, for the mass of opinion that accepts them we have looked into the matter with care, and we have found the evidence break down. The same reasoning and canons of criticism which convince me that Christ was crucified convince me at the same time that he was insufficiently crucified. I can only accept his death and resurrection at the cost of rejecting everything that I have been taught to hold most strongly. I can only accept the so-called testimony in support of these alleged facts at the cost of rejecting, or at any rate invalidating, all the testimony on which I have based all comfortable assurance of any kind whatsoever.

God and the Unknown

God is the unknown, and hence the nothing *qua* us. He is also the ensemble of all we know, and hence the everything *qua* us. So that the most absolute nothing and the most absolute everything are extremes that meet (like all other extremes) in God.

Men think they mean by God something like what Raffaelle and Michael Angelo have painted; unless this were so Raffaelle and Michael Angelo would not have painted as they did. But to get at our truer thoughts we should look at our less conscious and deliberate utterances. From these it has been gathered that God is our expression for all forces and powers which we do not understand, or with which we are unfamiliar, and for the highest ideal of wisdom, goodness and power which we can conceive, but for nothing else.

Thus God makes the grass grow because we do not understand how the air and earth and water near a piece of grass are seized by the grass and converted into more grass; but God does not mow the grass and make hay of it. It is Paul and Apollos who plant and water, but God who giveth the increase. We never say that God does anything which we can do ourselves, or ask him for anything which we know how to get in any other way. As soon as we understand a thing we remove it from the sphere of God's action.

As long as there is an unknown there will be a God for all practical purposes; the name of God has never yet been given to a known thing except by way of flattery, as to Roman Emperors, or through the attempt to symbolise the unknown generally, as in fetish worship, and then the priests had to tell the people that there was something more about the fetish than they knew of, or they would soon have ceased to think of it as God.

To understand a thing is to feel as though we could stand under or alongside of it in all its parts and form a picture of it in our minds throughout. We understand how a violin is made if our minds can follow the manufacture in all its detail and picture it to ourselves. If we feel that we can identify ourselves with the steam and machinery of a steam engine, so as to travel in imagination with the steam through all the pipes and valves, if we can see the movement of each part of the piston, connecting rod, &c., so as to be mentally one with both the steam and the mechanism throughout their whole action and construction, then we say we understand the steam engine, and the idea of God never crosses our minds in connection with it.

When we feel that we can neither do a thing ourselves, nor even learn to do it by reason of its intricacy and difficulty, and that no one else ever can or will, and yet we see the thing none the less done daily and hourly all round us, then we are not content to say we do not understand how the thing is done, we go further and ascribe the action to God. As soon as there is felt to be an unknown and apparently unknowable element, then, but not till then, does the idea God present itself to us. So at coroners' inquests juries never say the deceased died by the visitation of God if they know any of the more proximate causes.

It is not God, therefore, who sows the corn — we could sow corn ourselves, we can see the man with a bag in his hand walking over ploughed fields and sowing the corn broadcast — but it is God who made the man who goes about with the bag, and who makes the corn sprout, for we do not follow the processes that take place here.

As long as we knew nothing about what caused this or that weather we used to ascribe it to God's direct action and pray him to change it according to our wants: now that we know more about the weather there is a growing disinclination among clergymen to pray for rain or dry weather, while laymen look to nothing but the barometer. So people do not say God has shown them this or that when they have just seen it in the newspapers; they would only say that God had shown it them if it had come into their heads suddenly and after they had tried long and vainly to get at this particular point.

To lament that we cannot be more conscious of God and understand him better is much like lamenting that we are not more conscious of our circulation and digestion. Provided we live according to familiar laws of health, the less we think about circulation and digestion the better; and so with the ordinary rules of good conduct, the less we think about God the better.

To know God better is only to realise more fully how impossible it is that we should ever know him at all. I cannot tell which is the more childish — to deny him, or to attempt to define him.

Scylla and Charybdis

They are everywhere. Just now coming up Great Russell Street I loitered outside a print shop. There they were as usual — Hogarth's Idle and Virtuous Apprentices. The idle apprentice is certainly Scylla, but is not the virtuous apprentice just as much Charybdis? Is he so greatly preferable? Is not the right thing somewhere between the two? And does not the art of good living consist mainly in a fine perception of when to edge towards the idle and when towards the virtuous apprentice?

When John Bunyan (or Richard Baxter, or whoever it was) said "There went John Bunyan, but for the grace of God" (or whatever he did say), had he a right to be so cock-sure that the criminal on whom he was looking was not saying much the same thing as he looked upon John Bunyan? Does any one who knows me doubt that if I were offered my choice between a bishopric and a halter, I should choose the halter? I believe half the bishops would choose the halter themselves if they had to do it over again.

Philosophy

As a general rule philosophy is like stirring mud or not letting a sleeping dog lie. It is an attempt to deny, circumvent or otherwise escape from the consequences of the interlacing of the roots of things with one another. It professes to appease our ultimate "Why?" though in truth it is generally the solution of a *simplex ignotum* by a *complex ignotius*. This, at least, is my experience of everything that has been presented to me as philosophy. I have often had my "Why" answered with so much mystifying matter that I have left off pressing it through fatigue. But this is not having my ultimate "Why?" appeased. It is being knocked out of time.

Philosophy and Equal Temperament

It is with philosophy as with just intonation on a piano, if you get everything quite straight and on all fours in one department, in perfect tune, it is delightful so long as you keep well in the middle of the key; but as soon as you modulate you find the new key is out of tune and the more remotely you modulate the more out of tune you get. The only way is to distribute your error by equal temperament and leave common sense to make the correction in philosophy which the ear does instantaneously and involuntarily in music.

Hedging the Cuckoo

People will still keep trying to find some formula that shall hedge-in the cuckoo of mental phenomena to their satisfaction. Half the books — nay, all of them that deal with thought and its ways in the academic spirit — are but so many of these hedges in various stages of decay.

God and Philosophies

All philosophies, if you ride them home, are nonsense; but some are greater nonsense than others. It is perhaps because God does not set much store by or wish to encourage them that he has attached such very slender rewards to them.

Common Sense, Reason and Faith

Reason is not the ultimate test of truth nor is it the court of first instance.

For example: A man questions his own existence; he applies first to the court of mother-wit and is promptly told that he exists; he appeals next to reason and, after some wrangling, is told that the matter is very doubtful; he proceeds to the equity of that reasonable faith which inspires and transcends reason, and the judgment of the court of first instance is upheld while that of reason is reversed.

Nevertheless it is folly to appeal from reason to faith unless one is pretty sure of a verdict and, in most cases about which we dispute seriously, reason is as far as we need go.

The Credit System

The whole world is carried on on the credit system; if every one were to demand payment in hard cash, there would be universal bankruptcy. We think as we do mainly because other people think so. But if every one stands on every one else, what does the bottom man stand on? Faith is no foundation, for it rests in the end on reason. Reason is no foundation, for it rests upon faith.

Argument

We are not won by argument, which is like reading and writing and disappears when there is need of such vanity, or like colour that vanishes with too much light or shade, or like sound that becomes silence in the extremes. Argument is useless when there is either no conviction at all or a very strong conviction. It is a means of conviction and as such belongs to the means of conviction, not to the extremes. We are not won by arguments that we can analyse, but by tone and temper, by the manner which is the man himself.

Logic and Philosophy

When you have got all the rules and all the lore of philosophy and logic well into your head, and have spent years in getting to understand at any rate what they mean and have them at command, you will know less for practical purposes than one who has never studied logic or philosophy.

Science

If it tends to thicken the crust of ice on which, as it were, we are skating, it is all right. If it tries to find, or professes to have found, the solid ground at the bottom of the water, it is all wrong. Our business is with the thickening of this crust by extending our knowledge downward from above, as ice gets thicker while the frost lasts; we should not try to freeze upwards from the bottom.

Religion

A religion only means something so certainly posed that nothing can ever displace it. It is an attempt to settle first principles so authoritatively that no one need so much as even think of ever re-opening them for himself or feel any, even the faintest, misgiving upon the matter. It is an attempt to get an irrefragably safe investment, and this cannot be got, no matter how low the interest, which in the case of religion is about as low as it can be.

Any religion that cannot be founded on half a sheet of note-paper will be bottom-heavy, and this, in a matter so essentially of sentiment as religion, is as bad as being top-heavy in a material construction. It must of course catch on to reason, but the less it emphasises the fact the better.

Logic

Logic has no place save with that which can be defined in words. It has nothing to do, therefore, with those deeper questions that have got beyond words and consciousness. To apply logic here is as fatuous as to disregard it in cases where it is applicable. The difficulty lies, as it always does, on the border lines between the respective spheres of influence.

Logic and Faith

Logic is like the sword—those who appeal to it shall perish by it. Faith is appealing to the living God, and one may perish by that too, but somehow one would rather perish that way than the other, and one has got to perish sooner or later.

Common Sense and Philosophy

The voices of common sense and of high philosophy sometimes cross; but common sense is the unalterable canto fermo and philosophy is the variable counterpoint.

First Principles

It is said we can build no superstructure without a foundation of unshakable principles. There are no such principles. Or, if there be any, they are beyond our reach—we cannot fathom them; therefore, *qua* us, they have no existence, for there is no other "is not" than inconceivableness by ourselves. There is one thing certain, namely, that we can have nothing certain; therefore it is not certain that we can have nothing certain. We are as men who will insist on looking over the brink of a precipice; some few can gaze into the abyss below without losing their heads, but most men will grow dizzy and fall. The only thing to do is to glance at the chaos on which our thoughts are founded, recognise that it is a chaos and that, in the nature of things, no theoretically firm ground is even conceivable, and then to turn aside with the disgust, fear and horror of one who has been looking into his own entrails.

Even Euclid cannot lay a demonstrable premise, he requires postulates and axioms which transcend demonstration and without which he can do nothing. His superstructure is demonstration, his ground is faith. And so his *ultima ratio* is to tell a man that he is a fool by saying "Which is absurd." If his opponent chooses to hold out in spite of this, Euclid can do no more. Faith and authority are as necessary for him as for any one else. True, he does not want us to believe very much; his yoke is tolerably easy, and he will not call a man a fool until he will have public opinion generally on his side; but none the less does he begin with dogmatism and end with persecution.

There is nothing one cannot wrangle about. Sensible people will agree to a middle course founded upon a few general axioms and propositions about which, right or wrong, they will not think it worth while to wrangle for some time, and those who reject these can be put into mad-houses. The middle way may be as full of hidden rocks as the other ways are of manifest ones, but it is the pleasantest while we can keep to it and the dangers, being hidden, are less alarming.

In practice it is seldom very hard to do one's duty when one knows what it is, but it is sometimes exceedingly difficult to find this out. The difficulty is, however, often reducible into that of knowing what gives one pleasure, and this, though difficult, is a safer guide and more easily distinguished. In all cases of doubt, the promptings of a kindly disposition are more trustworthy than the conclusions of logic, and sense is better than science.

Why I should have been at the pains to write such truisms I know not.

XXI
Rebelliousness

God and Life

We regard these as two distinct things and say that the first made the second, much as, till lately, we regarded memory and heredity as two distinct things having less connection than even that supposed to exist between God and life. Now, however, that we know heredity to be only a necessary outcome, development and manifestation of memory — so that, given such a faculty as memory, the faculty of heredity follows as being inherent therein and bound to issue from it — in like manner presently, instead of seeing life as a thing created by God, we shall see God and life as one thing, there being no life without God nor God without life, where there is life there is God and where there is God there is life.

They say that God is love, but life and love are co-extensive; for hate is but a mode of love, as life and death lurk always in one another; and "God is life" is not far off saying "God is love." Again, they say, "Where there is life there is hope," but hope is of the essence of God, for it is faith and hope that have underlain all evolution.

God and Flesh

The course of true God never did run smooth. God to be of any use must be made manifest, and he can only be made manifest in and through flesh. And flesh to be of any use (except for eating) must be alive, and it can only be alive by being inspired of God. The trouble lies in the getting the flesh and the God together in the right proportions. There is lots of God and lots of flesh, but the flesh has always got too much God or too little, and the God has always too little flesh or too much.

Gods and Prophets

It is the manner of gods and prophets to begin: "Thou shalt have none other God or Prophet but me." If I were to start as a god or a prophet, I think I should take the line:

"Thou shalt not believe in me. Thou shalt not have me for a god. Thou shalt worship any damned thing thou likest except me." This should be my first and great commandment, and my second should be like unto it. [333]

Faith and Reason

The instinct towards brushing faith aside and being strictly reasonable is strong and natural; so also is the instinct towards brushing logic and consistency on one side if they become troublesome, in other words—so is the instinct towards basing action on a faith which is beyond reason. It is because both instincts are so natural that so many accept and so many reject Catholicism. The two go along for some time as very good friends and then fight; sometimes one beats and sometimes the other, but they always make it up again and jog along as before, for they have a great respect for one another.

God and the Devil

God's merits are so transcendent that it is not surprising his faults should be in reasonable proportion. The faults are, indeed, on such a scale that, when looked at without relation to the merits with which they are interwoven, they become so appalling that people shrink from ascribing them to the Deity and have invented the Devil, without seeing that there would be more excuse for God's killing the Devil, and so getting rid of evil, than there can be for his failing to be everything that he would like to be.

For God is not so white as he is painted, and he gets on better with the Devil than people think. The Devil is too useful for him to wish him ill and, in like manner, half the Devil's trade would be at an end should any great mishap bring God well down in the world. For all the mouths they make at one another they play into each other's hands and have got on so well as partners, playing Spenlow and Jorkins to one another, for so many years that there seems no reason why they should cease to do so. The conception of them as the one absolutely void of evil and the other of good is a vulgar notion taken from science whose priests have ever sought to get every idea and every substance pure of all alloy.

God and the Devil are about as four to three. There is enough preponderance of God to make it far safer to be on his side than on the Devil's, but the excess is not so great as his professional claqueurs pretend it is. It is like gambling at Monte Carlo; if you play long enough you are sure to lose, but now and again you may win a great deal of excellent money if you will only cease playing the moment you have won it.

Christianity

i

As an instrument of warfare against vice, or as a tool for making virtue, Christianity is a mere flint implement.

ii

Christianity is a woman's religion, invented by women and womanish men for themselves. The Church's one foundation is not Christ, as is commonly said, it is woman; and calling the Madonna the Queen of Heaven is only a poetical way of acknowledging that women are the main support of the priests.

iii

It is not the church in a village that is the source of the mischief, but the rectory. I would not touch a church from one end of England to the other.

iv

Christianity is only seriously pretended by some among the idle, bourgeois middle-classes. The working classes and the most cultured intelligence of the time reach by short cuts what the highways of our schools and universities mislead us from by many a winding bout, if they do not prevent our ever reaching it.

v

It is not easy to say which is the more obvious, the antecedent improbability of the Christian scheme and miracles, or the breakdown of the evidences on which these are supposed to rest. And yet Christianity has overrun the world.

vi

If there is any moral in Christianity, if there is anything to be learned from it, if the whole story is not profitless from first to last, it comes to this that a man should back his own opinion against the world's—and this is a very risky and immoral thing to do, but the Lord hath mercy on whom he will have mercy.

vii

Christianity is true in so far as it has fostered beauty and false in so far as it has fostered ugliness. It is therefore not a little true and not a little false.

viii

Christ said he came not to destroy but to fulfil—but he destroyed more than he fulfilled. Every system that is to live must both destroy and fulfil.

Miracles

They do more to unsettle faith in the existing order than to settle it in any other; similarly, missionaries are more valuable as underminers of old faiths than as propagators of new. Miracles are not impossible; nothing is impossible till we have got an incontrovertible first premise. The question is not "Are the Christian miracles possible?" but "Are they convenient? Do they fit comfortably with our other ideas?"

Wants and Creeds

As in the organic world there is no organ, so in the world of thought there is no thought, which may not be called into existence by long persistent effort. If a man wants either to believe or disbelieve the Christian miracles he can do so if he tries hard enough; but if he does not care whether he believes or disbelieves and simply wants to find out which side has the best of it, this he will find a more difficult matter. Nevertheless he will probably be able to do this too if he tries.

Faith

i

The reason why the early Christians held faith in such account was because they felt it to be a feat of such superhuman difficulty.

ii

You can do very little with faith, but you can do nothing without it.

iii

We are all agreed that too much faith is as bad as too little, and too little as bad as too much; but we differ as to what is too much and what too little.

iv

It is because both Catholics and myself make faith, not reason, the basis of our system that I am able to be easy in mind about not becoming a Catholic. Not that I ever wanted to become a Catholic, but I mean I believe I can beat them with their own weapons.

v

A man may have faith as a mountain, but he will not be able to say to a grain of mustard seed: "Be thou removed, and be thou cast into the sea" — not at least with any effect upon the mustard seed — unless he goes the right way to work by putting the mustard seed into his pocket and taking the train to Brighton.

vi

The just live by faith, but they not infrequently also die by it.

The Cuckoo and the Moon

The difference between the Christian and the Mahomedan is only as the difference between one who will turn his money when he first hears the cuckoo, but thinks it folly to do so on seeing the new moon, and one who will turn it religiously at the new moon, but will scout the notion that he need do so on hearing the cuckoo.

Buddhism

This seems to be a jumble of Christianity and *Life and Habit*.

Theist and Atheist

The fight between them is as to whether God shall be called God or shall have some other name.

The Peculiar People

The only people in England who really believe in God are the Peculiar People. Perhaps that is why they are called peculiar. See how belief in an anthropomorphic God divides allegiance and disturbs civil order as soon as it becomes vital.

Renan

There is an article on him in the *Times*, April 30, 1883, of the worst *Times* kind, and that is saying much. It appears he whines about his lost faith and professes to wish that he could believe as he believed when young. No sincere man will regret having attained a truer view concerning anything which he has ever believed. And then he talks about the difficulties of coming to disbelieve the Christian miracles as though it were a great intellectual feat. This is very childish. I hope no one will say I was sorry when I found out that there was no reason for believing in heaven and hell. My contempt for Renan has no limits. (Has he an accent to his name? I despise him too much to find out.)

The Spiritual Treadmill

The Church of England has something in her liturgy of the spiritual treadmill. It is a very nice treadmill no doubt, but Sunday after Sunday we keep step with the same old "We have left undone that which we ought to have done; And we have done those things which we ought not to have done" without making any progress. With the Church of Rome, I understand that those whose piety is sufficiently approved are told they may consider themselves as a finished article and that, except on some few rare festivals, they need no longer keep on going to church and confessing. The picture is completed and may be framed, glazed and hung up.

The Dim Religious Light

A light cannot be religious if it is not dim. Religion belongs to the twilight of our thoughts, just as business of all kinds to their full daylight. So a picture which may be impressive while seen in a dark light will not hold its own in a bright one.

The Greeks and Romans did not enquire into the evidences on which their belief that Minerva sprang full-armed from the brain of Jupiter was based. If they had written books of evidences to show how certainly it all happened, &c.—well, I suppose if they had had an endowed Church with some considerable prizes, they would have found means to hoodwink the public.

The Peace that Passeth Understanding

Yes. But as there is a peace more comfortable than any understanding, so also there is an understanding more covetable than any peace.

The New Testament

If it is a testamentary disposition at all, it is so drawn that it has given rise to incessant litigation during the last nearly two thousand years and seems likely to continue doing so for a good many years longer. It ought never to have been admitted to probate. Either the testator drew it himself, in which case we have another example of the folly of trying to make one's own will, or if he left it to the authors of the several books—this is like employing many lawyers to do the work of one.

Christ and the L. & N.W. Railway

Admitting for the moment that Christ can be said to have died for me in any sense, it is only pretended that he did so in the same sort of way as the London and North Western Railway was made for me. Granted that I am very glad the railway was made and use it when I find it convenient, I do not suppose that those who projected and made the line allowed me to enter into their thoughts; the debt of my gratitude is divided among so many that the amount due from each one is practically nil.

The Jumping Cat

God is only a less jumping kind of jumping cat; and those who worship God are still worshippers of the jumping cat all the time. There is no getting away from the jumping cat—if I climb up into heaven, it is there; if I go down to hell, it is there also; if I take the wings of the morning and remain in the uttermost parts of the sea, even there, and so on; it is about my path and about my bed and spieth out all my ways. It is the eternal underlying verity or the eternal underlying lie, as people may choose to call it.

Personified Science

Science is being daily more and more personified and anthropomorphised into a god. By and by they will say that science took our nature upon him, and sent down his only begotten son, Charles Darwin, or Huxley, into the world so that those who believe in him, &c.; and they will burn people for saying that science, after all, is only an expression for our ignorance of our own ignorance.

Science and Theology

We should endow neither; we should treat them as we treat conservatism and liberalism, encouraging both, so that they may keep watch upon one another, and letting them go in and out of power with the popular vote concerning them.

The world is better carried on upon the barrister principle of special pleading upon two sides before an impartial ignorant tribunal, to whom things have got to be explained, than it would be if nobody were to maintain any opinion in which he did not personally believe.

What we want is to reconcile both science and theology with sincerity and good breeding, to make our experts understand that they are nothing if they are not single-minded and urbane. Get them to understand this, and there will be no difficulty about reconciling science and theology.

The Church and the Supernatural

If we saw the Church wishing to back out of the supernatural and anxious to explain it away where possible, we would keep our disbelief in the supernatural in the background, as far as we could, and would explain away our rejection of the miracles, as far as was decent; furthermore we would approximate our language to theirs wherever possible, and insist on the points on which we are all agreed, rather than on points of difference; in fact, we would meet them half way and be only too glad to do it. I maintain that in my books I actually do this as much as is possible, but I shall try and do it still more. As a matter of fact, however, the Church clings to the miraculous element of Christianity more fondly than ever; she parades it more and more, and shows no sign of wishing to give up even the smallest part of it. It is this which makes us despair of being able to do anything with her and feel that either she or we must go.

Gratitude and Revenge

Gratitude is as much an evil to be minimised as revenge is. Justice, our law and our law courts are for the taming and regulating of revenge. Current prices and markets and commercial regulations are for the taming of gratitude and its reduction from a public nuisance to something which shall at least be tolerable. Revenge and gratitude are correlative terms. Our system of commerce is a protest against the unbridled licence of gratitude. Gratitude, in fact, like revenge, is a mistake unless under certain securities.

Cant and Hypocrisy

We should organise a legitimate channel for instincts so profound as these, just as we have found it necessary to do with lust and revenge by the institutions of marriage and the law courts. This is the *raison d'être* of the church. You kill a man just as much whether you murder him or hang him after the formalities of a trial. And so with lust and marriage, *mutatis mutandis*. So again with the professions of religion and medicine. You swindle a man as much when you sell him a drug of whose action you are ignorant, and tell him it will protect him from disease, as when you give him a bit of bread, which you assure him is the body of Jesus Christ, and then send a plate round for a subscription. You swindle him as much by these acts as if you picked his pocket, or obtained money from him under false pretences in any other way; but you swindle him according to the rules and in an authorised way.

Real Blasphemy

On one of our Sunday walks near London we passed a forlorn and dilapidated Primitive Methodist Chapel. The windows were a good deal broken and there was a notice up offering 10/- reward to any one who should give such information as should lead to the, &c. Cut in stone over the door was this inscription, and we thought it as good an example of real blasphemy as we had ever seen:

> When God makes up his last account
> Of holy children in his mount,
> 'Twill be an honour to appear
> As one new born and nourished here.

The English Church Abroad

People say you must not try to abolish Christianity until you have something better to put in its place. They might as well say we must not take away turnpikes and corn laws till we have some other hindrances to put in their place. Besides no one wants to abolish Christianity — all we want is not to be snubbed and bullied if we reject the miraculous part of it for ourselves.

At Biella an English clergyman asked if I was a Roman Catholic. I said, quite civilly, that I was not a Catholic.

He replied that he had asked me not if I was a Catholic but if I was a Roman Catholic. What was I? Was I an Anglican Catholic? So, seeing that he meant to argue, I replied:

"I do not know. I am a Londoner and of the same religion as people generally are in London."

This made him angry. He snorted:

"Oh, that's nothing at all;" and almost immediately left the table.

As much as possible I keep away from English-frequented hotels in Italy and Switzerland because I find that if I do not go to service on Sunday I am made uncomfortable. It is this bullying that I want to do away with. As regards Christianity I should hope and think that I am more Christian than not.

People ought to be allowed to leave their cards at church, instead of going inside. I have half a mind to try this next time I am in a foreign hotel among English people.

Drunkenness

When we were at Shrewsbury the other day, coming up the Abbey Foregate, we met a funeral and debated whether or not to take our hats off. We always do in Italy, that is to say in the country and in villages and small towns, but we have been told that it is not the custom to do so in large towns and in cities, which raises a question as to the exact figure that should be reached by the population of a place before one need not take off one's hat to a funeral in one of its streets. At Shrewsbury seeing no one doing it we thought it might look singular and kept ours on. My friend Mr. Phillips, the tailor, was in one carriage, I did not see him, but he saw me and afterwards told me he had pointed me out to a clergyman who was in the carriage with him.

"Oh," said the clergyman, "then that's the man who says England owes all her greatness to intoxication."

This is rather a free translation of what I did say; but it only shows how impossible it is to please those who do not wish to be pleased. Tennyson may talk about the slow sad hours that bring us all things ill and all good things from evil, because this is vague and indefinite; but I may not say that, in spite of the terrible consequences of drunkenness, man's intellectual development would not have reached its present stage without the stimulus of alcohol—which I believe to be both perfectly true and pretty generally admitted—because this is definite. I do not think I said more than this and am sure that no one can detest drunkenness more than I do. [343] It seems to me it will be wiser in me not to try to make headway at Shrewsbury.

Hell-Fire

If Vesuvius does not frighten those who live under it, is it likely that Hell-fire should frighten any reasonable person?

I met a traveller who had returned from Hades where he had conversed with Tantalus and with others of the shades. They all agreed that for the first six, or perhaps twelve, months they disliked their punishment very much; but after that, it was like shelling peas on a hot afternoon in July. They began by discovering (no doubt long after the fact had been apparent enough to every one else) that they had not been noticing what they were doing so much as usual, and that they had been even thinking of something else. From this moment, the automatic stage of action having set in, the progress towards always thinking of something else was rapid and they soon forgot that they were undergoing any punishment.

Tantalus did get a little something not infrequently; water stuck to the hairs of his body and he gathered it up in his hand; he also got many an apple when the wind was napping as it had to do sometimes. Perhaps he could have done with more, but he got enough to keep him going quite comfortably. His sufferings were nothing as compared with those of a needy heir to a fortune whose father, or whoever it may be, catches a dangerous bronchitis every winter but invariably recovers and lives to 91, while the heir survives him a month having been worn out with long expectation.

Sisyphus had never found any pleasure in life comparable to the delight of seeing his stone bound down-hill, and in so timing its rush as to inflict the greatest possible scare on any unwary shade who might be wandering below. He got so great and such varied amusement out of this that his labour had become the automatism of reflex action—which is, I understand, the name applied by men of science to all actions that are done without reflection. He was a pompous, ponderous old gentleman, very irritable and always thinking that the other shades were laughing at him or trying to take advantage of him. There were two, however, whom he hated with a fury that tormented him far more seriously than anything else ever did. The first of these was Archimedes who had instituted a series of experiments in regard to various questions connected with mechanics and had conceived a scheme by which he hoped to utilise the motive power of the stone for the purpose of lighting Hades with electricity. The other was Agamemnon, who took good care to keep out of the stone's way when it was more than a quarter of the distance up the slope, but who delighted in teasing Sisyphus so long as he considered it safe to do so. Many of the other shades took daily pleasure in gathering together about stone-time to enjoy the fun and to bet on how far the stone would roll.

As for Tityus—what is a bird more or less on a body that covers nine acres? He found the vultures a gentle stimulant to the liver without which it would have become congested.

Sir Isaac Newton was intensely interested in the hygrometric and barometric proceedings of the Danaids.

"At any rate," said one of them to my informant, "if we really are being punished, for goodness' sake don't say anything about it or we may be put to other work. You see, we must be doing something, and now we know how to do this, we don't want the bother of learning something new. You may be right, but we have not got to make our living by it, and what in the name of reason can it matter whether the sieves ever get full or not?"

My traveller reported much the same with regard to the eternal happiness on Mount Olympus. Hercules found Hebe a fool and could never get her off his everlasting knee. He would have sold his soul to find another Ægisthus.

So Jove saw all this and it set him thinking.

"It seems to me," said he, "that Olympus and Hades are both failures."

Then he summoned a council and the whole matter was thoroughly discussed. In the end Jove abdicated, and the gods came down from Olympus and assumed mortality. They had some years of very enjoyable Bohemian existence going about as a company of strolling players at French and Belgian town fairs; after which they died in the usual way, having discovered at last that it does not matter how high up or how low down you are, that happiness and misery are not absolute but depend on the direction in which you are tending and consist in a progression towards better or worse, and that pleasure, like pain and like everything that grows, holds in perfection but a little moment.

XXII
Reconciliation

Religion

By religion I mean a living sense that man proposes and God disposes, that we must watch and pray that we enter not into temptation, that he who thinketh he standeth must take heed lest he fall, and the countless other like elementary maxims which a man must hold as he holds life itself if he is to be a man at all.

If religion, then, is to be formulated and made tangible to the people, it can only be by means of symbols, counters and analogies, more or less misleading, for no man professes to have got to the root of the matter and to have seen the eternal underlying verity face to face—and even though he could see it he could not grip it and hold it and convey it to another who has not. Therefore either these feelings must be left altogether unexpressed and, if unexpressed, then soon undeveloped and atrophied, or they must be expressed by the help of images or idols—by the help of something not more actually true than a child's doll is to a child, but yet helpful to our weakness of understanding, as the doll no doubt gratifies and stimulates the motherly instinct in the child.

Therefore we ought not to cavil at the visible superstition and absurdity of much on which religion is made to rest, for the unknown can never be satisfactorily rendered into the known. To get the known from the unknown is to get something out of nothing, a thing which, though it is being done daily in every fraction of every second everywhere, is logically impossible of conception, and we can only think by logic, for what is not in logic is not in thought. So that the attempt to symbolise the unknown is certain to involve inconsistencies and absurdities of all kinds and it is childish to complain of their existence unless one is prepared to advocate the stifling of all religious sentiment, and this is like trying to stifle hunger or thirst. To be at all is to be religious more or less. There never was any man who did not feel that behind this world and above it and about it there is an unseen world greater and more incomprehensible than anything he can conceive, and this feeling, so profound and so universal, needs expression. If expressed it can only be so by the help of inconsistencies and errors. These, then, are not to be ordered impatiently out of court; they have grown up as the best guesses at truth that could be made at any given time, but they must become more or less obsolete as our knowledge of truth is enlarged. Things become known which were formerly unknown and, though this brings us no nearer to ultimate universal truth, yet it shows us that many of our guesses were wrong. Everything that catches on to realism and naturalism as much as Christianity does must be affected by any profound modification in our views of realism and naturalism.

God and Convenience

I do not know or care whether the expression "God" has scientific accuracy or no, nor yet whether it has theological value; I know nothing either of one or the other, beyond looking upon the recognised exponents both of science and theology with equal distrust; but for convenience, I am sure that there is nothing like it—I mean for convenience of getting quickly at the right or wrong of a matter. While you are fumbling away with your political economy or your biblical precepts to know whether you shall let old Mrs. So-and-so have 5/- or no, another, who has just asked himself which would be most well-pleasing in the sight of God, will be told in a moment that he should give her—or not give her—the 5/-. As a general rule she had better have the 5/- at once, but sometimes we must give God to understand that, though we should he very glad to do what he would have of us if we reasonably could, yet the present is one of those occasions on which we must decline to do so.

The World

Even the world, so mondain as it is, still holds instinctively and as a matter of faith unquestionable that those who have died by the altar are worthier than those who have lived by it, when to die was duty.

Blasphemy

I begin to understand now what Christ meant when he said that blasphemy against the Holy Ghost was unforgiveable, while speaking against the Son of Man might be forgiven. He must have meant that a man may be pardoned for being unable to believe in the Christian mythology, but that if he made light of that spirit which the common conscience of all men, whatever their particular creed, recognises as divine, there was no hope for him. No more there is.

Gaining One's Point

It is not he who gains the exact point in dispute who scores most in controversy, but he who has shown the most forbearance and the better temper.

The Voice of Common Sense

It is this, and not the Voice of the Lord, which maketh men to be of one mind in an house. But then, the Voice of the Lord is the voice of common sense which is shared by all that is.

Amendes Honorables

There is hardly an offence so great but if it be frankly apologised for it is easily both forgiven and forgotten. There is hardly an offence so small but it rankles if he who has committed it does not express proportionate regret. Expressions of regret help genuine regret and induce amendment of life, much as digging a channel helps water to flow, though it does not make the water. If a man refuses to make them and habitually indulges his own selfishness at the expense of what is due to other people, he is no better than a drunkard or a debauchee, and I have no more respect for him than I have for the others.

We all like to forgive, and we all love best not those who offend us least, nor those who have done most for us, but those who make it most easy for us to forgive them.

So a man may lose both his legs and live for years in health if the amputation has been clean and skilful, whereas a pea in his boot may set up irritation which must last as long as the pea is there and may in the end kill him.

Forgiveness and Retribution

It is no part of the bargain that we are never to commit trespasses. The bargain is that if we would be forgiven we must forgive them that trespass against us. Nor again is it part of the bargain that we are to let a man hob-nob with us when we know him to be a thorough blackguard, merely on the plea that unless we do so we shall not be forgiving him his trespasses. No hard and fast rule can be laid down, each case must be settled instinctively as it arises.

As a sinner I am interested in the principle of forgiveness; as sinned against, in that of retribution. I have what is to me a considerable vested interest in both these principles, but I should say I had more in forgiveness than in retribution. And so it probably is with most people or we should have had a clause in the Lord's prayer: "And pay out those who have sinned against us as they whom we have sinned against generally pay us out."

Inaccuracy

I am not sure that I do not begin to like the correction of a mistake, even when it involves my having shown much ignorance and stupidity, as well as I like hitting on a new idea. It does comfort one so to be able to feel sure that one knows how to tumble and how to retreat promptly and without chagrin. Being bowled over in inaccuracy, when I have tried to verify, makes me careful. But if I have not tried to verify and then turn out wrong, this, if I find it out, upsets me very much and I pray that I may be found out whenever I do it.

Jutland and "Waitee"

I made a mistake in *The Authoress of the Odyssey* [in a note on] when I said "Scheria means Jutland—a piece of land jutting out into the sea." Jutland means the Land of the Jutes.

And I made a mistake in *Alps and Sanctuaries* [Chap. III], speaking of the peasants in the Val Leventina knowing English, when I said "One English word has become universally adopted by the Ticinesi themselves. They say 'Waitee' just as we should say 'Wait' to stop some one from going away. It is abhorrent to them to end a word with a consonant so they have added 'ee,' but there can be no doubt about the origin of the word." The Avvocato Negri of Casale-Monferrato says that they have a word in their dialetto which, if ever written, would appear as "vuaitee," it means "stop" or "look here," and is used to attract attention. This, or something like it, no doubt is what they really say and has no more to do with waiting than Jutland has to do with jutting.

The Parables

The people do not act reasonably in a single instance. The sower was a bad sower; the shepherd who left his ninety and nine sheep in the wilderness was a foolish shepherd; the husbandman who would not have his corn weeded was no farmer—and so on. None of them go nearly on all fours, they halt so much as to have neither literary nor moral value to any but slipshod thinkers.

Granted, but are we not all slipshod thinkers?

The Irreligion of Orthodoxy

We do not fall foul of Christians for their religion, but for what we hold to be their want of religion—for the low views they take of God and of his glory, and for the unworthiness with which they try to serve him.

Society and Christianity

The burden of society is really a very light one. She does not require us to believe the Christian religion, she has very vague ideas as to what the Christian religion is, much less does she require us to practise it. She is quite satisfied if we do not obtrude our disbelief in it in an offensive manner. Surely this is no very grievous burden.

Sanctified by Faith

No matter how great a fraud a thing may have been or be, if it has passed through many minds an aroma of life attaches to it and it must be handled with a certain reverence. A thing or a thought becomes hallowed if it has been long and strongly believed in, for veneration, after a time, seems to get into the thing venerated. Look at Delphi—fraud of frauds, yet sanctified by centuries of hope and fear and faith. If greater knowledge shows Christianity to have been founded upon error, still greater knowledge shows that it was aiming at a truth.

Ourselves and the Clergy

As regards the best of the clergy, whether English or foreign, I feel that they and we mean in substance the same thing, and that the difference is only about the way this thing should be put and the evidence on which it should be considered to rest.

We say that they jeopardise the acceptance of the principles which they and we alike cordially regard as fundamental by basing them on assertions which a little investigation shows to be untenable. They reply that by declaring the assertions to be untenable we jeopardise the principles. We answer that this is not so and that moreover we can find better, safer and more obvious assertions on which to base them.

The Rules of Life

Whether it is right to say that one believes in God and Christianity without intending what one knows the hearer intends one to intend depends on how much or how little the hearer can understand. Life is not an exact science, it is an art. Just as the contention, excellent so far as it goes, that each is to do what is right in his own eyes leads, when ridden to death, to anarchy and chaos, so the contention that every one should be either self-effacing or truthful to the bitter end reduces life to an absurdity. If we seek real rather than technical truth, it is more true to be considerately untruthful within limits than to be inconsiderately truthful without them. What the limits are we generally know but cannot say.

There is an unbridgeable chasm between thought and words that we must jump as best we can, and it is just here that the two hitch on to one another. The higher rules of life transcend the sphere of language; they cannot be gotten by speech, neither shall logic be weighed for the price thereof. They have their being in the fear of the Lord and in the departing from evil without even knowing in words what the Lord is, nor the fear of the Lord, nor yet evil.

Common straightforwardness and kindliness are the highest points that man or woman can reach, but they should no more be made matters of conversation than should the lowest vices. Extremes meet here as elsewhere and the extremes of vice and virtue are alike common and unmentionable.

There is nothing for it but a very humble hope that from the Great Unknown Source our daily insight and daily strength may be given us with our daily bread. And what is this but Christianity, whether we believe that Jesus Christ rose from the dead or not? So that Christianity is like a man's soul—he who finds may lose it and he who loses may find it.

If, then, a man may be a Christian while believing himself hostile to all that some consider most essential in Christianity, may he not also be a free-thinker (in the common use of the word) while believing himself hostile to free-thought?

XXIII
Death

Fore-knowledge of Death

No one thinks he will escape death, so there is no disappointment and, as long as we know neither the when nor the how, the mere fact that we shall one day have to go does not much affect us; we do not care, even though we know vaguely that we have not long to live. The serious trouble begins when death becomes definite in time and shape. It is in precise fore-knowledge, rather than in sin, that the sting of death is to be found; and such fore-knowledge is generally withheld; though, strangely enough, many would have it if they could.

Continued Identity

I do not doubt that a person who will grow out of me as I now am, but of whom I know nothing now and in whom therefore I can take none but the vaguest interest, will one day undergo so sudden and complete a change that his friends must notice it and call him dead; but as I have no definite ideas concerning this person, not knowing whether he will be a man of 59 or 79 or any age between these two, so this person will, I am sure, have forgotten the very existence of me as I am at this present moment. If it is said that no matter how wide a difference of condition may exist between myself now and myself at the moment of death, or how complete the forgetfulness of connection on either side may be, yet the fact of the one's having grown out of the other by an infinite series of gradations makes the second personally identical with the first, then I say that the difference between the corpse and the till recently living body is not great enough, either in respect of material change or of want of memory concerning the earlier existence, to bar personal identity and prevent us from seeing the corpse as alive and a continuation of the man from whom it was developed, though having tastes and other characteristics very different from those it had while it was a man.

From this point of view there is no such thing as death—I mean no such thing as the death which we have commonly conceived of hitherto. A man is much more alive when he is what we call alive than when he is what we call dead; but no matter how much he is alive, he is still in part dead, and no matter how much he is dead, he is still in part alive, and his corpse-hood is connected with his living body-hood by gradations which even at the moment of death are ordinarily subtle; and the corpse does not forget the living body more completely than the living body has forgotten a thousand or a hundred thousand of its own previous states; so that we should see the corpse as a person, of greatly and abruptly changed habits it is true, but still of habits of some sort, for hair and nails continue to grow after death, and with an individuality which is as much identical with that of the person from whom it has arisen as this person was with himself as an embryo of a week old, or indeed more so.

If we have identity between the embryo and the octogenarian, we must have it also between the octogenarian and the corpse, and do away with death except as a rather striking change of thought and habit, greater indeed in degree than, but still, in kind, substantially the same as any of the changes which we have experienced from moment to moment throughout that fragment of existence which we commonly call our life; so that in sober seriousness there is no such thing as absolute death, just as there is no such thing as absolute life.

Either this, or we must keep death at the expense of personal identity, and deny identity between any two states which present considerable differences and neither of which has any fore-knowledge of, or recollection of the other. In this case, if there be death at all, it is some one else who dies and not we, because while we are alive we are not dead, and as soon as we are dead we are no longer ourselves.

So that it comes in the end to this, that either there is no such thing as death at all, or else that, if there is, it is some one else who dies and not we. We cannot blow hot and cold with the same breath. If we would retain personal identity at all, we must continue it beyond what we call death, in which case death ceases to be what we have hitherto thought it, that is to say, the end of our being. We cannot have both personal identity and death too.

Complete Death

To die completely, a person must not only forget but be forgotten, and he who is not forgotten is not dead. This is as old as *non omnis moriar* and a great deal older, but very few people realise it.

Life and Death

When I was young I used to think the only certain thing about life was that I should one day die. Now I think the only certain thing about life is that there is no such thing as death.

The Defeat of Death

There is nothing which at once affects a man so much and so little as his own death. It is a case in which the going-to-happen-ness of a thing is of greater importance than the actual thing itself which cannot be of importance to the man who dies, for Death cuts his own throat in the matter of hurting people. As a bee that can sting once but in the stinging dies, so Death is dead to him who is dead already. While he is shaking his wings, there is *brutum fulmen* but the man goes on living, frightened, perhaps, but unhurt; pain and sickness may hurt him but the moment Death strikes him both he and Death are beyond feeling. It is as though Death were born anew with every man; the two protect one another so long as they keep one another at arm's length, but if they once embrace it is all over with both.

The Torture of Death

The fabled pains of Tantalus, Sisyphus and all the rest of them show what an instinctive longing there is in all men both for end and endlessness of both good and ill, but as torture they are the merest mockery when compared with the fruitless chase to which poor Death has been condemned for ever and ever. Does it not seem as though he too must have committed some crime for which his sentence is to be for ever grasping after that which becomes non-existent the moment he grasps it? But then I suppose it would be with him as with the rest of the tortured, he must either die himself, which he has not done, or become used to it and enjoy the frightening as much as the killing. Any pain through which a man can live at all becomes unfelt as soon as it becomes habitual. Pain consists not in that which is now endured but in the strong memory of something better that is still recent. And so, happiness lies in the memory of a recent worse and the expectation of a better that is to come soon.

Ignorance of Death

i

The fear of death is instinctive because in so many past generations we have feared it. But how did we come to know what death is so that we should fear it? The answer is that we do not know what death is and that this is why we fear it.

ii

If a man know not life which he hath seen how shall he know death which he hath not seen?

iii

If a man has sent his teeth and his hair and perhaps two or three limbs to the grave before him, the presumption should be that, as he knows nothing further of these when they have once left him, so will he know nothing of the rest of him when it too is dead. The whole may surely be argued from the parts.

iv

To write about death is to write about that of which we have had little practical experience. We can write about conscious life, but we have no consciousness of the deaths we daily die. Besides, we cannot eat our cake and have it. We cannot have *tabulæ rasæ* and *tabulæ scriptæ* at the same time. We cannot be at once dead enough to be reasonably registered as such, and alive enough to be able to tell people all about it.

v

There will come a supreme moment in which there will be care neither for ourselves nor for others, but a complete abandon, a *sans souci* of unspeakable indifference, and this moment will never be taken from us; time cannot rob us of it but, as far as we are concerned, it will last for ever and ever without flying. So that, even for the most wretched and most guilty, there is a heaven at last where neither moth nor rust doth corrupt and where thieves do not break through nor steal. To himself every one is an immortal: he may know that he is going to die, but he can never know that he is dead.

vi

If life is an illusion, then so is death—the greatest of all illusions. If life must not be taken too seriously—then so neither must death.

vii

The dead are often just as living to us as the living are, only we cannot get them to believe it. They can come to us, but till we die we cannot go to them. To be dead is to be unable to understand that one is alive.

Dissolution

Death is the dissolving of a partnership, the partners to which survive and go elsewhere. It is the corruption or breaking up of that society which we have called Ourself. The corporation is at an end, both its soul and its body cease as a whole, but the immortal constituents do not cease and never will. The souls of some men transmigrate in great part into their children, but there is a large alloy in respect both of body and mind through sexual generation; the souls of other men migrate into books, pictures, music, or what not; and every one's mind migrates somewhere, whether remembered and admired or the reverse. The living souls of Handel, Shakespeare, Rembrandt, Giovanni Bellini and the other great ones appear and speak to us in their works with less alloy than they could ever speak through their children; but men's bodies disappear absolutely on death, except they be in some measure preserved in their children and in so far as harmonics of all that has been remain.

On death we do not lose life, we only lose individuality; we live henceforth in others not in ourselves. Our mistake has been in not seeing that death is indeed, like birth, a salient feature in the history of the individual, but one which wants exploding as the end of the individual, no less than birth wanted exploding as his beginning.

Dying is only a mode of forgetting. We shall see this more easily if we consider forgetting to be a mode of dying. So the ancients called their River of Death, Lethe—the River of Forgetfulness. They ought also to have called their River of Life, Mnemosyne—the River of Memory. We should learn to tune death a good deal flatter than according to received notions.

The Dislike of Death

We cannot like both life and death at once; no one can be expected to like two such opposite things at the same time; if we like life we must dislike death, and if we leave off disliking death we shall soon die. Death will always be more avoided than sought; for living involves effort, perceived or unperceived, central or departmental, and this will only be made by those who dislike the consequences of not making it more than the trouble of making it. A race, therefore, which is to exist at all must be a death-disliking race, for it is only at the cost of death that we can rid ourselves of all aversion to the idea of dying, so that the hunt after a philosophy which shall strip death of his terrors is like trying to find the philosopher's stone which cannot be found and which, if found, would defeat its own object.

Moreover, as a discovery which should rid us of the fear of death would be the vainest, so also it would be the most immoral of discoveries, for the very essence of morality is involved in the dislike (within reasonable limits) of death. Morality aims at a maximum of comfortable life and a minimum of death; if then, a minimum of death and a maximum of life were no longer held worth striving for, the whole fabric of morality would collapse, as indeed we have it on record that it is apt to do among classes that from one cause or another have come to live in disregard and expectation of death.

However much we may abuse death for robbing us of our friends—and there is no one who is not sooner or later hit hard in this respect—yet time heals these wounds sooner than we like to own; if the heyday of grief does not shortly kill outright, it passes; and I doubt whether most men, if they were to search their hearts, would not find that, could they command death for some single occasion, they would be more likely to bid him take than restore.

Moreover, death does not blight love as the accidents of time and life do. Even the fondest grow apart if parted; they cannot come together again, not in any closeness or for any long time. Can death do worse than this?

The memory of a love that has been cut short by death remains still fragrant though enfeebled, but no recollection of its past can keep sweet a love that has dried up and withered through accidents of time and life.

XXIV
The Life of the World to Come

Posthumous Life

i

To try to live in posterity is to be like an actor who leaps over the footlights and talks to the orchestra.

ii

He who wants posthumous fame is as one who would entail land, and tie up his money after his death as tightly and for as long a time as possible. Still we each of us in our own small way try to get what little posthumous fame we can.

The Test of Faith

Why should we be so avid of honourable and affectionate remembrance after death? Why should we hold this the one thing worth living or dying for? Why should all that we can know or feel seem but a very little thing as compared with that which we never either feel or know? What a reversal of all the canons of action which commonly guide mankind is there not here? But however this may be, if we have faith in the life after death we can have little in that which is before it, and if we have faith in this life we can have small faith in any other.

Nevertheless there is a deeply rooted conviction, even in many of those in whom its existence is least apparent, that honourable and affectionate remembrance after death with a full and certain hope that it will be ours is the highest prize to which the highest calling can aspire. Few pass through this world without feeling the vanity of all human ambitions; their faith may fail them here, but it will not fail them — not for a moment, never — if they possess it as regards posthumous respect and affection. The world may prove hollow but a well-earned good fame in death will never do so. And all men feel this whether they admit it to themselves or no.

Faith in this is easy enough. We are born with it. What is less easy is to possess one's soul in peace and not be shaken in faith and broken in spirit on seeing the way in which men crowd themselves, or are crowded, into honourable remembrance when, if the truth concerning them were known, no pit of oblivion should be deep enough for them. See, again, how many who have richly earned esteem never get it either before or after death. It is here that faith comes in. To see that the infinite corruptions of this life penetrate into and infect that which is to come, and yet to hold that even infamy after death, with obscure and penurious life before it, is a prize which will bring a man more peace at the last than all the good things of this life put together and joined with an immortality as lasting as Virgil's, provided the infamy and failure of the one be unmerited, as also the success and immortality of the other. Here is the test of faith—will you do your duty with all your might at any cost of goods or reputation either in this world or beyond the grave? If you will—well, the chances are 100 to 1 that you will become a faddist, a vegetarian and a teetotaller.

And suppose you escape this pit-fall too. Why should you try to be so much better than your neighbours? Who are you to think you may be worthy of so much good fortune? If you do, you may be sure that you do not deserve it.

And so on *ad infinitum*. Let us eat and drink neither forgetting nor remembering death unduly. The Lord hath mercy on whom he will have mercy and the less we think about it the better.

Starting again ad Infinitum

A man from the cradle to the grave is but the embryo of a being that may be born into the world of the dead who still live, or that may die so soon after entering it as to be practically still-born. The greater number of the seeds shed, whether by plants or animals, never germinate and of those that grow few reach maturity, so the greater number of those that reach death are still-born as regards the truest life of all—I mean the life that is lived after death in the thoughts and actions of posterity. Moreover of those who are born into and fill great places in this invisible world not one is immortal.

We should look on the body as the manifesto of the mind and on posterity as the manifesto of the dead that live after life. Each is the mechanism whereby the other exists.

Life, then, is not the having been born—it is rather an effort to be born. But why should some succeed in attaining to this future life and others fail? Why should some be born more than others? Why should not some one in a future state taunt Lazarus with having a good time now and tell him it will be the turn of Dives in some other and more remote hereafter? I must have it that neither are the good rewarded nor the bad punished in a future state, but every one must start anew quite irrespective of anything they have done here and must try his luck again and go on trying it again and again *ad infinitum*. Some of our lives, then, will be lucky and some unlucky and it will resolve itself into one long eternal life during which we shall change so much that we shall not remember our antecedents very far back (any more than we remember having been embryos) nor foresee our future very much, and during which we shall have our ups and downs *ad infinitum* — effecting a transformation scene at once as soon as circumstances become unbearable.

Nevertheless, some men's work does live longer than others. Some achieve what is very like immortality. Why should they have this piece of good fortune more than others? The answer is that it would be very unjust if they knew anything about it, or could enjoy it in any way, but they know nothing whatever about it, and you, the complainer, do profit by their labour, so that it is really you, the complainer, who get the fun, not they, and this should stop your mouth. The only thing they got was a little hope, which buoyed them up often when there was but little else that could do so.

Preparation for Death

That there is a life after death is as palpable as that there is a life before death — see the influence that the dead have over us — but this life is no more eternal than our present life.

Shakespeare and Homer may live long, but they will die some day, that is to say, they will become unknown as direct and efficient causes. Even so God himself dies, for to die is to change and to change is to die to what has gone before. If the units change the total must do so also.

As no one can say which egg or seed shall come to visible life and in its turn leave issue, so no one can say which of the millions of now visible lives shall enter into the afterlife on death, and which have but so little life as practically not to count. For most seeds end as seeds or as food for some alien being, and so with lives, by far the greater number are sterile, except in so far as they can be devoured as the food of some stronger life. The Handels and Shakespeares are the few seeds that grow — and even these die.

And the same uncertainty attaches to posthumous life as to pre-lethal. As no one can say how long another shall live, so no one can say how long or how short a time a reputation shall live. The most unpromising weakly-looking creatures sometimes live to ninety while strong robust men are carried off in their prime. And no one can say what a man shall enter into life for having done. Roughly, there is a sort of moral government whereby those who have done the best work live most enduringly, but it is subject to such exceptions that no one can say whether or no there shall not be an exception in his own case either in his favour or against him.

In this uncertainty a young writer had better act as though he had a reasonable chance of living, not perhaps very long, but still some little while after his death. Let him leave his notes fairly full and fairly tidy in all respects, without spending too much time about them. If they are wanted, there they are; if not wanted, there is no harm done. He might as well leave them as anything else. But let him write them in copying ink and have the copies kept in different places.

The Vates Sacer

Just as the kingdom of heaven cometh not by observation, so neither do one's own ideas, nor the good things one hears other people say; they fasten on us when we least want or expect them. It is enough if the kingdom of heaven be observed when it does come.

I do not read much; I look, listen, think and write. My most intimate friends are men of more insight, quicker wit, more playful fancy and, in all ways, abler men than I am, but you will find ten of them for one of me. I note what they say, think it over, adapt it and give it permanent form. They throw good things off as sparks; I collect them and turn them into warmth. But I could not do this if I did not sometimes throw out a spark or two myself.

Not only would Agamemnon be nothing without the *vates sacer* but there are always at least ten good heroes to one good chronicler, just as there are ten good authors to one good publisher. Bravery, wit and poetry abound in every village. Look at Mrs. Boss [the original of Mrs. Jupp in *The Way of All Flesh*] and at Joanna Mills [*Life and Letters of Dr. Butler*, I, 93]. There is not a village of 500 inhabitants in England but has its Mrs. Quickly and its Tom Jones. These good people never understand themselves, they go over their own heads, they speak in unknown tongues to those around them and the interpreter is the rarer and more important person. The *vates sacer* is the middleman of mind.

So rare is he and such spendthrifts are we of good things that people not only will not note what might well be noted but they will not even keep what others have noted, if they are to be at the pains of pigeon-holing it. It is less trouble to throw a brilliant letter into the fire than to put it into such form that it can be safely kept, quickly found and easily read. To this end a letter should be gummed, with the help of the edgings of stamps if necessary, to a strip, say an inch and a quarter wide, of stout hand-made paper. Two or three paper fasteners passed through these strips will bind fifty or sixty letters together, which, arranged in chronological order, can be quickly found and comfortably read. But how few will be at the small weekly trouble of clearing up their correspondence and leaving it in manageable shape! If we keep our letters at all we throw them higgledy-piggledy into a box and have done with them; let some one else arrange them when the owner is dead. The some one else comes and finds the fire an easy method of escaping the onus thrown upon him. So on go letters from Tilbrook, Merian, Marmaduke Lawson [364] —just as we throw our money away if the holding on to it involves even very moderate exertion.

On the other hand, if this instinct towards prodigality were not so great, beauty and wit would be smothered under their own selves. It is through the waste of wit that wit endures, like money, its main preciousness lies in its rarity—the more plentiful it is the cheaper does it become.

The Dictionary of National Biography

When I look at the articles on Handel, on Dr. Arnold, or indeed on almost any one whom I know anything about, I feel that such a work as the *Dictionary of National Biography* adds more terror to death than death of itself could inspire. That is one reason why I let myself go so unreservedly in these notes. If the colours in which I paint myself fail to please, at any rate I shall have had the laying them on myself.

The World

The world will, in the end, follow only those who have despised as well as served it.

Accumulated Dinners

The world and all that has ever been in it will one day be as much forgotten as what we ate for dinner forty years ago. Very likely, but the fact that we shall not remember much about a dinner forty years hence does not make it less agreeable now, and after all it is only the accumulation of these forgotten dinners that makes the dinner of forty years hence possible.

Judging the Dead

The dead should be judged as we judge criminals, impartially, but they should be allowed the benefit of a doubt. When no doubt exists they should be hanged out of hand for about a hundred years. After that time they may come down and move about under a cloud. After about 2000 years they may do what they like. If Nero murdered his mother—well, he murdered his mother and there's an end. The moral guilt of an action varies inversely as the squares of its distances in time and space, social, psychological, physiological or topographical, from ourselves. Not so its moral merit: this loses no lustre through time and distance.

Good is like gold, it will not rust or tarnish and it is rare, but there is some of it everywhere. Evil is like water, it abounds, is cheap, soon fouls, but runs itself clear of taint.

Myself and My Books

Bodily offspring I do not leave, but mental offspring I do. Well, my books do not have to be sent to school and college and then insist on going into the Church or take to drinking or marry their mother's maid.

My Son

I have often told my son that he must begin by finding me a wife to become his mother who shall satisfy both himself and me. But this is only one of the many rocks on which we have hitherto split. We should never have got on together; I should have had to cut him off with a shilling either for laughing at Homer, or for refusing to laugh at him, or both, or neither, but still cut him off. So I settled the matter long ago by turning a deaf ear to his importunities and sticking to it that I would not get him at all. Yet his thin ghost visits me at times and, though he knows that it is no use pestering me further, he looks at me so wistfully and reproachfully that I am half-inclined to turn tall, take my chance about his mother and ask him to let me get him after all. But I should show a clean pair of heels if he said "Yes."

Besides, he would probably be a girl.

Obscurity

When I am dead, do not let people say of me that I suffered from misrepresentation and neglect. I was neglected and misrepresented; very likely not half as much as I supposed but, nevertheless, to some extent neglected and misrepresented. I growl at this sometimes but, if the question were seriously put to me whether I would go on as I am or become famous in my own lifetime, I have no hesitation about which I should prefer. I will willingly pay the few hundreds of pounds which the neglect of my works costs me in order to be let alone and not plagued by the people who would come round me if I were known. The probability is that I shall remain after my death as obscure as I am now; if this be so, the obscurity will, no doubt, be merited, and if not, my books will work not only as well without my having been known in my lifetime but a great deal better; my follies and blunders will the better escape notice to the enhancing of the value of anything that may be found in books. The only two things I should greatly care about if I had more money are a few more country outings and a little more varied and better cooked food. [1882.]

P.S.—I have long since obtained everything that a reasonable man can wish for. [1895.]

Posthumous Honours

I see Cecil Rhodes has just been saying that he was a lucky man, inasmuch as such honours as are now being paid him generally come to a man after his death and not before it. This is all very well for a politician whose profession immerses him in public life, but the older I grow the more satisfied I am that there can be no greater misfortune for a man of letters or of contemplation than to be recognised in his own lifetime. Fortunately the greater man he is, and hence the greater the misfortune he would incur, the less likelihood there is that he will incur it. [1897.]

Posthumous Recognition

Shall I be remembered after death? I sometimes think and hope so. But I trust I may not be found out (if I ever am found out, and if I ought to be found out at all) before my death. It would bother me very much and I should be much happier and better as I am. [1880.]

P.S.—This note I leave unaltered. I am glad to see that I had so much sense thirteen years ago. What I thought then, I think now, only with greater confidence and confirmation. [1893.]

Analysis of the Sales of My Books

	Copies Sold	Cash Profit			Cash Loss			Total Profit			Total loss			Value of stock		
Erewhon	3843	62	10	10	—			69	3	10		—		6	13	0
The Fair Haven	442	—			41	2	2	—			27	18	2	13	4	0
Life and Habit	640	—			4	17	1½	7	19	1½	—			12	16	3
Evolution Old & New	541	—			103	11	10	—			89	13	10	13	18	0
Unconscious Memory	272	—			38	13	5	—			38	13	5	—		
Alps and Sanctuaries	332	—			113	6	4	—			110	18	4	22	8	0
Selections from Previous Works	120	—			51	4	10½	—			48	10	10½	2	14	0
Luck or Cunning?	284	—			41	6	4	—			13	18	10	27	7	6
Ex Voto	217	—			147	18	0	—			111	8	0	36	10	0
Life and Letters of Dr. Butler	201	—			216	18	0	—			193	18	0	23	0	0
The Authoress of the Odyssey	165	—			81	1	3	—			59	10	3	21	11	0
The Iliad in English Prose	157	—			89	4	8	—			77	6	8	11	18	0
A Holbein Card	6	—			8	1	9	—			8	1	9	—		
A Book of Essays	0	—			3	11	9	—			—			3	11	9
		62	10	10	960	17	6	77	2	11½	779	18	1½	195	11	6

To this must be added my book on the Sonnets in respect of which I have had no account as yet but am over a hundred pounds out of pocket by it so far—little of which, I fear, is ever likely to come back.

It will be noted that my public appears to be a declining one; I attribute this to the long course of practical boycott to which I have been subjected for so many years, or, if not boycott, of sneer, snarl and misrepresentation. I cannot help it, nor if the truth were known, am I at any pains to try to do so. [369]

Worth Doing

If I deserve to be remembered, it will be not so much for anything I have written, or for any new way of looking at old facts which I may have suggested, as for having shown that a man of no special ability, with no literary connections, not particularly laborious, fairly, but not supremely, accurate as far as he goes, and not travelling far either for his facts or from them, may yet, by being perfectly square, sticking to his point, not letting his temper run away with him, and biding his time, be a match for the most powerful literary and scientific coterie that England has ever known.

I hope it may be said of me that I discomfited an unscrupulous, self-seeking clique, and set a more wholesome example myself. To have done this is the best of all discoveries.

Doubt and Hope

I will not say that the more than coldness with which my books are received does not frighten me and make me distrust myself. It must do so. But every now and then I meet with such support as gives me hope again. Still, I know nothing. [1890.]

Unburying Cities

Of course I am jealous of the *éclat* that Flinders Petrie, Layard and Schliemann get for having unburied cities, but I do not see why I need be; the great thing is to unbury the city, and I believe I have unburied Scheria as effectually as Schliemann unburied Troy. [*The Authoress of the Odyssey.*] True, Scheria was above ground all the time and only wanted a little common sense to find it; nevertheless people have had all the facts before them for over 2500 years and have been looking more or less all the time without finding. I do not see why it is more meritorious to uncover physically with a spade than spiritually with a little of the very commonest common sense.

Apologia

i

When I am dead I would rather people thought me better than I was instead of worse; but if they think me worse, I cannot help it and, if it matters at all, it will matter more to them than to me. The one reputation I deprecate is that of having been ill-used. I deprecate this because it would tend to depress and discourage others from playing the game that I have played. I will therefore forestall misconception on this head.

As regards general good-fortune, I am nearly fifty-five years old and for the last thirty years have never been laid up with illness nor had any physical pain that I can remember, not even toothache. Except sometimes, when a little over-driven, I have had uninterrupted good health ever since I was about five-and-twenty.

Of mental suffering I have had my share—as who has not?—but most of what I have suffered has been, though I did not think so at the time, either imaginary, or unnecessary and, so far, it has been soon forgotten. It has been much less than it very easily might have been if the luck had not now and again gone with me, and probably I have suffered less than most people, take it all round. Like every one else, however, I have the scars of old wounds; very few of these wounds were caused by anything which was essential in the nature of things; most, if not all of them, have been due to faults of heart and head on my own part and on that of others which, one would have thought, might have been easily avoided if in practice it had not turned out otherwise.

For many years I was in a good deal of money difficulty, but since my father's death I have had no trouble on this score—greatly otherwise. Even when things were at their worst, I never missed my two months' summer Italian trip since 1876, except one year and then I went to Mont St. Michel and enjoyed it very much. It was those Italian trips that enabled me to weather the storm. At other times I am engrossed with work that fascinates me. I am surrounded by people to whom I am attached and who like me in return so far as I can judge. In Alfred [his clerk and attendant] I have the best body-guard and the most engaging of any man in London. I live quietly but happily. And if this is being ill-used I should like to know what being well-used is.

I do not deny, however, that I have been ill-used. I have been used abominably. The positive amount of good or ill fortune, however, is not the test of either the one or the other; the true measure lies in the relative proportion of each and the way in which they have been distributed, and by this I claim, after deducting all bad luck, to be left with a large balance of good.

Some people think I must be depressed and discouraged because my books do not make more noise; but, after all, whether people read my books or no is their affair, not mine. I know by my sales that few read my books. If I write at all, it follows that I want to be read and miss my mark if I am not. So also with *Narcissus*. Whatever I do falls dead, and I would rather people let me see that they liked it. To this extent I certainly am disappointed. I am sorry not to have wooed the public more successfully. But I have been told that winning and wearing generally take something of the gilt off the wooing, and I am disposed to acquiesce cheerfully in not finding myself so received as that I need woo no longer. If I were to succeed I should be bored to death by my success in a fortnight and so, I am convinced, would my friends. Retirement is to me a condition of being able to work at all. I would rather write more books and music than spend much time over what I have already written; nor do I see how I could get retirement if I were not to a certain extent unpopular.

It is this feeling on my own part—omnipresent with me when I am doing my best to please, that is to say, whenever I write—which is the cause why I do not, as people say, "get on." If I had greatly cared about getting on I think I could have done so. I think I could even now write an anonymous book that would take the public as much as *Erewhon* did. Perhaps I could not, but I think I could. The reason why I do not try is because I like doing other things better. What I most enjoy is running the view of evolution set forth in *Life and Habit* and making things less easy for the hacks of literature and science; or perhaps even more I enjoy taking snapshots and writing music, though aware that I had better not enquire whether this last is any good or not. In fact there is nothing I do that I do not enjoy so keenly that I cannot tear myself away from it, and people who thus indulge themselves cannot have things both ways. I am so intent upon pleasing myself that I have no time to cater for the public. Some of them like things in the same way as I do; that class of people I try to please as well as ever I can. With others I have no concern, and they know it so they have no concern with me. I do not believe there is any other explanation of my failure to get on than this, nor do I see that any further explanation is needed. [1890.]

ii

Two or three people have asked me to return to the subject of my supposed failure and explain it more fully from my own point of view. I have had the subject on my notes for some time and it has bored me so much that it has had a good deal to do with my not having kept my Note-Books posted recently.

Briefly, in order to scotch that snake, my failure has not been so great as people say it has. I believe my reputation stands well with the best people. Granted that it makes no noise, but I have not been willing to take the pains necessary to achieve what may be called guinea-pig review success, because, although I have been in financial difficulties, I did not seriously need success from a money point of view, and because I hated the kind of people I should have had to court and kow-tow to if I went in for that sort of thing. I could never have carried it through, even if I had tried, and instinctively declined to try. A man cannot be said to have failed, because he did not get what he did not try for. What I did try for I believe I have got as fully as any reasonable man can expect, and I have every hope that I shall get it still more both so long as I live and after I am dead.

If, however, people mean that I am to explain how it is I have not made more noise in spite of my own indolence in matter, the answer is that those who do not either push the themselves into noise, or give some one else a substantial interest in pushing them, never do get made a noise about. How can they? I was too lazy to go about from publisher to publisher and to decline to publish a book myself if I could not find some one to speculate in it. I could take any amount of trouble about writing a book but, so long as I could lay my hand on the money to bring it out with, I found publishers' antechambers so little to my taste that I soon tired and fell back on the short and easy method of publishing my book myself. Of course, therefore, it failed to sell. I know more about these things now, and will never publish a book at my own risk again, or at any rate I will send somebody else round the antechambers with it for a good while before I pay for publishing it.

I should have liked notoriety and financial success well enough if they could have been had for the asking, but I was not going to take any trouble about them and, as a natural consequence, I did not get them. If I had wanted them with the same passionate longing that has led me to pursue every enquiry that I ever have pursued, I should have got them fast enough. It is very rarely that I have failed to get what I have really tried for and, as a matter of fact, I believe I have been a great deal happier for not trying than I should have been if I had had notoriety thrust upon me.

I confess I should like my books to pay their expenses and put me a little in pocket besides—because I want to do more for Alfred than I see my way to doing. As a natural consequence of beginning to care I have begun to take pains, and am advising with the Society of Authors as to what will be my best course. Very likely they can do nothing for me, but at any rate I shall have tried.

One reason, and that the chief, why I have made no noise, is now explained. It remains to add that from first to last I have been unorthodox and militant in every book that I have written. I made enemies of the parsons once for all with my first two books. [*Erewhon* and *The Fair Haven*.] The evolution books made the Darwinians, and through them the scientific world in general, even more angry than *The Fair Haven* had made the clergy so that I had no friends, for the clerical and scientific people rule the roast between them.

I have chosen the fighting road rather than the hang-on-to-a-great-man road, and what can a man who does this look for except that people should try to silence him in whatever way they think will be most effectual? In my case they have thought it best to pretend that I am non-existent. It is no part of my business to complain of my opponents for choosing their own line; my business is to defeat them as best I can upon their own line, and I imagine I shall do most towards this by not allowing myself to be made unhappy merely because I am not fussed about, and by going on writing more books and adding to my pile.

My Work

Why should I write about this as though any one will wish to read what I write?

People sometimes give me to understand that it is a piece of ridiculous conceit on my part to jot down so many notes about myself, since it implies a confidence that I shall one day be regarded as an interesting person. I answer that neither I nor they can form any idea as to whether I shall be wanted when I am gone or no. The chances are that I shall not. I am quite aware of it. So the chances are that I shall not live to be 85; but I have no right to settle it so. If I do as Captain Don did [*Life of Dr. Butler*, I, opening of Chapter VIII], and invest every penny I have in an annuity that shall terminate when I am 89, who knows but that I may live on to 96, as he did, and have seven years without any income at all? I prefer the modest insurance of keeping up my notes which others may burn or no as they please.

I am not one of those who have travelled along a set road towards an end that I have foreseen and desired to reach. I have made a succession of jaunts or pleasure trips from meadow to meadow, but no long journey unless life itself be reckoned so. Nevertheless, I have strayed into no field in which I have not found a flower that was worth the finding, I have gone into no public place in which I have not found sovereigns lying about on the ground which people would not notice and be at the trouble of picking up. They have been things which any one else has had—or at any rate a very large number of people have had—as good a chance of picking up as I had. My finds have none of them come as the result of research or severe study, though they have generally given me plenty to do in the way of research and study as soon as I had got hold of them. I take it that these are the most interesting—or whatever the least offensive word may be:

1. The emphasising the analogies between crime and disease. [*Erewhon*.]

2. The emphasising also the analogies between the development of the organs of our bodies and of those which are not incorporate with our bodies and which we call tools or machines. [*Erewhon* and *Luck or Cunning*?]

3. The clearing up the history of the events in connection with the death, or rather crucifixion, of Jesus Christ; and a reasonable explanation, first, of the

belief on the part of the founders of Christianity that their master had risen from the dead and, secondly, of what might follow from belief in a single supposed miracle. [*The Evidence for the Resurrection of Jesus Christ, The Fair Haven* and *Erewhon Revisited*.]

4. The perception that personal identity cannot be denied between parents and offspring without at the same time denying it as between the different ages (and hence moments) in the life of the individual and, as a corollary on this, the ascription of the phenomena of heredity to the same source as those of memory. [*Life and Habit*.]

5. The tidying up the earlier history of the theory of evolution. [*Evolution Old and New*.]

6. The exposure and discomfiture of Charles Darwin and Wallace and their followers. [*Evolution Old and New, Unconscious Memory, Luck or Cunning*? and "The Deadlock in Darwinism" in the *Universal Review* republished in *Essays on Life, Art and Science*.] [376]

7. The perception of the principle that led organic life to split up into two main divisions, animal and vegetable. [*Alps and Sanctuaries*, close of Chapter XIII: *Luck or Cunning*?]

8. The perception that, if the kinetic theory is held good, our thought of a thing, whatever that thing may be, is in reality an exceedingly weak dilution of the actual thing itself. [Stated, but not fully developed, in *Luck or Cunning*? Chapter XIX, also in some of the foregoing notes.]

9. The restitution to Giovanni and Gentile Bellini of their portraits in the Louvre and the finding of five other portraits of these two painters of whom Crowe and Cavalcaselle and Layard maintain that we have no portrait. [Letters to the *Athenæum*, &c.]

10. The restoration to Holbein of the drawing in the Basel Museum called *La Danse*. [*Universal Review*, Nov., 1889.]

11. The calling attention to Gaudenzio Ferrari and putting him before the public with something like the emphasis that he deserves. [*Ex Voto*.]

12. The discovery of a life-sized statue of Leonardo da Vinci by Gaudenzio Ferrari. [*Ex Voto*.]

13. The unearthing of the Flemish sculptor Jean de Wespin (called Tabachetti in Italy) and of Giovanni Antonio Paracca. [*Ex Voto*.]

14. The finding out that the *Odyssey* was written at Trapani, the clearing up of the whole topography of the poem, and the demonstration, as it seems to me, that the poem was written by a woman and not by a man. Indeed, I may almost claim to have discovered the *Odyssey*, so altered does it become when my views of it are adopted. And robbing Homer of the *Odyssey* has

rendered the *Iliad* far more intelligible; besides, I have set the example of how he should be approached. [*The Authoress of the Odyssey*.]

15. The attempt to do justice to my grandfather by writing *The Life and Letters of Dr. Butler* for which, however, I had special facilities.

16. In *Narcissus* and *Ulysses* I made an attempt, the failure of which has yet to be shown, to return to the principles of Handel and take them up where he left off.

17. The elucidation of Shakespeare's *Sonnets*. [*Shakespeare's Sonnets Reconsidered*.]

I say nothing here about my novel [*The Way of All Flesh*] because it cannot be published till after my death; nor about my translations of the *Iliad* and the *Odyssey*. Nevertheless these three books also were a kind of picking up of sovereigns, for the novel contains records of things I saw happening rather than imaginary incidents, and the principles on which the translations are made were obvious to any one willing to take and use them.

The foregoing is the list of my "mares'-nests," and it is, I presume, this list which made Mr. Arthur Platt call me the Galileo of Mares'-Nests in his diatribe on my *Odyssey* theory in the *Classical Review*. I am not going to argue here that they are all, as I do not doubt, sound; what I want to say is that they are every one of them things that lay on the surface and open to any one else just as much as to me. Not one of them required any profundity of thought or extensive research; they only required that he who approached the various subjects with which they have to do should keep his eyes open and try to put himself in the position of the various people whom they involve. Above all, it was necessary to approach them without any preconceived theory and to be ready to throw over any conclusion the moment the evidence pointed against it. The reason why I have discarded so few theories that I have put forward — and at this moment I cannot recollect one from which there has been any serious attempt to dislodge me — is because I never allowed myself to form a theory at all till I found myself driven on to it whether I would or no. As long as it was possible to resist I resisted, and only yielded when I could not think that an intelligent jury under capable guidance would go with me if I resisted longer. I never went in search of any one of my theories; I never knew what it was going to be till I had found it; they came and found me, not I them. Such being my own experience, I begin to be pretty certain that other people have had much the same and that the soundest theories have come unsought and without much effort.

The conclusion, then, of the whole matter is that scientific and literary fortunes are, like money fortunes, made more by saving than in any other way — more through the exercise of the common vulgar essentials, such as sobriety and straightforwardness, than by the more showy enterprises that when they happen to succeed are called genius and when they fail, folly. The streets are full of sovereigns crying aloud for some one to come and pick them up, only the thick veil of our own insincerity and conceit hides them from us. He who can most tear this veil from in front of his eyes will be able to see most and to walk off with them.

I should say that the sooner I stop the better. If on my descent to the nether world I were to be met and welcomed by the shades of those to whom I have done a good turn while I was here, I should be received by a fairly illustrious crowd. There would be Giovanni and Gentile Bellini, Leonardo da Vinci, Gaudenzio Ferrari, Holbein, Tabachetti, Paracca and D'Enrico; the Authoress of the *Odyssey* would come and Homer with her; Dr. Butler would bring with him the many forgotten men and women to whom in my memoir I have given fresh life; there would be Buffon, Erasmus Darwin and Lamarck; Shakespeare also would be there and Handel. I could not wish to find myself in more congenial company and I shall not take it too much to heart if the shade of Charles Darwin glides gloomily away when it sees me coming.

XXV
Poems

Prefatory Note

i. *Translation from an Unpublished Work of Herodotus*

ii. *The Shield of Achilles, with Variations*

iii. *The Two Deans*

iv. *On the Italian Priesthood*

Butler wrote these four pieces while he was an undergraduate at St. John's College, Cambridge. He kept no copy of any of them, but his friend the Rev. Canon Joseph McCormick, D.D., Rector of St. James's, Piccadilly, kept copies in a note-book which he lent me. The only one that has appeared in print is "The Shield of Achilles," which Canon McCormick sent to The Eagle, *the magazine of St. John's College, Cambridge, and it was printed in the number for December* 1902, *about six months after Butler's death.*

"On the Italian Priesthood" is a rendering of the Italian epigram accompanying it which, with others under the heading "Astuzia, Inganno," is given in Raccolta di Proverbi Toscani di Giuseppe Giusti (*Firenze,* 1853).

v. *A Psalm of Montreal*

This was written in Canada in 1875. *Butler often recited it and gave copies of it to his friends. Knowing that Mr. Edward Clodd had had something to do with its appearance in the* Spectator *I wrote asking him to tell me what he remembered about it. He very kindly replied,* 29th October, 1905:

"The 'Psalm' was recited to me at the Century Club by Butler. He gave me a copy of it which I read to the late Chas. Anderson, Vicar of S. John's, Limehouse, who lent it to Matt. Arnold (when inspecting Anderson's Schools) who lent it to Richd. Holt Hutton who, with Butler's consent, printed it in the Spectator *of* 18th May, 1878."

The "Psalm of Montreal" was included in Selections from Previous Works (1884) *and in* Seven Sonnets, *etc.*

vi. *The Righteous Man*

Butler wrote this in 1876; *it has appeared before only in* 1879 *in the* Examiner, *where it formed part of the correspondence "A Clergyman's*

Doubts" of which the letter signed "Ethics" has already been given in this volume (see p. 304 ante). "The Righteous Man" was signed "X.Y.Z." and, in order to connect it with the discussion, Butler prefaced it with a note comparing it to the last six inches of a line of railway; there is no part of the road so ugly, so little travelled over, or so useless generally, but it is the end, at any rate, of a very long thing.

vii. *To Critics and Others.*

This was written in 1883 and has not hitherto been published.

viii. *For Narcissus*

These are printed for the first time. The pianoforte score of Narcissus *was published in 1888. The poem (A) was written because there was some discussion then going on in musical circles about additional accompaniments to the* Messiah *and we did not want any to be written for* Narcissus.

The poem (B) shows how Butler originally intended to open Part II with a kind of descriptive programme, but he changed his mind and did it differently.

ix. *A Translation Attempted in Consequence of a Challenge*

This translation into Homeric verse of a famous passage from Martin Chuzzlewit *was a by-product of Butler's work on the* Odyssey *and the* Iliad. *It was published in* The Eagle *in March, 1894, and was included in* Seven Sonnets.

I asked Butler who had challenged him to attempt the translation and he replied that he had thought of that and had settled that, if any one else were to ask the question, he should reply that the challenge came from me.

x. *In Memoriam H. R. F.*

This appears in print now for the first time. Hans Rudolf Faesch, a young Swiss from Basel, came to London in the autumn of 1893. He spent much of his time with us until 14th February, 1895, when he left for Singapore. We saw him off from Holborn Viaduct Station; he was not well and it was a stormy night. The next day Butler wrote this poem and, being persuaded that we should never see Hans Faesch again, called it an In Memoriam. Hans did not die on the journey, he arrived safely in Singapore and settled in the East where he carried on business. We exchanged letters with him frequently; he paid two visits to Europe and we saw him on both occasions. But he did not live long. He died in the autumn of 1903 at Vien Tiane in the Shan States, aged 32, having survived Butler by about a year and a half.

xi. *An Academic Exercise*

This has never been printed before. It is a Farewell, and that is why I have placed it next after the In Memoriam. The contrast between the two poems illustrates the contrast pointed out at the close of the note on "The Dislike of Death" (ante):

"The memory of a love that has been cut short by death remains still fragrant though enfeebled, but no recollection of its past can keep sweet a love that has dried up and withered through accidents of time and life."

In the ordinary course Butler would have talked this Sonnet over with me at the time he wrote it, that is in January, 1902; he may even have done so, but I think not. From 2nd January, 1902, until late in March, when he left London alone for Sicily, I was ill with pneumonia and remember very little of what happened then. Between his return in May and his death in June I am sure he did not mention the subject. Knowing the facts that underlie the preceding poem I can tell why Butler called it an In Memoriam; not knowing the facts that underlie this poem I cannot tell why Butler should have called it an Academic Exercise. It is his last Sonnet and is dated "Sund. Jan. 12th 1902," within six months of his death, at a time when he was depressed physically because his health was failing and mentally because he had been "editing his remains," reading and destroying old letters and brooding over the past. One of the subjects given in the section "Titles and Subjects" (ante) is "The diseases and ordinary causes of mortality among friendships." I suppose that he found among his letters something which awakened memories of a friendship of his earlier life – a friendship that had suffered from a disease, whether it recovered or died would not affect the sincerity of the emotions experienced by Butler at the time he believed the friendship to be virtually dead. I suppose the Sonnet to be an In Memoriam upon the apprehended death of a friendship as the preceding poem is an In Memoriam upon the apprehended death of a friend.

This may be wrong, but something of the kind seems necessary to explain why Butler should have called the Sonnet an Academic Exercise. No one who has read Shakespeare's Sonnets Reconsidered will require to be told that he disagreed contemptuously with those critics who believe that Shakespeare composed his Sonnets as academic exercises. It is certain that he wrote this, as he wrote his other Sonnets, in imitation of Shakespeare, not merely imitating the form but approaching the subject in the spirit in which he believed Shakespeare to have approached his subject. It follows therefore that he did not write this sonnet as an academic exercise, had he done so he would not have been imitating Shakespeare. If we assume that he was presenting his story as he presented the dialogue in "A Psalm of Montreal" in a form "perhaps true, perhaps imaginary, perhaps a little of the one and a little of the other," it would be quite in the manner of the author of The Fair Haven to burlesque the methods of the critics by ignoring the sincerity of the emotions and fixing on the little bit of inaccuracy in the facts. We may suppose him to be saying out loud to the critics: "You think Shakespeare's Sonnets were composed as academic exercises, do you? Very well then, now what do you make of this?" And adding aside to himself: "That will be good enough for them; they'll swallow anything."

xii. A Prayer

Extract from Butler's Note-Books under the date of February or March 1883:

"'Cleanse thou me from my secret sins.' I heard a man moralising on this and shocked him by saying demurely that I did not mind these so much, if I could get rid of those that were obvious to other people."

He wrote the sonnet in 1900 or 1901. In the first quatrain "spoken" does not rhyme with "open"; Butler knew this and would not alter it because there are similar assonances in Shakespeare, e.g. "open" and "broken" in Sonnet LXI.

xiii. Karma

I am responsible for grouping these three sonnets under this heading. The second one beginning "What is't to live" appears in Butler's Note-Book with the remark, "This wants much tinkering, but I cannot tinker it" — meaning that he was too much occupied with other things. He left the second line of the third of these sonnets thus:

"Them palpable to touch and view."

I have "tinkered" it by adding the two syllables "and clear" to make the line complete.

In writing this sonnet Butler was no doubt thinking of a note he made in 1891:

"It is often said that there is no bore like a clever bore. Clever people are always bores and always must be. That is, perhaps, why Shakespeare had to leave London — people could not stand him any longer."

xiv. The Life after Death

Butler began to write sonnets in 1898 when he was studying those of Shakespeare on which he published a book in the following year. (Shakespeare's Sonnets Reconsidered, &c.) He had gone to Flushing by himself and on his return wrote to me:

24 Aug. 1898. "Also at Flushing I wrote one myself, a poor innocent thing, but I was surprised to find how easily it came; if you like it I may write a few more."

The "poor innocent thing" was the sonnet beginning "Not on sad Stygian shore," the first of those I have grouped under the heading "The Life after Death." It appears in his notebooks with this introductory sentence:

"Having now learned Shakespeare's Sonnets by heart — and there are very few which I do not find I understand the better for having done this — on Saturday night last at the Hotel Zeeland at Flushing, finding myself in a meditative mood, I wrote the following with a good deal less trouble than I anticipated when I took pen and paper in hand. I hope I may improve it."

Of course I liked the sonnet very much and he did write "a few more" — among them the two on Handel which I have put after "Not on sad Stygian shore" because he intended that they should follow it. I am sure he would have wished this volume to close with these three sonnets, especially because the last two of them were inspired by Handel, who was never absent from his thoughts for long. Let me conclude these introductory remarks by reproducing a note made in 1883:

"Of all dead men Handel has had the largest place in my thoughts. In fact I should say that he and his music have been the central fact in my life ever since I was old enough to know of the existence of either life or music. All day long — whether I am

writing or painting or walking, but always — I have his music in my head; and if I lose sight of it and of him for an hour or two, as of course I sometimes do, this is as much as I do. I believe I am not exaggerating when I say that I have never been a day since I was 13 without having Handel in my mind many times over."

i — Translation from an Unpublished Work of Herodotus

And the Johnians practise their tub in the following manner: — They select 8 of the most serviceable freshmen and put these into a boat and to each one of them they give an oar; and, having told them to look at the backs of the men before them, they make them bend forward as far as they can and at the same moment, and, having put the end of the oar into the water, pull it back again in to them about the bottom of the ribs; and, if any of them does not do this or looks about him away from the back of the man before him, they curse him in the most terrible manner, but if he does what he is bidden they immediately cry out:

"Well pulled, number so-and-so."

For they do not call them by their names but by certain numbers, each man of them having a number allotted to him in accordance with his place in the boat, and the first man they call stroke, but the last man bow; and when they have done this for about 50 miles they come home again, and the rate they travel at is about 25 miles an hour; and let no one think that this is too great a rate for I could say many other wonderful things in addition concerning the rowing of the Johnians, but if a man wishes to know these things he must go and examine them himself. But when they have done they contrive some such a device as this, for they make them run many miles along the side of the river in order that they may accustom them to great fatigue, and many of them, being distressed in this way, fall down and die, but those who survive become very strong and receive gifts of cups from the others; and after the revolution of a year they have great races with their boats against those of the surrounding islanders, but the Johnians, both owing to the carefulness of the training and a natural disposition for rowing, are always victorious. In this way, then, the Johnians, I say, practise their tub.

ii — The Shield of Achilles — With Variations

And in it he placed the Fitzwilliam and King's College Chapel and the lofty towered church of the Great Saint Mary, which looketh towards the Senate House, and King's Parade and Trumpington Road and the Pitt Press and the divine opening of the Market Square and the beautiful flowing fountain which formerly Hobson laboured to make with skilful art; him did his father beget in the many-public-housed Trumpington from a slavey mother and taught him blameless works; and he, on the other hand, sprang up like a young shoot and many beautifully matched horses did he nourish in his stable, which used to convey his rich possessions to London and the various cities of the world; but oftentimes did he let them out to others and whensoever any one was desirous of hiring one of the long-tailed horses he took them in order, so that the labour was equal to all, wherefore do men now speak of the choice of the renowned Hobson. And in it he placed the close of the divine Parker, and many beautiful undergraduates were delighting their tender minds upon it playing cricket with one another; and a match was being played and two umpires were quarrelling with one another; the one saying that the batsman who was playing was out and the other declaring with all his might that he was not; and while they two were contending, reviling one another with abusive language, a ball came and hit one of them on the nose and the blood flowed out in a stream and darkness was covering his eyes, but the rest were crying out on all sides:

"Shy it up."

And he could not; him, then, was his companion addressing with scornful words:

"Arnold, why dost thou strive with me since I am much wiser? Did not I see his leg before the wicket and rightly declare him to be out? Thee, then, has Zeus now punished according to thy deserts and I will seek some other umpire of the game equally-participated-in-by-both-sides."

And in it he placed the Cam and many boats equally rowed on both sides were going up and down on the bosom of the deep rolling river and the coxswains were cheering on the men, for they were going to enter the contest of the scratchean fours; and three men were rowing together in a boat, strong and stout and determined in their hearts that they would either first break a blood vessel or earn for themselves the electroplated-Birmingham-manufactured magnificence of a pewter to stand on their ball tables in memorial of their strength, and from time to time drink from it the exhilarating streams of beer whensoever their dear heart should compel them; but the fourth was weak and unequally matched with the others and the coxswain was encouraging him and called him by name and spake cheering words:

"Smith, when thou hast begun the contest, be not flurried nor strive too hard against thy fate, look at the back of the man before thee and row with as much strength as the Fates spun out for thee on the day when thou fellest between the knees of thy mother, neither lose thine oar, but hold it tight with thy hands."

iii — The Two Deans

Scene: The Court of St. John's College, Cambridge. Enter the two deans on their way to morning chapel.

Junior Dean: Brother, I am much pleased with Samuel Butler,
I have observed him mightily of late;
Methinks that in his melancholy walk
And air subdued when'er he meeteth me
Lurks something more than in most other men.

Senior Dean: It is a good young man. I do bethink me
That once I walked behind him in the cloister,
He saw me not, but whispered to his fellow:
"Of all men who do dwell beneath the moon
I love and reverence most the senior Dean."

Junior Dean: One thing is passing strange, and yet I know not
How to condemn it; but in one plain brief word
He never comes to Sunday morning chapel.
Methinks he teacheth in some Sunday school,
Feeding the poor and starveling intellect
With wholesome knowledge, or on the Sabbath morn
He loves the country and the neighbouring spire
Of Madingley or Coton, or perchance
Amid some humble poor he spends the day
Conversing with them, learning all their cares,
Comforting them and easing them in sickness.
Oh 'tis a rare young man!

Senior Dean: I will advance him to some public post,
He shall be chapel clerk, some day a fellow,
Some day perhaps a Dean, but as thou sayst
He is indeed an excellent young man —

Enter Butler suddenly without a coat, or anything on his head, rushing through the cloisters, bearing a cup, a bottle of cider, four lemons, two nutmegs, half a pound of sugar and a nutmeg grater.

Curtain falls on the confusion of Butler and the horror-stricken dismay of the two deans.

iv — On the Italian Priesthood

(Con arte e con inganno, si vive mezzo l'anno;
Con inganno e con arte, si vive l'altra parte.)

In knavish art and gathering gear
They spend the one half of the year;
In gathering gear and knavish art
They somehow spend the other part.

v — A Psalm of Montreal

The City of Montreal is one of the most rising and, in many respects, most agreeable on the American continent, but its inhabitants are as yet too busy with commerce to care greatly about the masterpieces of old Greek Art. In the Montreal Museum of Natural History I came upon two plaster casts, one of the Antinous and the other of the Discobolus — not the good one, but in my poem, of course, I intend the good one — banished from public view to a room where were all manner of skins, plants, snakes, insects, etc., and, in the middle of these, an old man stuffing an owl.

"Ah," said I, "so you have some antiques here; why don't you put them where people can see them?"

"Well, sir," answered the custodian, "you see they are rather vulgar."

He then talked a great deal and said his brother did all Mr. Spurgeon's printing.

The dialogue — perhaps true, perhaps imaginary, perhaps a little of the one and a little of the other — between the writer and this old man gave rise to the lines that follow:

Stowed away in a Montreal lumber room
The Discobolus standeth and turneth his face to the wall;
Dusty, cobweb-covered, maimed and set at naught,
Beauty crieth in an attic and no man regardeth:
   O God! O Montreal!

Beautiful by night and day, beautiful in summer and winter,
Whole or maimed, always and alike beautiful —
He preacheth gospel of grace to the skin of owls
And to one who seasoneth the skins of Canadian owls:
   O God! O Montreal!

When I saw him I was wroth and I said, "O Discobolus!
Beautiful Discobolus, a Prince both among gods and men!
What doest thou here, how camest thou hither, Discobolus,
Preaching gospel in vain to the skins of owls?"
   O God! O Montreal!

And I turned to the man of skins and said unto him, "O thou man of skins,
Wherefore hast thou done thus to shame the beauty of the Discobolus?"
But the Lord had hardened the heart of the man of skins
And he answered, "My brother-in-law is haberdasher to Mr. Spurgeon."
   O God! O Montreal!

"The Discobolus is put here because he is vulgar —
He has neither vest nor pants with which to cover his limbs;

I, Sir, am a person of most respectable connections
My brother-in-law is haberdasher to Mr. Spurgeon."
    O God! O Montreal!

    Then I said, "O brother-in-law to Mr. Spurgeon's haberdasher,
Who seasonest also the skins of Canadian owls,
Thou callest trousers 'pants,' whereas I call them 'trousers,'
Therefore thou art in hell-fire and may the Lord pity thee!"
    O God! O Montreal!

    "Preferrest thou the gospel of Montreal to the gospel of Hellas,
The gospel of thy connection with Mr. Spurgeon's haberdashery to the
gospel of the Discobolus?"
Yet none the less blasphemed he beauty saying, "The Discobolus hath no
gospel,
But my brother-in-law is haberdasher to Mr. Spurgeon."
    O God! O Montreal!

vi — The Righteous Man

    The righteous man will rob none but the defenceless,
Whatsoever can reckon with him he will neither plunder nor kill;
He will steal an egg from a hen or a lamb from an ewe,
For his sheep and his hens cannot reckon with him hereafter —
They live not in any odour of defencefulness:
Therefore right is with the righteous man, and he taketh advantage
righteously,
Praising God and plundering.

    The righteous man will enslave his horse and his dog,
Making them serve him for their bare keep and for nothing further,
Shooting them, selling them for vivisection when they can no longer profit
him,
Backbiting them and beating them if they fail to please him;
For his horse and his dog can bring no action for damages,
Wherefore, then, should he not enslave them,
shoot them, sell them for vivisection?

    But the righteous man will not plunder the defenceful —
Not if he be alone and unarmed — for his conscience will smite him;
He will not rob a she-bear of her cubs, nor an eagle of her eaglets —
Unless he have a rifle to purge him from the fear of sin:
Then may he shoot rejoicing in innocency — from ambush or a safe distance;
Or he will beguile them, lay poison for them, keep no faith with them;
For what faith is there with that which cannot reckon hereafter,

Neither by itself, nor by another, nor by any residuum of ill consequences?
Surely, where weakness is utter, honour ceaseth.

Nay, I will do what is right in the eye of him who can harm me,
And not in those of him who cannot call me to account.
Therefore yield me up thy pretty wings, O humming-bird!
Sing for me in a prison, O lark!
Pay me thy rent, O widow! for it is mine.
Where there is reckoning there is sin,
And where there is no reckoning sin is not.

vii — To Critics and Others

O Critics, cultured Critics!
Who will praise me after I am dead,
Who will see in me both more and less than I intended,
But who will swear that whatever it was it was all perfectly right:
You will think you are better than the people who, when I was alive, swore
that whatever I did was wrong
And damned my books for me as fast as I could write them;
But you will not be better, you will be just the same, neither better nor
worse,
And you will go for some future Butler as your fathers have gone for me.
Oh! How I should have hated you!

But you, Nice People!
Who will be sick of me because the critics thrust me down your throats,
But who would take me willingly enough if you were not bored about me,
Or if you could have the cream of me — and surely this should suffice:
Please remember that, if I were living, I should be upon your side
And should hate those who imposed me either on myself or others;
Therefore, I pray you, neglect me, burlesque me, boil me down, do whatever
you like with me,
But do not think that, if I were living, I should not aid and abet you.
There is nothing that even Shakespeare would enjoy
more than a good burlesque of *Hamlet*.

viii—For *Narcissus*

(A)

(To be written in front of the orchestral score.)

May he be damned for evermore
Who tampers with Narcissus' score;
May he by poisonous snakes be bitten

Who writes more parts than what we've written.
We tried to make our music clear
For those who sing and those who hear,
Not lost and muddled up and drowned
In over-done orchestral sound;
So kindly leave the work alone
Or do it as we want it done.

(B)

Part II

Symphony

(During which the audience is requested to think as follows:)

An aged lady taken ill
Desires to reconstruct her will;
I see the servants hurrying for
The family solicitor;
Post-haste he comes and with him brings
The usual necessary things.
With common form and driving quill
He draws the first part of the will,
The more sonorous solemn sounds
Denote a hundred thousand pounds,
This trifle is the main bequest,
Old friends and servants take the rest.
'Tis done! I see her sign her name,
I see the attestors do the same.
Who is the happy legatee?
In the next number you will see.

ix — A Translation

(Attempted in consequence of a challenge.)

"'Mrs. Harris,' I says to her, 'dont name the charge, for if I could afford to
lay all my feller creeturs out for nothink I would gladly do it; sich is the love I
bear 'em. But what I always says to them as has the management of matters,
Mrs. Harris,'" — here she kept her eye on Mr. Pecksniff — "'be they gents or be
they ladies — is, Dont ask me whether I wont take none, or whether I will, but
leave the bottle on the chimley piece, and let me put my lips to it when I am
so dispoged.'" (*Martin Chuzzlewit*, Chap. XIX).

"ως εφατ αυταρ εγώ μιν αμειβομένη προσέειπον,
'δαιμονίη, Ἀρρισσιαδέω αλοχ' αντιθέοιο,
μη θην δη περι μίσθον ανείρεο, μὴδ' ονόμαζε

τοίη γάρ τοι εγων αγανη και ηπίη ειμί,
η κεν λαον απαντ' ει μοι δύναμίς γε παρείη,
σίτου επηετανου βιότου θ' αλις ενδον εόντος,
ασπασίως και αμισθος εουσα περιστείλαιμι
[εν λέκτρῳ λέξασα τανηλεγέος θανάτοιο
αυτή, ος κε θάνῃσι βροτων και πότμον επίσπῃ]
αλλ' εκ τοι ερέω συ δ' ενι φρεσι βάλλεο σῇσιν'" —
οσσε δέ οι Πεξνειφον εσέδρακον ασκελες αιεί —
"'κείνοισιν γαρ πασι πιφαυσκομένη αγορεύω
ειτ' ανδο' ειτε γυναιχ' οτέῳ τάδε εργα μέμηλεν,
ω φίλε, τίπτε συ ταυτα μ' ανείρεαι; ουδέ τί σε χρη
ιδμέναι η εθέλω πίνειν μέθυ, ηε και ουχί
ει δ' αγ' επ' εσχάροφιν κάταθες δέπας ηδέος οινου,
οφρ' εν χερσιν ελω πίνουσά τε τερπομένη τε,
χείλεά τε προσθεισ' οπόταν φίλον ητορ ανώγῃ.'"

x — In Memoriam

Feb. 14th, 1895

To

H. R. F.

Out, out, out into the night,
With the wind bitter North East and the sea rough;
You have a racking cough and your lungs are weak,
But out, out into the night you go,
  So guide you and guard you Heaven and fare you well!

    We have been three lights to one another and now we are two,
For you go far and alone into the darkness;
But the light in you was stronger and clearer than ours,
For you came straighter from God and, whereas we had learned,
You had never forgotten. Three minutes more and then
Out, out into the night you go,
  So guide you and guard you Heaven and fare you well!

    Never a cross look, never a thought,
Never a word that had better been left unspoken;
We gave you the best we had, such as it was,
It pleased you well, for you smiled and nodded your head;
And now, out, out into the night you go,
  So guide you and guard you Heaven and fare you well!

    You said we were a little weak that the three of us wept,
Are we then weak if we laugh when we are glad?

When men are under the knife let them roar as they will,
So that they flinch not.
Therefore let tears flow on, for so long as we live
No such second sorrow shall ever draw nigh us,
Till one of us two leaves the other alone
And goes out, out, out into the night,
  So guard the one that is left, O God, and fare him well!

      Yet for the great bitterness of this grief
We three, you and he and I,
May pass into the hearts of like true comrades hereafter,
In whom we may weep anew and yet comfort them,
As they too pass out, out, out into the night,
  So guide them and guard them Heaven and fare them well!

      . . .

      The minutes have flown and he whom we loved is gone,
The like of whom we never again shall see;
The wind is heavy with snow and the sea rough,
He has a racking cough and his lungs are weak.
Hand in hand we watch the train as it glides
Out, out, out into the night.
  So take him into thy holy keeping, O Lord,
  And guide him and guard him ever, and fare him well!

xi — An Academic Exercise

      We were two lovers standing sadly by
While our two loves lay dead upon the ground;
Each love had striven not to be first to die,
But each was gashed with many a cruel wound.
Said I: "Your love was false while mine was true."
Aflood with tears he cried: "It was not so,
'Twas your false love my true love falsely slew —
For 'twas your love that was the first to go."
Thus did we stand and said no more for shame
Till I, seeing his cheek so wan and wet,
Sobbed thus: "So be it; my love shall bear the blame;
Let us inter them honourably." And yet
  I swear by all truth human and divine
  'Twas his that in its death throes murdered mine.

xii — A Prayer

      Searcher of souls, you who in heaven abide,
To whom the secrets of all hearts are open,

Though I do lie to all the world beside,
From me to these no falsehood shall be spoken.
Cleanse me not, Lord, I say, from secret sin
But from those faults which he who runs can see,
'Tis these that torture me, O Lord, begin
With these and let the hidden vices be;
If you must cleanse these too, at any rate
Deal with the seen sins first, 'tis only reason,
They being so gross, to let the others wait
The leisure of some more convenient season;
    And cleanse not all even then, leave me a few,
    I would not be—not quite—so pure as you.

xiii—Karma

(A)

    Who paints a picture, writes a play or book
Which others read while he's asleep in bed
O' the other side of the world—when they o'erlook
His page the sleeper might as well be dead;
What knows he of his distant unfelt life?
What knows he of the thoughts his thoughts are raising,
The life his life is giving, or the strife
Concerning him—some cavilling, some praising?
Yet which is most alive, he who's asleep
Or his quick spirit in some other place,
Or score of other places, that doth keep
Attention fixed and sleep from others chase?
    Which is the "he"—the "he" that sleeps, or "he"
    That his own "he" can neither feel nor see?

(B)

    What is't to live, if not to pull the strings
Of thought that pull those grosser strings whereby
We pull our limbs to pull material things
Into such shape as in our thoughts doth lie?
Who pulls the strings that pull an agent's hand,
The action's counted his, so, we being gone,
The deeds that others do by our command,
Albeit we know them not, are still our own.
He lives who does and he who does still lives,
Whether he wots of his own deeds or no.
Who knows the beating of his heart, that drives

Blood to each part, or how his limbs did grow?
  If life be naught but knowing, then each breath
  We draw unheeded must be reckon'd death.

    (C)

    "Men's work we have," quoth one, "but we want them—
Them, palpable to touch and clear to view."
Is it so nothing, then, to have the gem
But we must weep to have the setting too?
Body is a chest wherein the tools abide
With which the craftsman works as best he can
And, as the chest the tools within doth hide,
So doth the body crib and hide the man.
Nay, though great Shakespeare stood in flesh before us,
Should heaven on importunity release him,
Is it so certain that he might not bore us,
So sure but we ourselves might fail to please him?
  Who prays to have the moon full soon would pray,
  Once it were his, to have it taken away.

xiv — The Life After Death

    (A)

Μέλλοντα ταυτα

    Not on sad Stygian shore, nor in clear sheen
Of far Elysian plain, shall we meet those
Among the dead whose pupils we have been,
Nor those great shades whom we have held as foes;
No meadow of asphodel our feet shall tread,
Nor shall we look each other in the face
To love or hate each other being dead,
Hoping some praise, or fearing some disgrace.
We shall not argue saying "'Twas thus" or "Thus,"
Our argument's whole drift we shall forget;
Who's right, who's wrong, 'twill be all one to us;
We shall not even know that we have met.
  Yet meet we shall, and part, and meet again,
  Where dead men meet, on lips of living men.

    (B)

HANDEL

    There doth great Handel live, imperious still,
Invisible and impalpable as air,

But forcing flesh and blood to work his will
Effectually as though his flesh were there;
He who gave eyes to ears and showed in sound
All thoughts and things in earth or heaven above.
From fire and hailstones running along the ground
To Galatea grieving for her love;
He who could show to all unseeing eyes
Glad shepherds watching o'er their flocks by night,
Or Iphis angel-wafted to the skies,
Or Jordan standing as an heap upright—
     He'll meet both Jones and me and clap or hiss us
     Vicariously for having writ *Narcissus*.

     (C)

     HANDEL

     Father of my poor music—if such small
Offspring as mine, so born out of due time,
So scorn'd, can be called fatherful at all,
Or dare to thy high sonship's rank to climb—
Best lov'd of all the dead whom I love best,
Though I love many another dearly too,
You in my heart take rank above the rest;
King of those kings that most control me, you,
You were about my path, about my bed
In boyhood always and, where'er I be,
Whate'er I think or do, you, in my head,
Ground-bass to all my thoughts, are still with me;
     Methinks the very worms will find some strain
     Of yours still lingering in my wasted brain.

Footnotes

[16] "The doctrine preached by Weismann was that to start with the body and inquire how its characters got into the germ was to view the sequence from the wrong end; the proper starting point was the germ, and the real question was not 'How do the characters of the organism get into the germ-cell *which it* produces?' but 'How are the characters of an organism represented in the germ *which produces it?*' Or, as Samuel Butler has it, the proper statement of the relation between successive generations is not to say that a hen produces another hen through the medium of an egg, but to say that a hen is merely an egg's way of producing another egg." *Breeding and the Mendelian Discovery*, by A. D. Darbishire. Cassell & Co., 1911.

"It has, I believe, been often remarked that a hen is only an egg's way of making another egg." *Life and Habit*, Trübner & Co., 1878, chapter viii,.

And compare the idea underlying "The World of the Unborn" in *Erewhon*.

[26] The two chapters entitled "The Rights of Animals" and "The Rights of Vegetables" appeared first in the new and revised edition of *Erewhon* 1901 and form part of the additions referred to in the preface to that book.

[30] On the Alps
It is reported thou didst eat strange flesh,
Which some did die to look on: and all this —
It wounds thine honour that I speak it now —
Was borne so like a soldier, that thy cheek
So much as lank'd not. — *Ant. & Cleop.*, I. iv. 66–71.

[31] *Walks in the Regions of Science and Faith*, by Harvey Goodwin, D.D., Lord Bishop of Carlisle. John Murray, 1883.

[32a] This quotation occurs on the title page of *Charles Dickens and Rochester* by Robert Langton. Chapman & Hall, 1880. Reprinted with additions from the Papers of the Manchester Literary Club, Vol. VI, 1880. But the italics are Butler's.

[32b] This is Butler's note as he left it. He made it just about the time he hit upon the theory that the *Odyssey* was written by a woman. If it had caught his eye after that theory had become established in his mind, he would have edited it so as to avoid speaking of Homer as the author of the poem.

[41] *Life and Habit* is dated 1878, but it actually appeared on Butler's birthday, 4th December, 1877.

[92] The five notes here amalgamated together into "Croesus and his Kitchen-Maid" were to have been part of an article for the *Universal Review*, but, before Butler wrote it, the review died. I suppose, but I do not now remember, that the article would have been about Mind and Matter or Organs and Tools, and, possibly, all the concluding notes of this group, beginning with "Our Cells," would have been introduced as illustrations.

[106] Cf. the note "Reproduction," ante.

[107] *Evolution Old & New,*.

[128] *Twelve Voluntaries and Fugues for the Organ or Harpsichord with Rules for Tuning*. By the celebrated Mr. Handel. Butler had a copy of this book and gave it to the British Museum (Press Mark, e. 1089). We showed the rules to Rockstro, who said they were very interesting and probably authentic; they would tune the instrument in one of the mean tone temperaments.

[131] Mr. Kemp lived in Barnard's Inn on my staircase. He was in the box-office at Drury Lane Theatre. See a further note about him on post.

[136] If I remember right, the original Jubilee sixpence had to be altered because it was so like a half-sovereign that, on being gilded, it passed as one.

[147] Raffaelle's picture "The Virgin and child attended by S. John the Baptist and S. Nicholas of Bari" (commonly known as the "Madonna degli Ansidei"), No. 1171, Room VI in the National Gallery, London, was purchased in 1885. Butler made this note in the same year; he revised the note in 1897 but, owing to changes in the gallery and in the attributions, I have found it necessary to modernise his descriptions of the other pictures with gold thread work so as to make them agree with the descriptions now (1912) on the pictures themselves.

[151] Cf. the passage in *Alps and Sanctuaries*, chapter XIII, beginning "The question whether it is better to abide quiet and take advantages of opportunities that come or to go further afield in search of them is one of the oldest which living beings have had to deal with. . . . The schism still lasts and has resulted in two great sects—animals and plants."

[153] Prince was my cat when I lived in Barnard's Inn. He used to stray into Mr. Kemp's rooms on my landing (see ante). Mrs. Kemp's sister brought her child to see them, and the child, playing with Prince one day, made a discovery and exclaimed:

"Oh! it's got pins in its toes."

Butler put this into *The Way of all Flesh*.

[162] Philippians i. 15–18:—

Some indeed preach Christ even of envy and strife; and some also of good will:

The one preach Christ of contention, not sincerely, supposing to add affliction to my bonds:

But the other of love, knowing that I am set for the defence of the gospel.

What then? notwithstanding, every way, whether in pretence, or in truth, Christ is preached; and I therein do rejoice, yea, and will rejoice.

[176] *Narcissus*, "Should Riches mate with Love."

[235] Butler gave this as a subject to Mr. E. P. Larken who made it into a short story entitled "The Priest's Bargain," which appeared in the *Pall Mall Magazine*, May, 1897.

[203] All things have I seen in the days of my vanity: there is a just man that perisheth in his righteousness, and there is a wicked man that prolongeth his life in his wickedness.

Be not righteous over much; neither make thyself over wise: why shouldest thou destroy thyself?

Be not over much wicked, neither be thou foolish: why shouldest thou die before thy time? (Eccles. vii. 15, 16, 17).

[204] Cf. "Imaginary Worlds," post.

[225] "So, again, it is said that when Andromeda and Perseus had travelled but a little way from the rock where Andromeda had so long been chained, she began upbraiding him with the loss of her dragon who, on the whole, she said, had been very good to her. The only things we really hate are unfamiliar things." *Life & Habit*, Chapter viii,/9.

[251] This note is one of those that appeared in the *New Quarterly Review*. The Hon. Mrs. Richard Grosvenor did not see it there, but a few years later I lent her my copy. She wrote to me 31 December, 1911.

> "The notes are delightful. By the way I can add to one. When
> Mr. Butler came to tell me he was going to stay with Dr.
> Creighton, he told me that Alfred had decided he might go on
> finding the little flake of tobacco in the letter. Then he asked me
> if I would lend him a prayer-book as he thought the bishop's man
> ought to find one in his portmanteau when he unpacked, the visit
> being from a Saturday to Monday. I fetched one and he said:

"'Is it cut?'"

[261] "Ramblings in Cheapside" in *Essays on Life, Art and Science*.

[263] Edmund Gurney, author of *The Power of Sound*, and Secretary of the Society for Psychical Research.

[279] Cf. Wamba's explanation of the Saxon swine being converted into Norman pork on their death. *Ivanhoe*, Chap. I.

[282] See "A Medieval Girl School" in *Essays on Life, Art & Science*.

[333] "Above all things, let no unwary reader do me the injustice of believing in *me*. In that I write at all I am among the damned. If he must believe in anything, let him believe in the music of Handel, the painting of Giovanni Bellini, and in the thirteenth chapter of St. Paul's First Epistle to the Corinthians" (*Life and Habit*, close of chapter II).

[343] "No one can hate drunkenness more than I do, but I am confident the human intellect owes its superiority over that of the lower animals in great measure to the stimulus which alcohol has given to imagination — imagination being little else than another name for illusion" (*Alps and Sanctuaries*, chapter III).

[364] There are letters from these people in *The Life and Letters of Dr. Samuel Butler*.

[369] Butler made this note in 1899 before the publication of *Shakespeare's Sonnets Reconsidered*, which was published in the same year. *The Odyssey Rendered info English Prose* appeared in 1900 and *Erewhon Revisited*, the last book published in his lifetime, in 1901. He made no analysis of the sales of these three books, nor of the sales of *A First Year in Canterbury Settlement* published in 1863, nor of his pamphlet *The Evidence for the Resurrection*, published in 1865. *The Way of all Flesh* and *Essays on Life, Art, and Science* were not published till after his death. I do not know what he means by *A Book of Essays*, unless it may be that he incurred an outlay of £3 11s. 9d. in connection with a projected republication of his articles in the *Universal Review* or of some of his Italian articles about the *Odyssey*.

[376] Butler had two separate grounds of complaint against Charles Darwin, one scientific, the other personal. With regard to the personal quarrel some facts came to light after Butler's death and the subject is dealt with in a pamphlet entitled *Charles Darwin and Samuel Butler: A Step towards Reconciliation*, by Henry Festing Jones (A. C. Fifield, 1911).